Passing the Buck

Kathryn Harrison

Passing the Buck:
Federalism and Canadian
Environmental Policy

UBCPress / Vancouver

Printed in Canada on acid-free paper ∞

ISBN 0-7748-0557-9 (hardcover)
ISBN 0-7748-0558-7 (paperback)

Canadian Cataloguing in Publication Data

Harrison, Kathryn, 1958-
 Passing the Buck

 Includes bibliographical references and index.
 ISBN 0-7748-0557-9 (bound) – ISBN 0-7748-0558-7 (pbk.)

1. Environmental policy – Canada. 2. Federal-provincial relations – Canada.
I. Title.

HC120.E5H37 1996   363.7´00971   C96-910451-0

This book has been published with the help of a grant from the Social Science Federation of Canada, using funds provided by the Social Sciences and Humanities Research Council of Canada.

Funding has also been provided by the University of British Columbia's K.D. Srivastava Fund.

UBC Press gratefully acknowledges the ongoing support to its publishing program from the Canada Council, the Province of British Columbia Cultural Services Branch, and the Department of Communications of the Government of Canada.

UBC Press
University of British Columbia
6344 Memorial Road
Vancouver, BC V6T 1Z2
(604) 822-3259
Fax: 1-800-668-0821
E-mail: orders@ubcpress.ubc.ca
http://www.ubcpress.ubc.ca

For George and Sophie

Contents

Acknowledgments / ix

1 Introduction: Federalism and Environmental Policy / 3

2 Federalism, Policy-Making, and Intergovernmental Politics / 12

3 The Constitutional Framework: Constraints and Opportunities / 31

4 The Emergence of Federal Involvement, 1969-72 / 55

5 The Federal Retreat, 1972-85 / 81

6 The Second Wave: The Re-emergence of the Federal Role, 1985-95 / 115

7 Conclusions / 162

Notes / 178

Bibliography / 216

Index / 229

Acknowledgments

This book could not have been completed without the assistance I received from many sources. A graduate fellowship from the Social Sciences and Humanities Research Council of Canada supported my work on the first draft of this book, while a research grant from the same Council assisted me at the revision stage. A research grant from the Science Council of British Columbia funded the travel I undertook to conduct interviews. Finally, this book has been published with the help of a grant from the Social Science Federation of Canada, using funds provided by the Social Sciences and Humanities Research Council of Canada.

Some of the material in this book has appeared in a previous form. Parts of the chapter entitled 'Federalism, Environmental Protection, and Blame Avoidance,' in Miriam Smith and François Rocher (eds.), *New Trends in Canadian Federalism,* are reprinted with permission from Broadview Press. Parts of Chapter 6 appear in a chapter entitled 'Prospects for Harmonization in Environmental Policy,' in Douglas Brown and Janet Hiebert (eds.), *Canada: The State of the Federation, 1994,* and are reprinted with the permission of the Institute of Intergovernmental Relations at Queen's University.

I am indebted to several dozen federal and provincial officials, industry representatives, and members of environmental groups who generously gave their time to interviews. While their names are not listed in order to maintain confidentiality, their anonymity in no way reflects the extent of their contribution. Sincere thanks are also owed to Andrew Fabro, the librarian for Environment Canada's Pacific and Yukon Region, who cheerfully tracked down the innumerable documents I requested; to Willem Maas and Aaron Delaney for their research assistance; and to Kent Weaver, whose E-mail messages were a source of insightful and challenging questions. Jean Wilson at UBC Press has been a supportive and, above all, patient colleague. I am especially grateful to the three members of my

Ph.D. dissertation committee: Peter Nemetz, Richard Johnston, and particularly Alan Cairns. My work has been strengthened not only by Professor Cairns's challenging questions, but by the inspiring example of his own scholarship, which served as the basis for a lively hypothetical conversation with him as I wrote.

Finally, my most profound debt is to my family. My husband and colleague, George Hoberg, has been a source of never-ending support from the inception of this project; he has been a sounding board for ideas, a reader of first drafts, a graphics consultant, and a source of encouragement whenever my confidence or enthusiasm flagged. Our daughter Sophie arrived on the scene in time for the revisions. While I had some difficulty interpreting Sophie's middle-of-the-night editorial advice, her very existence is a profound reminder for me of the importance of preserving our planet's resources for future generations. I hope that this book represents a small contribution toward that goal.

Passing the Buck

1
Introduction: Federalism and Environmental Policy

Within Canada the renewed salience of environmental issues in recent years has given rise to legislative and regulatory initiatives by both the federal and provincial governments and, not coincidentally, to increased inter-governmental conflict. Jurisdictional disputes have emerged over the Quebec government's James Bay hydro development, the Al-Pac pulp mill and Oldman River dam in Alberta, and the Rafferty-Alameda dam in Saskatchewan, to name but a few. As a result, questions concerning the appropriate balance of federal and provincial roles in environmental policy have assumed increasing prominence.

This book considers how the current division of federal and provincial responsibilities for environmental policy evolved, and the implications of this arrangement for the protection of the environment. The case of environmental protection is also used to explore the relationship between federalism and public policy more generally.

In light of recent developments, it is striking that there actually were remarkably few intergovernmental disputes over environmental matters until recently. As late as 1989, scholarly publications praised the cooperative atmosphere of federal-provincial relations in the environmental field.[1] The degree of cooperation achieved in environmental protection between the early 1970s and the late 1980s was particularly noteworthy given the often hostile climate of federal-provincial relations in other fields, including energy policy and constitutional reform, during the same period.

The challenge, then, is to account for both the recent intergovernmental conflicts concerning environmental issues, and the cooperative tenor of federal-provincial relations that prevailed previously. It will be argued that the low level of federal-provincial conflict between the early 1970s and the late 1980s reflected the fact that the federal government did not challenge provincial dominance in the field. In 1980, Thompson concluded that 'a summary of federal/provincial regulations shows provincial control over environmental matters being exercised against a background of minimum federal interference.'[2] Until recently, the federal government mainly played a supportive role conducting research, offering technical expertise, regulating automobile emissions, and encouraging the provinces to adopt consistent national standards. In contrast, provincial governments assumed the role of 'front line' protectors of the environment. They set standards for environmental and effluent quality, issued permits for individual polluters, and enforced both provincial and federal standards.

Two explanations for the historically weak federal role have been offered: constitutional constraints and provincial resistance. A number of authors suggest that the federal government was constrained by limited constitutional authority.[3] These authors generally agree that the provinces have strong claims to jurisdiction over the environment within their borders. They have considerable authority both by virtue of their legislative jurisdiction over 'property and civil rights' and their ownership of Crown resources. In contrast, federal jurisdiction over the environment is indirect and uncertain. Although most legal scholars believe that the federal government has at least some authority when it comes to environmental problems that cross international and interprovincial borders or that threaten public health, the limits of that authority are unclear.

The problem with the constitutional constraint argument, however, is that uncertain authority has not always prevented the federal government from becoming involved before. Why would the federal government display such self-restraint with respect to environmental issues when it did not do so with respect to health care, post-secondary education, or oil-pricing? In fact, legal scholars argue that the federal government has taken a surprisingly limited view of its own environmental powers.[4] Federal authority concerning the environment remains unclear twenty years after the passage of the first wave of environmental statutes largely because successive federal governments have declined to test the limits of that authority.

The constitutional constraint argument also fails to account for the disruption of intergovernmental harmony that occurred in the late 1980s, when the federal government proposed to play a more active role in the environmental field. Although subsequent chapters consider two landmark Supreme Court decisions that did serve to clarify and strengthen federal jurisdictional claims, it is significant that those decisions followed, rather than preceded, federal assertions of jurisdiction in the form of new environmental statutes.

Franson and Lucas suggest that 'the excuse of constitutional difficulties is used as a smokescreen to hide a basic unwillingness on the part of those involved to take the actions that are necessary.'[5] Along with other legal scholars, they attribute the federal timidity of the 1970s and early 1980s to an unwillingness to confront the provinces, which were highly protective of their jurisdiction over natural resources.[6] Again, however, it is noteworthy that the federal government was not so reluctant to provoke the provinces in other fields during that same period. For instance, when questions arose about which level of government could tax windfall profits from the oil industry, the federal government did not hesitate to challenge provincial authority with respect to natural resources. One is left to wonder why provincial resistance in the environmental field was singularly successful.

Like the constitutional constraint argument, the provincial resistance argument fails to account for the changes that occurred in both the balance of federal and provincial roles and federal-provincial relations in the late 1980s. There is no evidence suggesting that the provinces invited recent federal jurisdictional aggressiveness by 'letting down their guard.' Indeed, the intergovernmental conflicts that ensued demonstrate that the same provinces were as defensive as ever of their authority concerning natural resources.

While not denying the existence of either constitutional limitations or resistance from at least some of the provinces, I argue that the explanation for federal and provincial roles in environmental protection is not complete without considering governments' electoral incentives to extend or defend their jurisdiction over the environment in the first place. Environmental protection typically involves diffuse benefits and concentrated costs, and thus offers few political benefits but significant political costs.[7] One can expect the opponents of environmental regulation to be better organized, informed, and funded than the beneficiaries. Moreover, since environmental protection typically involves the imposition of costs on business, strengthening environmental standards can run counter to voters' concerns about the economy and unemployment. Thus, the absence of electoral incentives, rather than constitutional constraints or provincial opposition per se, may explain why the federal government did not pursue a larger role in environmental protection throughout the 1970s and early 1980s. The reality may be closer to a federal surrender than the provincial victory implied by many authors.

Why then have provincial governments been so eager to defend their environmental jurisdiction? A crucial difference between the federal and provincial perspectives is that the provinces are the owners of virtually all

Crown resources. Both orders of government would be expected to respond preferentially to the concentrated interests of resource development industries rather than the diffuse interests of the beneficiaries of resource conservation and protection. However, in the provinces' case, their ability to do so is inextricably tied to their authority to control the rate and terms of resource exploitation. Thus, the provinces can be expected to defend their jurisdiction over natural resources, not so much to protect them as to manage their exploitation.

Public opinion, and thus electoral incentives, are not static. The explanation for periods of heightened intergovernmental tension lies in cycles of public attention to environmental issues. During two relatively brief periods in which environmental issues attracted considerable public attention – in the early 1970s and again in the late 1980s – the federal government did in fact adopt a more expansive view of its environmental jurisdiction, despite constitutional uncertainty and objections from a number of provinces. Analysis of the withering of federal environmental programs as the first wave of public attention to the environment declined over the course of the 1970s thus can offer important lessons as the second wave ebbs in the early 1990s.

Federalism and Public Policy

In recent years there has been renewed interest in how institutions affect public policy by shaping the opportunities and incentives available to different political actors.[8] It is argued that it is not only the strength of the players, but also the 'rules of the game' that determine policy outcomes. One of the most fundamental rules of the game in Canadian politics is federalism and the associated division of powers between federal and provincial governments. Indeed, long before the movement to 'bring the state back in' to studies of politics, there was an extensive literature on the implications of federalism for public policy in Canada.

Although the state arguably has been well entrenched in Canadian political science all along, the literature offers disparate views on the relationship between federalism and public policy.[9] Many of the theories that have been offered directly conflict with each other. For instance, Professor Cairns's imagery of dirigiste governments competing to expand their jurisdiction[10] contrasts with Cameron and other authors' arguments that the vetoes and obstruction in the federal system constrain the scope of public policy.[11] There is disagreement between scholars like Trudeau, who argue that federalism promotes diversity and innovation,[12] and political economists who see interprovincial competition for investment inevitably leading to conservative policy outcomes.[13] And, there is debate over whether federalism promotes 'an ineradicable tendency to conflict' in the form of intergovernmental turf wars,[14] or is instead the stuff of collusive back room deals.[15]

Part of the apparent incoherence of the literature lies in the fact that different authors have been asking different questions. One vein of the literature explores the implications of assigning responsibility to either the federal or the provincial governments, while another explores the implications of overlapping federal and provincial jurisdiction. However, even within the first vein disagreements remain over whether the advantages of provincial jurisdiction outweigh those of federal jurisdiction in a given policy field.

In the environmental field, proponents of provincial responsibility emphasize that diversity promotes innovation ('ten heads are better than one'),[16] that provincial governments have a more intimate knowledge of local environmental problems and can tailor solutions to local circumstances accordingly,[17] and that diverse provincial policies better satisfy geographically diverse citizen preferences concerning environmental protection.[18] Advocates of federal responsibility, on the other hand, emphasize economies of scale in studying environmental problems and developing technically complex standards,[19] the ability of the federal government to respond to interprovincial spill-overs, the potentially greater resistance of the federal government to regionally dominant interests,[20] and the importance of national standards to overcome a potential 'race to the bottom' driven by interprovincial competition for investment.

More recently, scholars have acknowledged that we seldom face an either/or proposition between federal and provincial responsibility. More often than not both levels of government are involved in a given policy field. However, just as scholars have offered competing views concerning federal versus provincial jurisdiction, they also disagree about the implications of overlapping jurisdiction. Norrie, Simeon, and Krasnick have summarized the literature in terms of two distinct models of intergovernmental relations: competition and collaboration.[21] Advocates of the collaborative model stress the complementarity of joint federal-provincial action,[22] and the disadvantages of unilateralism, including unnecessary duplication,[23] the potential for obstruction (should independently devised federal and provincial policies conflict), intergovernmental conflict, and competitive expansion.[24] In contrast, advocates of competition argue that unilateralism promotes healthy federal-provincial competition to satisfy voters,[25] and facilitates oversight of each level of government by the other,[26] while joint decision-making entails undemocratic collusion. Involvement of multiple governments may create a 'joint decision trap' that allows any one government to veto a decision,[27] thus leading to the lowest common denominator, rather than the 'best of both worlds.'

Students of Canadian federalism disagree over whether intergovernmental competition or collaboration is likely to prevail, and over which outcome is to be preferred. However, one assumption implicit in the literature is that both levels of government invariably seek to expand or at least fully exploit their available jurisdiction.[28] Norrie, Simeon, and Krasnick assert that 'responding to new citizen needs, governments expanded to occupy the full "jurisdictional potential" allocated to them under the Constitution, and indeed sought to extend their reach beyond it.'[29] Similarly, Stevenson observes that governments 'seek to expand their authority and to increase their popularity with little concern for the formal boundaries of their jurisdiction.'[30] Perhaps the most extreme statements to this effect can be found in the work of Alan Cairns, who portrays federal and provincial governments as 'pyramids of bureaucratic power and ambition' capped by 'protectionist and expansionist' political authorities, 'steadily extending their tentacles of control, regulation, and manipulation into society.'[31] While there is no denying the dramatic growth of the scope of government activity over the past several decades, the question remains whether that growth has been indiscriminate, or whether one or both levels of government have declined to act in certain fields even while seeking to extend their jurisdiction in others. Moreover, during the current period of budgetary restraint, it is timely to examine temporal changes that cause governments to be more jurisdictionally aggressive during some periods than in others.

It is accepted wisdom that governments within the federal system seek both to claim credit and to avoid blame.[32] However, to date students of Canadian federalism have been more attentive to opportunities for credit claiming than to blame avoidance. It is true that some authors have in passing noted opportunities for governments to shirk responsibility within the federal system.[33] Certainly, environmentalists have long complained of 'jurisdictional buck-passing' in the environmental field.[34] However, the intergovernmental dynamics in less contentious policy fields have received relatively little scholarly attention, perhaps reflecting a preoccupation with conflict among political scientists.

The central argument of this volume is that the implications of federalism for public policy and intergovernmental relations are very different when both levels of government are eager to pursue their own programs, as compared to when one or both is content to vacate the field. To a large degree, government attitudes toward their available jurisdiction, and the type of intergovernmental dynamics that emerge in a given policy field, depend on the political costs and benefits of the policy in question. In effect, there is less need to 'bring the state back in' to Canadian scholarship on federalism and public policy than to bring society back in, to reconsider societal influences on governmental strategies of action *and of inaction* within the federal system. The argument here is not that institutions do not matter. Indeed, this book is preoccupied with the implications of one particular institution – federalism. Rather, it is that institutional analysis cannot proceed independently of social analysis.

The Study

This study uses the case of environmental protection to explore the phenomenon of policy inaction within Canadian federalism. The specific questions addressed – why has the division of federal and provincial responsibilities for environmental protection evolved as it has, and what are the implications of different federal-provincial arrangements for protection of the environment – are primarily empirical, rather than normative. Although those seeking simple policy prescriptions thus will be disappointed, I believe that empirical research need not be detached from normative analysis. Those of us who are concerned about the environment will have greater success in reforming public policy if we begin from an empirically grounded understanding of the factors that influence existing policies and institutional arrangements.

As virtually all human activity has some impact on the environment, it was necessary to narrow the focus of the study somewhat. The primary concern of this book is environmental protection policy, that is, policies to maintain or enhance the quality of the environment. Policies to conserve or allocate the quantity of natural resources will not generally be addressed. In addition, the book focuses primarily on the role of the federal government, rather than particular provincial governments, as public attention to the environment waxed and waned over a twenty-six-year period from 1969 to 1995. However, close attention is paid to provincial reactions to federal initiatives and to federal-provincial relations concerning the environment. Both because the theoretical argument of the book concerns environmental policy-making in the context of overlapping jurisdiction, and because the bulk of the population and associated environmental problems are concentrated in southern Canada, the research focused on the federal government's role within 'federal Canada,' that is, within the provinces. No effort has been made to investigate federal environmental protection efforts offshore or in the northern territories in any depth.

Various documentary sources were used in the research, including secondary literature, case law, newspapers, federal and provincial government reports, and legislative debates. However, a critical source of information, particularly concerning federal-provincial relations, was unstructured interviews conducted with seventy-six individuals. As summarized in Table 1.1, within government, they ranged from former ministers of the environment to technical specialists. In addition, spokespersons for the pulp and paper industry, representing an industry subject to overlapping national and provincial regulations, and environmental groups across the country were interviewed. Interviewees were guaranteed confidentiality, with the exception of several politicians who agreed to be interviewed 'on the record.'

Table 1.1

Sources of interviews for study

	Federal	Provincial	Other
Former ministers	2	3	
Environmental departments:			
Senior executives	3	4	
Federal-provincial relations specialists	5	8	
Technical specialists	19	9	
Other departments	6	4	
Pulp and paper industry			8
Environmental groups			5
Total	35	28	13

Interviews were conducted in Ottawa and in five provinces: British Columbia, Alberta, Ontario, Quebec, and New Brunswick. Each of the five provinces chosen brings unique characteristics to the study. Ontario is the largest and, historically, wealthiest province, which is thus less constrained by resource and scale limitations. In contrast, New Brunswick is included as a representative of the smaller and more economically vulnerable provinces. Quebec is included because governments of that province historically have been defensive of their jurisdiction in order to promote the province's distinctive identity. Both Alberta and British Columbia have natural resource based economies, and their provincial governments often have been aggressive in defending provincial jurisdiction over natural resources.

Outline of the Book

The theoretical chapter that follows explores in greater depth the implications of public opinion and interest group pressure for policy choices within the federal state and federal-provincial relations. The body of the book then traces the evolution of the federal role in environmental protection over a twenty-six-year period from 1969 to 1995. Chapter 3 reviews federal and provincial governments' sources of constitutional authority with respect to the environment, while Chapters 4 to 6 trace federal environmental policy and federal-provincial relations over three periods corresponding to the emergence of federal involvement (1969 to 1972), the federal retreat (1972 to 1985), and the resurgence of the federal role (1985 to 1995). The concluding chapter then returns to the broad themes introduced in this first chapter and speculates on future directions in Canadian federalism and environmental policy.

2
Federalism, Policy-Making, and Intergovernmental Politics

The point of departure for this chapter is Mancur Olson's insight that organizations established to pursue collective goods and information about public goods are themselves public goods.[1] Individuals who are diffusely affected by a public policy, whether winners or losers, are unlikely to organize to pursue their shared political goals, or even to inform themselves about the nature of the costs and benefits they bear. In contrast, individuals with a great deal at stake are more likely to overcome the obstacles to collective action in light of the resulting bias in both interest group activity and citizens' levels of awareness. It follows that democratic governments, motivated to claim credit and avoid blame from voters, would be inclined to pursue policies with concentrated benefits and to resist policies with concentrated costs. This insight has important implications for environmental protection, which typically benefits the public at large at the expense of a few regulated firms or individuals.

Wilson has built on Olson's insight by observing that policies characterized by different distributions of costs and benefits tend to evoke different types of politics.[2] Wilson argues that policies such as environmental protection, with diffuse benefits and concentrated costs, are likely to elicit very different politics than those where, for instance, both 'winners' and 'losers' are concentrated. Following Wilson's example, I argue here that policies with different distributions of costs and benefits are likely to provoke different *intergovernmental* politics. The purpose of this chapter is to explore how intergovernmental relations and, more generally, the implications of federalism for public policy, depend on the distribution of costs and benefits of a proposed policy.

This chapter proceeds in five sections. This first analyzes the relationship between distribution of costs and benefits, public opinion, and environmental policy. With that analysis as a foundation, the next three sections seek to extend its insights to the subject of federalism and environmental policy. The second and third sections discuss the implications of electoral considerations for the federal and the provincial governments' roles in environmental protection. The fourth section then considers the implications of federal and provincial incentives for intergovernmental relations. Finally, the fifth section considers the influence of factors other than public pressures on federal and provincial policy-making.

The Politics of Environmental Protection

Before going further, it is useful to distinguish between government functions: taxation, spending, service provision, and regulation.[3] Taxation and spending are familiar and require no explanation. Service provision is, in a sense, a special type of spending in which government uses public funds to directly provide a service to its constituents, rather than indirectly providing the service by giving constituents money. Regulation can be broadly defined as rules of behaviour backed up by the legitimate sanctions of the state.[4] In effect, rather than providing a public service itself, either directly or indirectly, the government exercises its coercive powers to force someone else to provide the service and to pay for it. Thus, an important characteristic of regulation is that the costs borne by government to administer the program tend to be small relative to the costs borne by the private sector.

Regulation typically is perceived as imposing concentrated costs on regulated industries in order to confer diffuse benefits on the public. One would not expect governments to pursue such regulatory policies aggressively, since those affected by diffuse benefits generally would be uninformed, unorganized, and thus unappreciative, while regulated interests would be well organized and unyielding in their opposition. However, regulation also can be used to deliver concentrated benefits at diffuse cost. Regulations such as those establishing agricultural marketing boards are actively sought by those who would be regulated.[5] In such cases, the diffuse victims of regulation are unorganized and uninformed, allowing government to purchase the beneficiaries' support with consumers' dollars.[6]

All else being equal, one would expect governments to prefer diffusely applied taxes, spending programs that deliver concentrated benefits, and regulations that impose diffuse costs to achieve concentrated benefits.[7] The absolute magnitude of costs and benefits can also come into play, however. Even diffuse costs can add up and cause taxpayers to revolt at the ballot box. In addition, the particular identity of winners and losers may be relevant. Policies that appear to reward undeserving interests may provoke opposition, even if the costs are widely diffused.[8]

Where does environmental policy fit within the preceding discussion? A government seeking to protect the environment can choose among the governing instruments described above. An analogy commonly offered is that of motivating a donkey to pull a cart with either a stick or a carrot. The 'stick' corresponds to the use of both the traditional 'command and control' form of regulation and incentive-based approaches, such as marketable permits and discharge fees.[9] The 'carrot' corresponds to, for example, government spending to subsidize pollution abatement costs. However, spending is best seen as a supplement rather than an alternative to regulation, since subsidies alone cannot eliminate regulated interests' economic incentive to pollute.[10] Governments also can choose to pull the hypothetical cart themselves, by relying on public enterprise. However, given the ubiquity of activities that affect the environment, this approach would entail an implausible degree of public ownership. In the end, some form of regulation, possibly supplemented by subsidies or public enterprise, is necessary to overcome economically rational polluting behaviour.

Environmental regulation presents a classic case of diffuse benefits and concentrated costs. In general, the public at large benefits from improvements in environmental quality, while the costs are borne by a smaller number of regulated firms or individuals. An Olsonian analysis suggests that the opponents of environmental protection are likely to be better organized and better informed than the beneficiaries. Moreover, those most directly harmed by environmental regulation tend to hold privileged positions in society. Regulated industries can offer politicians more than just votes or even campaign contributions. They create jobs, and thus offer extremely valuable indirect benefits. As a result, one would expect governments generally to be more responsive to the concentrated interests, that is, to the polluters. The logic of collective action is heavily weighted against strong environmental policy.

As Farber notes, 'the Olson paradigm appears to have a straightforward implication for environmental legislation: there should not be any.'[11] If that is the case, then why do governments ever adopt environmental protection policies? A number of explanations have been offered. First, however improbable it might seem to Olson, numerous environmental groups have emerged since the 1960s to pursue policies that involve diffuse benefits. Scholars seeking to explain the emergence of such groups have emphasized the importance of external (foundation or government) funding,[12] as well as the presence of 'policy entrepreneurs' who derive personal satisfaction from pursuing collective benefits. Although only a minority of those who would benefit from environmental protection are persuaded by policy entrepreneurs to actually join environmental groups, the substantial number that do join nonetheless provide an important voice for the interests of an otherwise silent constituency. Moreover, environmental groups provide information that 'rational' individuals diffusely affected by environmental regulation would not take the trouble to seek. Thus, these groups stimulate greater attentiveness to environmental issues even among non-members. The presence of an active environmental community effectively serves to concentrate the interests of those diffusely affected by environmental policy.

Although more sophisticated interest group theory can account for the emergence of interest groups representing diffuse interests, it nonetheless predicts that such groups will remain weak relative to those representing concentrated interests, a proposition for which there is considerable empirical support.[13] Moreover, in Canada the first generation of environmental statutes passed in the early 1970s coincided with, rather than followed, the emergence of organized environmental groups, and thus cannot be attributed to their influence.[14] In sum, interest group politics offers at best an incomplete explanation for the emergence of environmental protection policies.

Others have argued that governments adopt environmental policies primarily in response to rent-seeking industries. For instance, Elliott, Ackerman, and Millian argue convincingly that US federal government involvement in air pollution control was a response to lobbying by the coal and auto industries for consistent national standards (although their argument begs the question of what prompted the state standards).[15] Along a similar vein, Emond argues that the earliest Canadian provincial environmental statutes were passed to protect polluters from private litigation under common law.[16] Although this argument is persuasive in the case of some regulated industries, it fails to account for the breadth of environmental statutes or the very real costs that have been imposed on many sectors of industry that not only did not pursue environmental regulation, but actively opposed it.

Still others have implied that environmental statutes are all 'smoke and mirrors.' The incentives for those diffusely affected by regulations to remain ill-informed create ample opportunities for symbolic politics. Governments can claim credit for protecting the environment and at the same time avoid blame from regulated interests either by offering subsidies to cover the costs of regulation, or by simply neglecting to enforce regulations after exalting their stringency. There is considerable evidence that governments do both. Hartle for one argues that, in practice, most regulated interests have been 'gummed rather than bitten' by ostensibly strict regulations.[17]

The question remains, however, whether subsidies and weak enforcement reflect conscious strategies adopted by governments at the outset, or merely after-the-fact responses to persistent political opposition by regulated interests. The latter is more plausible, particularly with respect to non-enforcement. If weak enforcement were planned from the outset governments would either have to bear the brunt of industry wrath anyway until the laxity of enforcement became apparent or, alternatively, risk letting regulated interests in on the plan from the start. Even if there were sufficient trust between government and business to keep such a conspiracy quiet – a very big 'if' – it is far from obvious that regulated industries would welcome the prospect of being 'gummed,' even if not 'bitten.' Despite reassurances from the current government, regulated industries would not know, once legislation or regulations were in place, if a future government might be more inclined to enforce them.

The most compelling explanation for environmental policy is that public opinion occasionally overcomes the obstacles to collective action, thus transforming politicians' incentives. In his classic article on 'the issue attention cycle,' Downs offers the environment as an example of the propensity for issues to come and go from the political agenda as public attention waxes and wanes.[18]

Although the odds are weighted against public attention to environmental issues, a rare combination of effective political entrepreneurship and unusual events that capture the media's attention can cause even those diffusely affected to sit up and take note, and that leads electorally minded politicians to do the same. Although poorly informed, the beneficiaries of environmental regulation nonetheless substantially outnumber the victims. Thus, relatively small changes in levels of public awareness can transform the balance of political costs and benefits.[19] Farber argues that 'politics alternates between normal periods, in which public attention to an issue is weak, and extraordinary periods, in which the issue has high salience for the public. In those extraordinary periods when broad segments of the public are intensely involved with an issue, legislators find themselves in the spotlight, and their positions shift closer to those of the public at large.'[20]

Similarly, Baumgartner and Jones argue that American politics is characterized by 'punctuated equilibria.' Public indifference facilitates long periods of relative stability, dominated by 'policy monopolies' of politicians and interest groups. However, those stable periods are punctuated by intervals of rapid change, in which interests previously excluded from the policy monopoly succeed in mobilizing attention of the broader public and redefining the issue.[21]

Peters and Hogwood offer empirical support for the claim that legislators respond to Downsian cycles in public attention. In eleven of twelve policy sectors studied by the authors, the peak in government organizational activity occurred either in the same period or immediately following the peak in issue salience as measured by public opinion polls.[22]

To date, there have been two such peaks when the North American public has turned its attention to the environment, the first around 1970 and the second around 1990. However, given the diffuseness of the benefits of environmental protection, such high levels of salience have been difficult to sustain. It is not sufficient for members of the public merely to prefer a cleaner environment; they must also be familiar with government policies and be willing to weigh the government's performance on environmental issues heavily at election time. Whatever the origins of these unusual periods of public interest (a complex question that will not be examined here), the logic of collective action suggests that they will be exceptional and short-lived. In fact, as discussed in greater depth in Chapters 4 and 6, both the first and second 'green waves' crested with the onset of economic problems, as public attention returned to 'bread and butter' issues like unemployment and inflation. This trend is consistent with Peltzman's argument that 'regulation will tend to be more heavily weighted toward "producer protection" in depressions and toward "consumer protection" in expansions.'[23]

In summary, one would expect that most of the time, when environmental issues do not capture public attention, governments will decline to impose stringent environmental regulations in response to prevailing interest group pressures. Reluctance will be the norm. Although governments are more likely to pass environmental laws and regulations during exceptional periods of high salience of environmental problems, aggressiveness is by no means guaranteed even then. Rather, governments may attempt to assuage public demands during such periods with purely symbolic statutes.

The fact that governments choose to exercise certain powers and to neglect others based on their calculus of electoral costs and benefits is not an artifact of federalism. Unitary governments face similar choices. The causes of federal and provincial governments' anticipated disinclination to pursue environmental protection lie in public inattention to environmental issues and the resulting influence exercised by business interests relative to environmental groups. However, federal and provincial politicians devise their individual policies within the context of a federal system, which facilitates some responses and constrains others. The next three sections thus consider the implications of federalism for federal and provincial environmental policy, and the implications of federal and provincial attitudes for federal-provincial relations.

The Federal Role: Blame Avoidance

Before going further, it is important to distinguish between policy and jurisdiction. Constitutional jurisdiction is the capacity to make policy. It does not compel a government to take any particular course of action or, for that matter, to take any action at all. However, it is anticipated that federal and provincial governments' policy objectives would influence their attitudes toward their constitutional jurisdiction. Just as some policies are more politically appealing than others, some fields of jurisdiction are worth fighting for, while others are willingly vacated. One would expect governments to value jurisdiction that allows them to pursue politically attractive policies, and to disregard or even concede jurisdiction associated with electoral blame. Thus, the distribution of costs and benefits inherent in different policy fields can help to explain the inclination of governments to exercise, enlarge, defend, or surrender their constitutional resources.

However, one cannot assume that government attitudes about particular policies always translate directly into attitudes toward jurisdiction for several reasons. First, policies can be changed much more easily than jurisdiction. It is one thing to neglect a field of jurisdiction that currently holds no appeal, but quite another to surrender it permanently via constitutional amendment. It is thus important to distinguish between governments' positions concerning constitutional reform and their jurisdictional claims within the existing constitutional framework. Breton has labelled these two activities constitutional decision-making and 'in period' decision-making. Although governments are likely to behave in a risk averse manner when they are engaged in questions of constitutional design, 'in period' they would be expected to value jurisdiction that enables them to pursue politically appealing policies, and to be more inclined to neglect or informally concede jurisdiction associated with politically unappealing policies.[24]

Second, constitutional jurisdiction is typically broad and does not imply particular policy objectives. The constitution confers two main types of jurisdiction: authority over subjects, such as fisheries and education, and authority to exercise governing instruments, such as taxation.[25] Since the subject headings are broad and the instruments authorized for a wide variety of purposes, governments may value their jurisdiction for a number of purposes. A related issue is that of spill-overs between constitutional responsibilities. Whether or not a government has jurisdiction over one policy field may be relevant to its decision to seek or exercise jurisdiction in another area. For instance, Banting argues that the provinces were willing to agree to formally concede authority over welfare programs to the federal government via constitutional amendment because they did not have adequate powers of taxation to deliver the programs themselves.[26] It is thus essential to consider the broader political context in which governments evaluate their jurisdiction.

These last points are especially relevant in explaining the provinces' attitudes toward their environmental jurisdiction. As will be discussed in the next chapter, the constitutional heads of power that provide provincial governments with authority to protect the environment also provide authority to exploit natural resources and thus promote economic growth or diversification. Historically, provincial governments have relied heavily on Crown resources to pursue economic development and provide an important source of provincial revenues. The provinces thus are likely to remain protective of environmental jurisdiction, even during periods of public inattentiveness, since their authority to protect the environment is intimately tied to their ownership and control of natural resources. However, their intent would be to defend their authority to direct and profit from the exploitation of natural resources, rather than to conserve and protect them.

In contrast to provincial jurisdiction, federal authority over the environment is indirect and less closely tied to the exploitation of natural resources. Thus, the federal government normally would be expected to take a narrow view of its own jurisdiction, and by default to concede the environmental field to the provinces. However, trends in public interest in environmental issues can be expected to provoke shifts in the respective roles of the federal and provincial governments. Although federal involvement is more likely to emerge during periods of heightened salience, when voters are paying attention, the balance of federal and provincial roles is likely to shift back toward the provinces during periods of public apathy. Simeon and Robinson have observed that 'federal form follows state function.'[27] In other words, as federal and provincial governments are driven by electoral interests to cultivate certain fields of jurisdiction and to leave others fallow, the combination of social problems and the policies that emerge in response to them will gradually transform the face of Canadian federalism. Thus, as the balance of federal and provincial government roles evolves in response to their selective assertions of environmental jurisdiction, public policy in effect shapes the federal state.

At the same time, the converse is also true. Federalism can shape public policy when federal and provincial governments operate strategically within the federal context. Constitutional ambiguity and overlapping jurisdiction provide an opportunity for either level of government to avoid responsibility for environmental protection by pleading inadequate authority and 'passing the buck' to the other level. However, for the reasons discussed above, in the Canadian context the federal government is more likely than the provinces to take a narrow view of its environmental jurisdiction and avail itself of opportunities for interjurisdictional buck-passing. Thus, rather than merely conceding the field by default, the federal government may actively relinquish the lead role to the provinces in order to avoid electoral blame.[28]

Whenever inequities in political power exist, whether as a result of the distribution of resources or the nature of the costs and benefits associated with a particular policy, federalism has the potential to create a dynamic of competitive credit claiming in some cases and blame avoidance in others. Federalism thus could exacerbate governments' tendency to oversupply private goods that involve concentrated benefits, and to undersupply public goods that demand the imposition of concentrated costs. In the case of environmental policy, the former is clearly a much greater concern.

The Provincial Role: Policy-Making Amid Provincial Interdependence

The federal context can also shape provincial environmental policy. A critical implication of federalism from a provincial government's perspective is that there typically will be several provinces seeking to achieve similar environmental objectives at the same time. In devising environmental policies, provincial governments may be interdependent in several ways, thus creating opportunities for strategic behaviour. First, physical spillovers of pollutants between jurisdictions create a situation in which a downwind or downstream province is dependent on its neighbour to mitigate environmental impacts. The neighbour has few incentives to impose costs on polluting industries within its borders, and indeed has considerable incentives to take advantage of a situation in which its constituents do not incur the full cost of their actions.[29] However, the significance of this type of interdependence is mitigated by the size of Canadian provinces, which allows many immediate environmental problems to be effectively contained within provincial borders.

Perhaps more significant than ecological interdependence are the implications of economic interdependence. The fear is that interprovincial competition for investment will deter provinces from regulating polluting firms. In his seminal work on fiscal federalism, Oates argues that subnational jurisdictions are limited in their ability to pursue redistributive policies, such as progressive taxation and welfare benefits, because they are constrained by the mobility of individual citizens.[30] Wealthy citizens will tend to migrate away from jurisdictions with high taxes, while the poor will migrate toward those offering generous welfare benefits. As a result, individual provinces or municipalities will be driven to impose lower taxes and to offer less generous welfare benefits than their citizens really want. Recent studies offer empirical support for the dynamic postulated by Oates. In a study of US state welfare benefits levels, Peterson and Rom demonstrate that the poor do migrate in search of higher benefits, and that states wary of becoming 'welfare magnets' resist offering more generous welfare benefits than neighbouring jurisdictions.[31] Similarly, Burns and Beamer conducted an extensive analysis of the determinants of US state welfare spending that showed that for every $1.00 that a neighbouring state decreases welfare benefits, the average state trims its own benefits by $0.56.[32]

Just as subnational governments may find their efforts to redistribute wealth limited by citizen mobility, they also may find their efforts to enact regulations that impose costs on industry constrained by the threat of capital mobility. To the extent that individual provinces compete to attract new investment and to retain existing employers, they face incentives to offer weaker environmental standards than neighbouring jurisdictions. In the worst case, this dynamic could degenerate to a 'race to the bottom,' in which individual provinces compete for industry by offering progressively weaker regulatory standards.[33]

Markusen, Morey, and Olewiler have offered a formal model of this dynamic, in which two jurisdictions compete for a limited supply of investment capital.[34] The authors conclude that, to the extent that the two jurisdictions respond strategically to each other's policies, inefficient outcomes can occur in which a polluting industry benefits from competitive bidding between jurisdictions, and residents of both jurisdictions suffer from excessive pollution.

On the other hand, other authors argue that interprovincial competition for jobs may be quite healthy.[35] Although these authors acknowledge a tradeoff between job creation and environmental protection, they stress that voters care about both. These authors argue that it is entirely appropriate that a province with a high unemployment rate should have weaker environmental standards than its wealthy neighbour, since residents of the poor province undoubtedly place a higher value on job creation than their wealthy neighbours. For this reason, Zerbe argues that the migration of polluting industries to jurisdictions with weaker standards can be seen as 'a desirable equilibrating process.'[36]

A critical assumption in this model of efficient interjurisdictional competition is that local jurisdictions are 'price takers' with respect to investment capital.[37] In other words, although the environmental standards chosen by any one jurisdiction will affect the availability of jobs in that jurisdiction, there are so many other jurisdictions for investors to choose among that no one jurisdiction's policies will perceptibly affect the competitive position of its neighbours. Similarly, it is assumed that individual investors are so small that they cannot individually influence a jurisdiction's environmental standards. In effect, the authors defined away the problem of strategic behaviour by assuming an infinite number of jurisdictions and investors. Reality undoubtedly lies somewhere between the models that depict two jurisdictions caught in a prisoners' dilemma and those that depict an infinite number of jurisdictions in healthy competition with each other. However, ten provinces falls considerably short of an infinite number of jurisdictions, and thus some measure of provincial interdependence is quite conceivable. Indeed, a study I conducted of provincial interactions in environmental standard setting for the pulp and paper industry revealed considerable reluctance on the part of individual provinces to regulate unilaterally lest they be undercut by other provinces.[38]

Intergovernmental competition is inefficient whenever governments compete to cater to unduly influential voters, whether environmentalists or industry. Thus, to the extent that provincial governments compete to satisfy environmental groups that do not represent widespread voter preferences, a 'race to the top' with respect to environmental standards could ensue, which would be no more efficient than a race to the bottom. Such competition could emerge during periods of high salience of environmental issues. As increased public attention increases the political benefits of environmental protection relative to job protection, the interprovincial game could be transformed from a race to the bottom to a race to the top, with provinces competing to issue more stringent environmental standards.[39]

However, if one compares the political resources available to regulated industries and environmental groups, it is clear that undue industry influence is a much greater concern. As already discussed, regulated industries would be expected to be better informed and better organized than their opponents because of the concentrated costs and diffuse benefits of environmental regulation. As a further reflection of the obstacles to collective action, pressure groups representing regulated interests are likely to be better funded than those representing the public interest, and thus in a

position to spend more on the regulatory battle and to offer more generous campaign contributions to individual politicians and political parties.

Most important, however, is the indirect benefit that industry provides
to politicians by creating and maintaining jobs. The prospect of a plant
laying off some or all of its employees in response to the costs of environmental regulations is a powerful threat that environmental groups cannot
hope to match. The comparable claim, that workers dissatisfied with poor
environmental quality will weaken the economy by moving en masse to
another jurisdiction simply is not credible.[40]

Authors troubled by the implications of interprovincial competition for
investment tend to emphasize the role of the federal government in overcoming destructive interprovincial competition.[41] Brander suggests that
'the central government might well act as a broker in helping provincial
governments solve games of coordination, or it might even take a stronger
position and impose a code of conduct with the force of law.'[42] A question
that has received scant attention, however, is what incentives encourage
the federal government to take either approach to address the problem of
provincial interdependence? Oates treats the federal government as a
'benevolent despot' and fails to question either the federal government's
ability to recognize or willingness to overcome the dilemma of provincial
interdependence.[43] Similarly, in their economic analysis of federal states,
Breton and Scott acknowledge various inefficiencies of political 'markets,'
but nonetheless are generally optimistic that democratic accountability
will produce an efficient division of powers.[44]

Other authors adopt a less sanguine view of intergovernmental competition. Contrary to Breton and Scott's assumption, voters and interest
groups do have preferences when it comes to which level of government
should be responsible for particular policies. Mashaw and Rose-Ackerman
argue that regulated firms will prefer local jurisdiction inasmuch as they
can wrest concessions from local governments using the threat of capital
mobility.[45] Similarly, residents of provinces that benefit from the imposition of spillovers on neighbouring provinces may oppose federal
involvement, even if they would have supported comparable national
policies in a unitary state.[46] These authors depart from earlier work in rec-
ognizing that locally dominant groups obtain the support of local
governments not only in pursuing their desired policies but in obstructing
national regulations.[47] In effect, the very imbalances of political power
that lead one to call for federal involvement may also prevent that result
from occurring.

The federal government faces pressures from voters, interest groups, and
provincial governments. In light of the obstacles to collective action and

the resulting imbalance of political resources discussed earlier in this chapter, it is quite conceivable that regulated interests will dominate at both the local level and at the national level. Moreover, to the extent that regulated industries recruit provincial governments to act in their interest, the federal government will face additional opposition from the provinces. Thus, it is by no means obvious that the federal government will be willing to step in to resolve problems associated with interprovincial economic interdependence. Federal involvement is more likely to emerge, however, in periods of pronounced public attentiveness, when the level of environmental awareness among the beneficiaries of environmental protection may be high enough to overcome opposition from those who will bear the costs.

Implications for Federal-Provincial Relations

Federal and provincial governments' attitudes toward their jurisdiction have important implications for their attitudes toward each other. One would expect very different intergovernmental relations when both levels of government value their jurisdiction compared to when one or both is content to leave a field vacant. Federal and provincial governments may compete for opportunities to win friends, but they seldom compete for the honour of making enemies.

The preceding sections have argued that if a particular policy offers concentrated benefits, federal and provincial governments alike would tend to take a broader view of their jurisdiction. Since both levels of government are more likely to be active in a politically attractive policy field, there is greater potential for intergovernmental competition. Thus, during periods of heightened salience of environmental issues, federal and provincial governments might enter into competition to impress voters with their 'green' credentials.

At the same time, politically appealing policies will likely provoke each level of government to seek to enlarge its own jurisdiction and to defend this jurisdiction against incursions by the other level. Thus, elevated public interest in environmental issues could also provoke conflict in the form of federal-provincial 'turf wars.' Moreover, since we anticipate considerable governmental reticence even during periods of public attentiveness to the environment, it is possible that only one level will be prompted to pursue more aggressive environmental protection policies. This exacerbates the potential for federal-provincial conflict during periods of public attentiveness, although in this case along a green-brown, rather green-green axis. Intergovernmental cooperation would also be difficult to sustain during periods of elevated environmental concern, since governments responding to a demanding and dissatisfied public can benefit from attributing past failures to each other.

During 'normal' periods when the public is inattentive to environmental issues, however, environmental protection offers politicians the promise of more blame than credit. The federal government would be expected to take a narrow view of its environmental jurisdiction, while provincial governments would be inclined to fortify their jurisdiction for purposes of natural resource exploitation. Since federal and provincial views of their jurisdiction thus would be compatible, intergovernmental relations concerning the environment should be relatively cooperative. However, the incentive faced by both levels of government to deflect occasional demands for resolution of high profile environmental problems does create the potential for interludes of intergovernmental finger-pointing, even during periods of low salience of environmental issues. It is noteworthy, though, that because federal and provincial governments do not directly oppose each other in seeking re-election, it may be possible for them to 'circle the wagons' to collectively resist politically unappealing demands.[48]

Political Decision-Making in Context

The discussion thus far has depicted federal and provincial governments as devising strategies based primarily on the electoral costs and benefits of individual policies. In reality, governments operate in a more complex environment, in which personal and institutional preferences come into play, politicians' and bureaucrats' preferences diverge, and governments are not merely recipients but moulders of public opinion. Moreover, governments' choices concerning particular policies are shaped by the broader constitutional and political context. This section considers each of these factors in turn.

Politicians Have Personal and Institutional Objectives

Clearly, re-election is not the sole motive of individual politicians nor governments. Legislators have both selfish interests and altruistic motives that reflect their personal values, either of which may conflict with their electoral interests. Ideological or moral ideals may be especially influential in the case of political parties that have a solid base of support but little hope of forming a government, and thus face less temptation to accede to prevailing opinion. Their influence may be particularly significant during periods of minority government.

Legislators' policy preferences also may be influenced by their institutional context. As office holders, individuals may seek to defend or strengthen the office itself. And, as administrators of large organizations, they may seek to defend the interests of their employees. Thus, in intergovernmental relations, governments may choose to pursue their long-term interests as governments, even when these conflict with the near-term electoral interests of the governing party.

Personal or institutional preferences do not present a problem for a theory of governmental behaviour based on electoral calculus to the extent that politicians' personal and electoral motives coincide. But which motives will prevail when politicians' personal or institutional interests conflict with electoral interests? In such cases, one would expect the fact that politicians' personal goals cannot all be achieved in one term to ensure that, on balance, electoral considerations will prevail. Without re-election, even well-meaning legislators will be unable to pursue their 'good policy' objectives.

Governments Are Not Monolithic

Thus far, this chapter has adopted the language of executive federalism in depicting governments as unitary actors. It has been assumed that the traditions of party and cabinet solidarity allow cabinet to speak with a single voice on behalf of the government as a whole. However, as Schultz has demonstrated, intragovernmental politics can influence government positions in intergovernmental relations.[49] For instance, there may be important differences between the positions of departments that respond to different constituencies. Intragovernmental politics could be particularly significant in situations where the environment department seeks to regulate the activities of another department within the same government. Although in theory any differences would be resolved within cabinet, with both sides adhering to the government position thereafter, in practice, the 'losers' in an intragovernmental struggle may look to outside constituencies or the other level of government for support.

Notwithstanding norms of ministerial responsibility and the professional public service, there also can be important differences between bureaucrats and politicians. Wood has demonstrated in the US context that bureaucrats have considerable means to elude constraints imposed by their political sovereigns.[50]

Bureaucrats' and politicians' interests are most likely to diverge following a peak in issue salience. Downs hypothesized that each issue attention cycle would leave a legacy in the form of new legislation and government institutions.[51] Given administrative tools and statutory mandates, zealous bureaucrats in environmental protection departments may be inclined to exercise their authority more aggressively than would politicians seeking to avoid blame from regulated interests. On the other hand, officials concerned with enforcement of environmental laws typically have regular and ongoing contact with regulated firms and only minimal involvement with groups representing the beneficiaries of environmental regulation. Consequently, they may develop sympathies for regulated interests that are quite consistent with the goals of their electorally motivated political masters.

It is an empirical question to what degree bureaucrats' interests depart from those of their ministers and also to what degree they are able to elude accountability to the executive. While the development of a theory of intragovernmental relations is beyond the scope of this study, an effort is made in subsequent chapters to remain mindful of the influence of executive versus bureaucracy and interdepartmental differences.

Governments Influence Public Opinion

Governments are not merely passive recipients of the demands of the electorate. They can actively shape public perceptions of the costs and benefits of different policies through selective and timely dissemination of information. Moreover, Canadian governments have often influenced public opinion indirectly by playing an active role in creating and maintaining interest groups.[52] Compared to their US counterparts, they have been quite generous in providing core funding to private groups. Although there have been no studies of the funding of Canadian environmental groups, the more influential groups' heavy reliance on membership dues, direct mail fund-raising, door-to-door canvassing, and product sales suggests that they are less dependent on government funding than other categories of public interest groups, such as women's groups, aboriginal groups, and multicultural organizations. In fact, Doern and Conway report that in the late 1980s, annual federal government funding to environmental groups was only about $150,000.[53]

The possibility that governments exert substantial control over public opinion presents a fundamental challenge to the approach of this book, which depicts politicians primarily as recipients of public and interest group demands. An important test of this counter-argument can be found during periods of low salience of environmental issues. The fact that there are many more beneficiaries of environmental protection than victims creates an incentive for either enterprising governments or opposition parties to rekindle public interest in the environment. From a politician's perspective, there are many friends out there to be made, if only they can be made aware of their own interests. Subsequent chapters examine the extent to which government and opposition politicians seek to mobilize public interest in the environment.

Political and Constitutional Context Matters

Governments do not develop individual policies in a vacuum. The political implications of any one policy are assessed by each government in light of its full array of policies. There may be synergies or conflicts between policies that force a rethinking of any one proposal. Similarly, intergovernmental relations in one policy area could spill over into another area. In effect, governments are simultaneously engaged in a variety of overlapping political 'games,' with their constituents and with each other. For that reason, governments may adopt strategies that are different from those one would anticipate from an analysis of only one game.[54]

To further complicate matters, both federal and provincial games are played at several different levels, each with its own characteristic players, arenas, and stakes. Political games not only overlap, they are nested within larger games. A distinction between constitutional and 'in period' decision-making has already been noted. The latter can be further subdivided. The following chapters thus consider four levels of government decision-making relevant to environmental protection: constitution-making, legislation, standard setting, and enforcement. Governments' choices at each level are constrained by previous decisions at higher levels.

The context of each game can be significant. At the legislative level, federal and provincial roles evolve in response to emerging policy problems within broad but meaningful boundaries established by the constitution. The players enjoy considerable flexibility, but the game is not entirely without rules. Although it is argued that federal and provincial governments devise their policy objectives largely based on electoral calculus, the constitutional division of powers provides each level of government with strong or weak resources relative to the subject area in question.

Similarly, at the regulatory level, the executive cannot issue regulations unless they are authorized by legislation. However, within the context of that legislation considerable discretion typically remains. Just as constitutional fields can be left fallow, governments need not employ their legislative authority to pass regulations, nor enforce their regulations once passed. The chapters that follow attempt to strike a balance between analysis of governments' discretionary choices at each level and awareness of the constraints imposed by previous decisions at other levels.

Summary

The central focus of this chapter has been the relationship between the distribution of the costs and benefits, public and interest group pressures, and environmental protection. It has been argued that because the benefits of environmental protection tend to be diffuse and the costs concentrated, opponents of environmental regulation generally tend to be better funded and organized, and thus more politically influential, than the beneficiaries. As a result, governments normally would not be inclined to aggressively pursue environmental protection, except perhaps during periods of heightened salience of environmental issues.

Turning first to the federal government, federal politicians are expected to take a relatively narrow view of their environmental jurisdiction during 'normal' periods in which the public is inattentive to environmental issues. Overlapping jurisdiction exacerbates the federal government's predisposition to avoid imposing concentrated costs by providing a convenient escape from a politically unpleasant responsibility. Thus, during normal periods of low salience of environmental issues, the federal government is expected to avoid blame by claiming inadequate jurisdiction and deflecting demands for environmental protection to the provinces. Federal politicians may take a broader view of their environmental authority during exceptional periods of elevated public interest, but this is by no means inevitable. Considerable reluctance is likely to remain, and there may be a tendency to rely on symbolic measures. However, in general one would anticipate shifts in the balance of federal and provincial roles in environmental protection, with the federal role increasing during periods of public attentiveness and subsiding during normal periods of low salience.

With respect to the provinces, it is anticipated that, unlike the federal government, provincial governments will be defensive of their jurisdiction even during periods of low salience of environmental issues. This is because provincial jurisdiction over the environment is closely tied to the provinces' ability to exploit natural resources. Indeed, provincial governments may be more resistant than the federal government to increased public attentiveness to the environment in light of their role as developers of natural resources. Federalism can have a negative impact on provincial environmental policy by fostering interprovincial competition for investment, especially in the absence of a strong federal presence. The threat of capital mobility by regulated interests can exacerbate provincial governments' unwillingness to impose the costs of environmental regulation.

Finally, it is anticipated that federal-provincial relations concerning the environment normally will be relatively cooperative, since the federal government is not expected to challenge provincial jurisdiction during 'normal' periods of public inattention. However, during brief periods of heightened salience of environmental issues, intergovernmental competition and conflict are more likely to emerge.

3
The Constitutional Framework: Constraints and Opportunities

The central argument of this book – that the relationship between federalism and public policy depends on the distribution of costs and benefits of the particular policy in question – does not imply that the constitutional division of powers is unimportant. The constitution establishes the structure within which governments, interest groups, and individual citizens evaluate their political options. However, on many questions the written constitution is ambiguous or silent, leaving considerable room for interpretation by various political actors as well as the courts.

The evolving interpretation of the constitution reflects not only how the judiciary views the constitution, but also the nature of the cases brought before the courts. Since challenges to the constitutionality of laws are most often raised by defendants charged under them, governments normally must take some sort of positive action for their laws to be interpreted by the courts.[1] In other words, governments not only must pass laws that test the limits of their jurisdiction – they must also implement them.

Clearly, a decision to take a constitutional chance by exercising unclear jurisdiction would not be taken lightly by any government, given the finality of judicial decisions. Once the Supreme Court has ruled on a question concerning the division of powers, any gain or loss of contested jurisdiction is ostensibly permanent, barring constitutional amendment.[2] Before taking such an all-or-nothing risk, government leaders would weigh a number of factors. First, the likelihood of winning in court would be assessed on the basis of the strength of the constitutional claims and counterclaims, and the perceived receptiveness of the Court.

The potential for several types of costs also would be considered. The very action of contesting jurisdiction could provoke federal-provincial conflict if representatives of the challenged level of government are protective of the same field of jurisdiction. The intergovernmental dispute could spill over into other policy areas. The delays incurred in obtaining judicial clarification constitute another cost. Finally, there are the potential costs of losing in court, including political embarrassment[3] and, more importantly, a permanent constraint on policy options.

The potential gains and losses of provoking judicial clarification of contested jurisdiction would be weighed against the expected benefits to be gained from intergovernmental accommodation. Risk averse federal and provincial governments often have reached mutually advantageous agreements through informal bargaining, effectively bypassing formal tests of jurisdiction. Although the gains from such a strategy are likely to be less than those of winning jurisdiction in court, even small gains by informal means are preferable to losing in court.

All else being equal, governments would be deterred from testing uncertain jurisdiction the weaker the constitutional arguments, the more hostile the courts, the more cooperative the other level of government, and the more plausible the case of making acceptable gains via informal bargaining. However, a factor overlooked by those who have emphasized these forces in the environmental context is the attractiveness of the jurisdiction itself. The less valued the jurisdiction, the less likely that the benefits of taking a chance will outweigh the potential costs. At the limit, if a policy offers net political costs rather than benefits, a government has no incentive to test the constitutional waters, even if legal victory would be virtually certain and politically painless.

This chapter reviews the constitutional basis of federal and provincial authority in the field of environmental protection in order to explore the opportunities and constraints faced by both levels of government. In particular, the chapter addresses the question: how great are the constitutional risks of involvement in environmental protection for federal and provincial governments?

Sources of Provincial Authority

Since pollution was not a prominent issue in 1867, it is hardly surprising that responsibility for environmental protection was not explicitly allocated to either the federal or provincial legislatures by the BNA Act. In light of this omission, both federal and provincial authority with respect to environmental protection is derivative of other fields of jurisdiction that are explicitly mentioned in the constitution. Since almost every aspect of human endeavour has some environmental impact, 'the powers that may be used to combat environmental degradation are liberally sprinkled through the heads of power given to each level of government.'[4]

The result is a substantial degree of overlap between federal and provincial powers concerning the environment, since both levels of government have jurisdiction founded on different constitutional heads of power. Furthermore, since both levels of government rely on implied constitutional authority in protecting the environment, pending judicial clarification, there is considerable uncertainty concerning the limits of each level's jurisdiction. Governments can find authority to protect the environment both in their capacity as owners of public property and their capacity as legislators, each of which is discussed in turn below.

There is little disagreement that the provinces have extensive jurisdiction over the environment both as a result of strong legislative powers and extensive proprietary powers with respect to natural resources. Provincial natural resource assets are extensive. With the exception of national parks and other federal properties, Section 109 of the constitution confers upon the provinces ownership of all lands, mines, and minerals in the public domain within their borders.[5] The section does not mention water, fish, or wildlife since according to common law doctrine those resources cannot be owned in their natural state. However, ownership of land does convey extensive rights of access to these common property resources. Thus, as owners of the beds of most water bodies, provincial governments can exercise considerable control over the quality of water resources within their borders.[6]

Thompson and Eddy have noted that 'ownership confers a form of jurisdiction over resources that is scarcely less far-reaching than legislative jurisdiction.'[7] The provinces have the same extensive rights as private property owners to use, lease, or sell their property. Historically, royalties from the sale or lease of Crown resources have been an important source of provincial revenues in many provinces; as a result, those provinces have been highly protective of their proprietary jurisdiction over resources. Ownership of natural resources also confers extensive authority to conserve and protect those resources.[8] Like any other property owner, the provinces can specify conditions in contracts granting access to their resources in order to promote conservation. In addition, they can legislate with respect to provincial Crown resources by virtue of Section 92(5), which grants the provinces legislative authority over the 'management and sale of public lands.'

Historically, the courts have guarded against federal legislative encroachment in areas of provincial proprietary authority.[9] However, a series of Supreme Court decisions in the late 1970s suggested greater willingness on the part of the Court to allow encroachment by federal legislative powers, particularly the trade and commerce power, over provincial prerogatives with respect to Crown resources.[10] The more recent *Oldman Dam* and *Grand Council of Crees* cases, discussed below, also affirm the Court's willingness to interpret federal powers generously, despite conflict with provincial ownership of resources.

In addition to proprietary powers, the provinces also have several important sources of legislative authority over natural resources. Of the enumerated provincial heads of power, the most significant with respect to the environment is Section 92(13), which grants authority over 'Property and Civil Rights in the Province.' The courts have interpreted Section 92(13) broadly, essentially creating a residual regulatory power.[11] This power is reinforced by Section 92(10), which grants authority over 'Local Works and Undertakings,' and Section 92(16), which grants authority over 'Matters of a merely local or private Nature in the Province.' Significantly, the combination of proprietary powers and legislative jurisdiction over property and civil rights gives the provinces authority to legislate with respect to both publicly and privately owned resources within the province.

Section 92A of the constitution, added in 1982, affirms provincial jurisdiction over the exploration, development, conservation, and management of non-renewable natural resources, as well as forestry and sites and facilities for generation of hydroelectricity. Although the section gave the provinces important new powers to levy indirect taxes on those resources, in other respects, S.92A affirmed rather than extended well-established provincial jurisdiction over natural resources.[12] In any case, the section has limited impact on environmental protection since, with the exception of forestry and hydro sites, renewable resources were consciously excluded.[13]

Although provincial proprietary and legislative powers with respect to the environment are extensive, they are nonetheless constrained in several respects. First, the heads of power in Section 92 all contain a caveat limiting provincial powers to matters within the province. A province cannot pass laws primarily intended to have extraprovincial effect.[14] Thus, it has no legal capacity to control sources of environmental contaminants beyond its borders that affect the quality of the environment within the province.

Second, the provinces cannot legislate in areas of exclusive federal authority. However, provincial legislation will be found invalid only if the courts consider it to be primarily concerned with a matter within the exclusive jurisdiction of the federal government. In light of the breadth of provincial legislative and proprietary jurisdiction with respect to natural resources, federal jurisdiction seldom has prevented the provinces from passing legislation to protect the environment. However, exclusive federal control over certain subjects, such as harbours and airports, can create lacunae in provincial regulatory strategies.

Federal immunity from provincial laws presents a third restriction on provincial authority. Although the extent of interjurisdictional immunity remains unclear, the courts have tended to grant the federal government and its undertakings greater immunity from provincial and municipal laws than vice versa.[15]

Federal preeminence is a fourth restriction on provincial authority. In the event of a conflict, provincial laws must yield to federal law, even if both are supported by valid constitutional authority. However, it is noteworthy that the courts have adopted a relatively narrow interpretation of 'conflict' in the environmental field. For instance, it is not considered a conflict if the two levels of governments establish different effluent standards, since the existence of more stringent standards established by one jurisdiction does not prevent compliance with the weaker standards of the other.[16] Although federal preeminence thus does not prevent the provinces from promulgating environmental standards stricter than those of the federal government, more stringent federal standards nevertheless could frustrate a provincial government's intent if its own weaker standards were designed to strike a particular balance between competing environmental and economic objectives. At the extreme, if a province chooses to exercise its jurisdiction by exploiting rather than protecting natural resources, concurrent federal environmental standards could be a severe impediment to provincial policy objectives.

Unlike the limits to provincial powers discussed above, which concern federal constraints on the provinces' autonomy, the fifth restriction is imposed by the legal claims of provincial residents. All provinces except Quebec are subject to certain citizens' rights of access to natural resources under common law.[17] The Charter of Rights and Freedoms, which applies in all provinces, also may limit governments' prerogatives with respect to environmental protection. Although it appears unlikely that the courts would interpret the Charter so as to create a substantive right to a clean environment, rights to due process granted by the Charter may be used by polluters charged with environmental offenses.[18]

Sources of Federal Authority

Unlike the 'property and civil rights' clause, which gives the provinces extensive regulatory powers concerning the environment, the federal government's environmental jurisdiction is more indirect and uncertain. However, in light of the ubiquity of impacts of human activity on the environment, some authority over the environment is associated with almost every federal head of power.

Federal Proprietary Powers

Like the provinces, the federal government has extensive powers with respect to its own property. In addition to its proprietary powers to conserve or exploit federal Crown resources, Section 91(1A) grants the federal government authority to legislate with respect to its own resources. (The section is comparable to Section 92(5), which grants the provinces authority to legislate with respect to their own property.) Federal ownership is most extensive offshore[19] and in the territories, where the federal government's authority is comparable to that of the provinces within their borders. Various laws, including the Arctic Waters Pollution Prevention Act and the Northern Inland Waters Act, rely on those proprietary powers. However, as noted in Chapter 1, since the primary focus of this book is on federal environmental policy within the provinces, federal environmental protection activities offshore and in the territories are not examined in any depth in the following chapters.

Federal property within the provinces is much less significant than in the North. Section 108 of the constitution grants the federal government ownership of assets such as canals and harbours.[20] In addition, other federal properties, including park lands, have been acquired since Confederation. The federal government formally has exercised its proprietary powers with respect to these holdings in a number of statutes that prohibit pollution of harbours and parks.[21] However, the fact that federal holdings are scattered throughout the provinces means that federal proprietary powers do not offer a basis for comprehensive efforts to protect the environment, except in the northern territories.

Federal Legislative Powers

Federal legislative powers can be divided into two categories: sectoral and global.[22] Sectoral powers to protect the environment are associated with federal authority over specific subject areas, such as fisheries, navigation, and agriculture. Environmental authority associated with these powers is circumscribed because it must relate to the specific subject at hand. Global heads of power have the potential to support a more far-reaching federal role in environmental protection by virtue of touching on a broader range of activities or subjects. The most important of those are federal authority with respect to criminal law and trade and commerce, as well as the residual power to make laws concerning 'Peace, Order, and good Government.'

Sectoral Powers

Section 91(12) gives the federal government exclusive legislative jurisdiction with respect to 'Sea Coast and Inland Fisheries.' The section authorizes the federal government to adopt measures to preserve fish and fish habitat, providing the federal government with an important opportunity to regulate water pollution. Although the courts have been careful to ensure that federal pollution control efforts under the Fisheries Act maintain a close connection to the federal fisheries power,[23] the fact that most waters are frequented by fish and, with few exceptions, water pollutants are harmful to fish, nevertheless gives the federal government considerable authority to control water pollution through its fisheries power. In practice, the federal government has relied heavily on its fisheries power to accomplish environmental objectives. Indeed, Thompson observes that 'protection of fish and fish habitat became the surrogate in Canada for federal protection of the environment.'[24]

In the early years of Confederation, constitutional references to the Privy Council were employed on several occasions to resolve conflicts between federal and provincial powers over fisheries.[25] Since the federal government has relied heavily on its fisheries jurisdiction in controlling water pollution, the accommodation eventually reached between federal and provincial jurisdiction concerning fisheries has important implications for federal powers over environmental protection and thus merits further attention here.

The essence of the problem is that although the constitution grants the federal government authority to regulate fisheries, it simultaneously grants the provinces, as owners of the beds of water bodies, extensive ownership rights to the fish themselves.[26] The combination of federal legislative and provincial proprietary powers concerning fisheries creates practical difficulties. For instance, although the federal government can specify a maximum catch, only the provinces have the authority to implement that limit by allocating fishing licenses. This problem was largely resolved when the federal government delegated administrative authority with respect to inland fisheries to all provinces but Nova Scotia, Newfoundland, and Prince Edward Island through a series of federal-provincial agreements. Parisien argues that the federal government's willingness to cede its administrative authority not only reflects the awkwardness of the separation of powers, but also the fact that only the provinces' jurisdiction offered the potential to generate revenues.[27]

Divided jurisdiction presents less of a problem in tidal waters, where federal legislative powers are not constrained by provincial ownership of resources.[28] This has led to different accommodations of federal and provincial powers in fresh and salt water. The federal government has retained complete control over coastal fisheries, as well as anadromous species (i.e., those like salmon that spend their adult lives in the ocean but migrate inland to spawn) in both fresh and salt water. In provinces where there is a federal-provincial agreement, federal and provincial officials divide their inland jurisdiction according to the type of fish at issue: 'federal fish' (anadromous species) or 'provincial fish' (all others). Since the federal government has relied heavily on its jurisdiction over fisheries to accomplish its water pollution control objectives, in practice this division of federal and provincial responsibilities concerning fisheries has carried through to the field of environmental protection, with the federal government playing a larger role in water pollution control wherever 'federal fish' are present.

Several other sectoral powers are relevant to environmental protection, though none compare in significance to the fisheries power. The federal government has exclusive authority with respect to 'Navigation and Shipping' under Section 91(10). As interpreted by the courts, the section supports a federal role in any body of water that can be navigated or made navigable.[29] The federal government thus has veto power over dams, bridges, and other developments that might affect the flow of water or otherwise obstruct navigation. However, the navigation and shipping power has limited utility with respect to pollution control, although jurisdiction over shipping does grant the federal government authority to regulate air and water pollution from vessels.

Section 132 of the constitution gives the federal government legislative authority to implement treaties entered into by the British Empire on Canada's behalf. A 1937 decision of the Privy Council held that the section does not provide federal authority to implement international treaties negotiated by Canada as a sovereign country.[30] However, there has been speculation (discussed below) that authority to implement newer treaties concerning international environmental matters might be found within the federal power to make laws for the 'Peace, Order, and good Government' of Canada. Two 'Empire treaties' with relevance to environmental protection are the Migratory Birds Convention and the International Boundary Waters Treaty. The latter's provision that neither the United States nor Canada shall pollute boundary waters to the injury of health or property in the other country could be a potent regulatory weapon for the federal government. But, in practice the implementing legislation carries little practical force as it does not confer responsibility on any federal department or agency to actually ensure that the treaty's obligations are met.[31]

Section 95 establishes concurrent federal and provincial jurisdiction with respect to agriculture, subject to federal preeminence. The power is important because it establishes federal authority to regulate pesticides, a significant source of environmental contamination. Section 91(24), which establishes federal jurisdiction with respect to 'Indians, and Lands reserved for the Indians,' gives the federal government regulatory control over reserve lands and indirect jurisdiction over projects off-reserve that have environmental impacts on Aboriginal peoples. Section 91(6), establishing federal power over 'The Census and Statistics,' authorizes federal research and environmental monitoring, and probably also confers federal powers to compel individuals or firms to release information relevant to environmental protection.[32] Finally, Section 92(10)(a) gives the federal government exclusive authority with respect to interprovincial 'Works and Undertakings.' It is the basis for federal jurisdiction over interprovincial transport, and thus, would support federal environmental regulations concerning trucking companies and railways. However, since water bodies and the air that cross provincial boundaries are not considered 'works' in the constitutional sense, the section does not confer broader powers over transboundary environmental problems.

Although in general the federal government has formally exercised the environmental jurisdiction associated with its sectoral and proprietary powers by passing legislation, it has not done so aggressively. With the exception of the fisheries power, responsibility for implementing legislation based on these powers generally has been left to line departments, such as agriculture and transport, which have objectives that are tangential if not antithetical to environmental protection. As a result, the impact to date of sectorally based environmental legislation has been limited at best.

Global Powers

Federal heads of power that have the potential to support a more far-reaching role include trade and commerce, criminal law, taxation, spending, and 'Peace, Order and good Government.' The federal power over international and interprovincial trade and commerce under Section 91(2) could support a strong federal role in the control of toxic substances. The clause has been given more expansive interpretation by the courts in recent years, suggesting that it could buttress the federal role in environmental protection.[33] For instance, in *National Leasing Ltd.* v. *General Motors of Canada Ltd.*, the Supreme Court upheld a federal regulatory regime on the grounds that exclusive provincial jurisdiction could result in havens for unfair competition. While the case did not concern environmental regulation, application of similar logic to the environmental field suggests that the courts may also be willing to countenance federal environmental regulations to preclude provincial 'pollution havens.'[34]

The Supreme Court's 1994 *Grand Council of Crees* decision directly addresses the issue of environmental jurisdiction associated with the trade and commerce power.[35] The case concerned the authority of the National Energy Board (NEB) to grant Hydro Quebec a license to export power from the planned second phase of its James Bay development subject to two conditions: that the project be subjected to an environmental assessment prior to construction, in accordance with federal procedures, and that the completed facility comply with all relevant federal environmental standards and guidelines. The Supreme Court upheld the conditional license over the objections of Hydro Quebec and the Attorney General of Quebec.

The *Grand Council of Crees* decision indicates that federal environmental authority associated with the trade and commerce power is indeed broad. Following the precedent of *Oldman Dam*, discussed below, the Court condoned federal reliance on the trade and commerce power to pursue environmental objectives. Moreover, the Court condoned NEB's imposition of environmental conditions on the entire project, even though only part of the power was to be exported, and even though the Court acknowledged that the project would eventually be built anyway to satisfy domestic demand. The decision implies that the federal government may have authority to impose environmental criteria, not just on hydroelectric facilities, but on a wide range of manufacturing facilities that export even a fraction of their products internationally or interprovincially.

To date, the federal government has relied on the trade and commerce power to regulate fuel additives, automobile emissions, and phosphates in detergents. However, Mellon and her co-authors argue that the effectiveness of federal efforts to control auto emissions has been hampered because the federal government has relied exclusively on its trade and commerce power, rather than asserting broader authority under 'Peace, Order, and good Government' given the transboundary nature of automobile emissions. As it stands, federal regulations only apply to manufacturers or importers of new automobiles, leaving regulation of emissions from vehicles in use to the provinces.[36]

Section 91(3) establishes unlimited federal taxation powers. Taxation can be used as an environmental policy instrument by federal or provincial governments in two ways: tax exemptions and credits can be offered as subsidies to encourage environmentally sound behaviour, and emission fees can be used as a regulatory tool to discourage undesirable behaviour. Federal reliance on taxation powers could be overruled as an invasion of provincial jurisdiction, however, if the courts perceive the real intent of federal taxation to be pollution control, rather than generation of revenues. (On the other hand, provincial emission fees could be found invalid if the courts perceive them as a form of indirect tax, rather than as an exercise of provincial jurisdiction over 'property and civil rights.') In this respect, pollution taxes are probably more constitutionally vulnerable than tax expenditures, since recipients of subsidies are less likely to challenge their constitutional validity than are those subject to new taxes.

The federal taxation power has been used on occasion to subsidize pollution abatement. For instance, in 1965, accelerated depreciation of pollution control equipment was first authorized under the Income Tax Regulations. However, 'pollution taxes' have never been used as a regulatory instrument by the federal government, though they have been authorized since 1970 under the Canada Water Act.

Closely related to federal taxation powers is the controversial federal spending power. Although not explicitly mentioned in the constitution, the spending power is often justified on the basis of a combination of unlimited federal powers of taxation, federal proprietary powers, and the federal government's authority to legislate with respect to its own assets. To date, the spending power has been used to support Environment Canada's extensive environmental monitoring and research activities. The power of the purse also has been used to provide loans or subsidies for pollution abatement directly to polluters. Municipalities were first offered forgivable loans for sewage treatment facilities in 1961. Federal grants and loans for pollution abatement have also been provided to the pulp and paper industry and non-ferrous smelters. However, in striking contrast to the US federal government, the Canadian federal government has not subsidized provincial administration of environmental programs, either conditionally or unconditionally. Although the federal spending power has been used to support the federal government's own programs and to subsidize polluters, it has not been used to strong-arm the provinces.

Section 91(27) of the constitution gives the federal government exclusive authority with respect to 'Criminal Law.' While allowing Parliament considerable scope to define criminal activity, the courts nevertheless insist that the subject of legislation based on S.91(27) be 'essentially criminal.' Parliament cannot 'invade the proper sphere of the provincial legislature by simply adopting the guise or disguise of criminal legislation.'[37] However, there are indications that the courts would consider threats to public health resulting from environmental contamination to be an appropriate matter for the criminal law. Relying on the criminal law power, the Supreme Court upheld both the federal Hazardous Products

Act[38] and a federal statute to prevent adulteration of foods, suggesting that the Court might be equally willing to uphold criminal penalties for 'adulteration' of the environment.[39]

The criminal law power is limited in several respects as a basis for environmental protection, however. First, the constitutional boundaries of 'criminal' behaviour are unclear. It is not known whether the courts would consider only wanton acts of pollution that directly endanger health to be criminal behaviour, or whether commonplace activities that merely contribute to public health hazards also would be considered appropriate matters for regulation under the criminal law power.

Second, the federal government may be constrained by the availability of policy instruments under the criminal law power. The criminal law power is usually described as 'prohibitive' rather than 'regulatory,' on the grounds that behaviour that is truly criminal would be prohibited rather than merely restricted.[40] However, Franson and Lucas argue that, because the Supreme Court has upheld federal authority under the criminal law power to establish legal schemes to prevent crime as well as to punish criminals, 'most practical pollution control schemes could probably be brought within this holding.'[41]

Third, reliance on the criminal law presents a number of enforcement problems. Remedies available under the criminal law are limited to criminal rather than civil sanctions, creating the prospect of 'overkill' for relatively minor offenses.[42] In addition, the high standard of proof required in criminal law, where the prosecution must establish guilt 'beyond a reasonable doubt,' is problematic in environmental cases, where there typically is a high degree of scientific uncertainty.[43] For that reason, Thompson argues that the civil law criterion of 'balance of probabilities' is a more appropriate standard of proof for environmental law.[44]

Finally, although the criminal law power establishes relatively clear authority with respect to environmental threats to public health, its utility is less clear with respect to protection of the quality of environment for commercial uses or protection of aesthetic values. Despite its limitations and uncertainties, the authority to control hazards to human health afforded by the criminal law power nevertheless makes it an important weapon in the federal environmental arsenal. The federal government's willingness to use its criminal law power for purposes of environmental regulation is discussed in some detail in subsequent chapters.

The Limits of Peace, Order, and Good Government
The extent of federal authority with respect to the environment under the residual power to make laws for 'the Peace, Order, and good Government

of Canada' is 'notoriously controversial.'[45] In interpreting the preamble of Section 91, the courts have relied on two doctrines. The national emergency doctrine has been used to uphold far-reaching federal jurisdiction during times of national crisis. In contrast, the courts have relied on the national concern doctrine in granting the federal government authority over matters not mentioned among the listed heads of power, but considered by the courts to be 'beyond local or provincial concerns or interests [which] must from [their] inherent nature be the concern of the Dominion as a whole.'[46]

Under the national emergency doctrine, the federal government clearly would have extensive, though only temporary, powers in the event of an environmental crisis of national or international proportions. However, as Gibson argues, 'the courts are not likely to cry "emergency" as often as the ecologists.'[47] Despite high levels of public concern, it is doubtful that the courts would find current environmental conditions to constitute a national emergency.

A debate over the extent of federal authority over the environment afforded by the national concern doctrine has raged since environment issues rose to prominence in the late 1960s. In the absence of judicial clarification, speculation has been rampant. Although there is consensus that Section 91 provides support for some federal involvement in environmental protection, there is substantial disagreement over the extent of federal authority.

Air pollution does not respect political borders, ocean waters and many river systems are interjurisdictional, and toxic substances migrate through the food chain and the environment, without regard to political jurisdiction. This physical mobility of pollutants has led many to conclude that environmental protection is a coherent subject that is inherently a 'national concern,' thus justifying a federal response to a wide range of environmental problems.[48]

Other scholars, particularly those from Quebec, envision a more limited federal role confined to discrete interjurisdictional environmental problems. They argue that pollution control normally is a local or provincial matter, most appropriately the subject of provincial jurisdiction over 'property and civil rights.'[49] Lederman, among others, argues that pollution control simply does not have sufficient 'factual unity' to be treated as a single subject under the national concern doctrine.[50] Underlying many authors' caution is a fear that assignment of a subject so pervasive as the environment to the federal government would allow the federal government to dominate many of the enumerated provincial powers in Section 92. Thus, Beaudoin argues that 'recourir a la théorie de l'intérêt national en matière de lutte anti-pollution c'est accepter l'avènement de l'état uni-taire à plus ou moins court terme.'[51]

The strongest argument for federal jurisdiction clearly can be made in the case of interjurisdictional pollution. With respect to international environmental matters, the weakness of federal treaty powers under Section 132 has generated scholarly interest in potential federal powers to implement international agreements under the 'Peace, Order, and good Government' clause. Gibson argues that the existence of an international treaty might be taken as evidence that a subject is a matter of national concern, an argument indirectly given support by the Supreme Court in the *Crown Zellerbach* case (discussed below).[52]

Trends in the international environmental agenda thus may have important implications for the federal government's role. During the 1970s, North American attention shifted from discrete, local incidents of transboundary pollution to regional transboundary problems, such as acid rain and Great Lakes pollution. More recently, international attention has turned to global environmental problems, such as global warming and deterioration of the ozone layer. If a federal treaty power concerning trans-boundary environmental problems can be supported by the 'Peace, Order, and good Government' clause, the emergence of global environmental concerns could have important ramifications not only for the extent of federal involvement in environmental protection, but for the fundamen-tal division of powers. Attempts to address global warming, for example, could entail policy responses that touch on most aspects of life in indus-trialized societies, many of which now fall within provincial jurisdiction.

With respect to transboundary environmental concerns within Canada, jurisdiction over interprovincial waters has received the most scholarly attention. While some legal scholars are convinced that water quality in interprovincial rivers is beyond the competence of any single province, and therefore properly within federal jurisdiction,[53] others are reluctant to draw conclusions in the absence of clearer signals from the courts.[54] Most commentators agree that some federal role is justified to prevent or regu-late interprovincial spillovers. However, that leaves many questions unanswered. Is federal authority limited to control of individual sources that can be shown to have an adverse impact on another jurisdiction? Or does the very fact that a river is interprovincial justify federal regulation of all discharges into it? If so, would federal authority extend to the entire drainage basin of which an interprovincial river is a small part, on the grounds that contaminants are mobile throughout the basin?

Some scholars have argued in favour of federal jurisdiction even with respect to resources entirely contained within provincial borders. For instance, Gibson stresses not the physical mobility of pollutants, but the economic mobility of polluters. He argues that protection of the environment could be considered a 'national concern' because provinces that must compete for investment by polluting industries are incapable of unilaterally protecting the environment within their borders.[55] In effect, he asserts that the threat of an interprovincial race to the bottom is sufficient constitutional justification for federal involvement.

Judicial Interpretation of Peace, Order, and Good Government

There are surprisingly few indications of how the courts interpret federal powers under the 'Peace, Order, and good Government' clause. With respect to air quality, in 1982, the Manitoba Queen's Bench relied on the national concern doctrine in upholding federal regulations issued under the Clean Air Act concerning emission of air pollutants. The Court held that because air contaminants do not respect provincial boundaries, control of air quality clearly is a matter beyond private or local concern.[56] It is noteworthy that the Court did not demand proof that individual sources affected by the regulations had interprovincial impacts; rather, the Court found the entire subject of air pollution control to be within federal jurisdiction under 'Peace, Order, and good Government.' The Court also found the regulations supportable under the federal criminal law power, on the grounds that the intent was to control hazards to public health, even though the approach was clearly regulatory rather than prohibitive. The Court's generosity is noteworthy since, as discussed in Chapter 4, the federal government studiously avoided reliance on 'Peace, Order, and good Government' in drafting the act.

With respect to water quality, Rueggeberg and Thompson observe that 'the field of interprovincial water law is as yet "up for grabs" in Canada.'[57] To date, there has been only one relevant Supreme Court case with confusing multiple judgements. The 1975 *Interprovincial Co-operatives* decision concerned the constitutionality of a Manitoba statute that purported to establish liability for acts of pollution committed in Ontario and Saskatchewan that had detrimental effects in Manitoba.[58] Since the question before the Court concerned the constitutionality of provincial rather than federal actions, the Court did not directly address the limits of the federal government's jurisdiction. However, each of the written judgments indirectly addressed the question of federal authority in interjurisdictional waters.

A narrow majority found the Manitoba statute to be ultra vires. Three justices concluded that Manitoba could not legislate with respect to actions committed in another province because the matter of interprovincial pollution falls exclusively within federal jurisdiction under the 'Peace, Order, and good Government' power. The willingness of these three judges to confer such broad authority on the federal government is striking; the argument of exclusive federal jurisdiction was not advanced by either side in the dispute nor by any of the intervenors, including the federal government itself.[59] In fact, the federal government joined Ontario and Quebec in arguing in favour of provincial jurisdiction![60]

The other member of the majority expressed concern with the apparently limitless federal role in interprovincial waters foreseen by his colleagues. However, even he alluded to an extensive federal role in stating that 'the overall authority seized with the regulation and control of pollution in interprovincial waters ... rests with Parliament.'[61] Although the three dissenting judges would have upheld the Manitoba statute, they too hinted at a substantial concurrent federal role in stating that, 'if any regulatory authority to have interprovincial effect is to exist in respect of pollution of interprovincial waters, it would have to be established under federal legislation.'[62]

The 1988 *Crown Zellerbach* decision by the Supreme Court concerning pollution of coastal waters offers further evidence of the Court's willingness to rely on the national concern doctrine. In a four to three decision, the Court upheld a federal regulatory scheme to control ocean dumping authorized by the Ocean Dumping Control Act, after finding marine pollution to be a valid matter of national concern.[63] The case provided a stark test of federal powers under 'Peace, Order, and good Government' since a previous decision had determined that the bed of the watercourse in question, Johnstone Strait, belongs to the province of British Columbia.

The majority decision, delivered by Justice LeDain, enunciated two tests for the national concern doctrine. First, a matter must have 'singleness, distinctiveness and indivisibility' clearly distinguishing it from matters of provincial concern. In assessing a matter's 'singleness,' LeDain's decision suggests that it is relevant to consider the potential for extraprovincial impacts should individual provinces fail to adequately address a problem. Second, a finding of federal jurisdiction must have a 'scale of impact on provincial jurisdiction that is reconcilable with the fundamental distribution of legislative power under the Constitution.'[64] The majority concluded, with surprisingly little discussion, that the subject of marine pollution met the first test. For this they faced heavy criticism from the dissenting opinion.[65] Nor did they dwell on the second test, concerning the scale of impact on the division of powers, even though the decision would appear to grant exclusive control of marine pollution to the federal government.[66]

The dissent, written by Justice LaForest, is wary of the impact on the distribution of powers of assigning the federal government powers over environmental protection under the auspices of the 'Peace, Order, and good Government' clause. LaForest rejects the majority's conclusion concerning the distinctiveness of marine pollution in light of the interrelatedness of ecosystems, and argues that, since all physical activities have some environmental impact, allocating matters of environmental protection to the federal government 'would effectively gut provincial legislative jurisdiction.'[67]

Although the minority would have struck down the federal legislation, the dissenting opinion nevertheless envisions substantial federal jurisdiction with respect to the environment. Consistent with his earlier scholarly publications, LaForest does not question federal authority to regulate pollution in inland waters if there are extraprovincial impacts.[68] Moreover, LaForest offers a generous reading of previous decisions, including the *Interprovincial Co-operatives* and *Canada Metal* cases, noting that 'a combination of the federal legislative power and the criminal power could go a long way toward prohibiting the pollution of internal waters as well as those in territorial waters and the high seas.'[69] He continues, 'in fact, as I see it, the potential breadth of federal power to control pollution by use of its general power is so great that even without resort to the specific argument made by the appellant, the constitutional challenge in the end may be the development of judicial strategies to confine its ambit.'[70]

Does the *Crown Zellerbach* decision indicate that the courts will use the national concern doctrine to find federal jurisdiction over environmental matters? Lucas concludes that 'large chunks of the broad "environment" subject now appear to be fair game for federal legislators.'[71] Elsewhere he argues that the decision 'opens the way for a back door federal approach to regulation of provincial natural resource development, conservation and management.'[72] While a single decision cannot fully elucidate the scope of federal jurisdiction under the 'Peace, Order, and good Government' clause, the *Crown Zellerbach* case does indicate the Supreme Court's willingness to concede federal powers with respect to international and interprovincial pollution. Furthermore, it demonstrates the Court's willingness to turn to the 'Peace, Order, and good Government' power in exploring the limits of federal authority with respect to the environment, rather than confining its review to the federal government's more circumscribed sectoral powers.

Perhaps the most significant constitutional case to date has been the 1992 Supreme Court decision concerning the Oldman River dam. At issue was a federal regulation concerning environmental impact assessments.

The federal government first began to perform environmental assessments in 1974. However, federal policy was not codified in regulations until 1984, when the Environmental Impact Assessment and Review Process (EARP) Guidelines Order was issued under the authority of the Department of the Environment Act. The intent of the EARP Guidelines Order was to ensure that the government's own projects, those that receive substantial federal government funding, and those that could have an impact on an area of federal responsibility, such as fisheries or navigation, were subjected to an early and thorough environmental review. The regulation thus relied on a variety of federal powers, including sectoral and proprietary powers and the spending power.

In a landmark 1989 case, environmental groups were successful in asking the court to force the federal government to perform an environmental assessment of the Rafferty and Alameda dams being built by the Saskatchewan government on the Souris river.[73] The Federal Court ruled that because a federal license was required for the project, the Souris being an international river, the federal government was required by the terms of its own EARP Guidelines Order to perform an environmental review. The federal government previously had assumed that it could exercise discretion in interpreting its own regulation. Although the government's flexible intent was indicated by the use of the word 'Guidelines' in the title of the EARP regulation, the appearance of the word shall (as in 'the Minister shall') throughout the regulation was the basis for the Court's more forceful interpretation. In effect, the Court ruled that the government had chosen to regulate itself, however unintentionally, and that it therefore must abide by its own regulation.

Soon after that decision, the Federal Court of Appeal adopted a similar approach in a case concerning the Oldman River dam, which was being constructed by the province of Alberta.[74] However, in the *Oldman Dam* case, the Court extended the *Rafferty-Alameda* decision in concluding that, even though no federal license was required from the Department of Fisheries and Oceans for the project, the federal government nevertheless was required to perform an environmental assessment under the terms of its Guidelines Order, because the development would affect fish habitat, an area of exclusive federal jurisdiction. In light of the potential for almost any project to impinge on some area of federal jurisdiction, the effect of the *Oldman* decision was to greatly extend the conditions under which federal environmental reviews could be considered mandatory. (The profound political implications of this decision are examined in Chapter 6.)

The province of Alberta subsequently appealed the *Oldman Dam* decision to the Supreme Court. The provinces of Quebec, New Brunswick,

British Columbia, Saskatchewan, and Newfoundland intervened in support of Alberta, while Manitoba and the Northwest Territories argued in support of federal involvement. The case raised a number of questions of administrative law. Particularly notable was the issue of whether the federal government was in fact compelled to comply with its own regulation.[75] On that question alone, the federal government joined with Alberta in the appeal. In response, the majority's decision, which was delivered by Justice LaForest on behalf of seven of eight Supreme Court justices, did restrict the scope of the lower court decision somewhat.[76] Although the Supreme Court held that the Minister of Transport was bound to comply with the EARP regulation, the Court reversed the Appeals Court's similar finding concerning the Minister of Fisheries, holding that the EARP Guidelines Order applies only if a minister has an 'affirmative duty' to make a discrete regulatory decision.

Of greater import to this chapter, the *Oldman Dam* case also raised significant constitutional issues concerning both sectoral and global authority over the environment. Alberta, joined by Newfoundland, New Brunswick, British Columbia, Quebec, and Saskatchewan, argued that the EARP regulation overstepped the constitutional authority of the federal government. Following Lederman's example, those provinces argued that environmental protection does not have sufficient 'factual unity' to justify federal intervention under the 'Peace, Order, and good Government' clause. With respect to enumerated powers, the provinces depicted the EARP Guidelines Order as a 'constitutional Trojan horse,' through which the federal government sought to invade exclusive provincial jurisdiction under the pretext of narrow fields of jurisdiction, such as fisheries and navigation. Interestingly, Manitoba and the Northwest Territories, both of which are situated downstream of the Alberta dam, argued in support of federal jurisdiction.

The Court was unanimous on the constitutional questions, even though Justice Stevenson disagreed with his colleagues on questions of administrative law. Given the scope of the decision, it is perhaps not surprising that conflicting interpretations of its implications have been offered. It is generally agreed that in upholding the EARP Guidelines Order, the Supreme Court embraced a broad view of the environment. The decision asserted that 'quite simply, the environment comprises all that is around us and as such must be a part of what actuates many decisions of any moment.'[77] The Court rejected the characterization offered by the Alberta government that the dam was a 'provincial project' by virtue of being 'primarily subject to provincial regulation.'[78] Instead, the Court affirmed that the environment is too broad to be considered a coherent subject of jurisdiction belonging to either the federal or provincial level of government; rather, environmental authority is associated to varying degrees with both provincial and federal heads of power. There is disagreement among legal scholars, however, as to whether or not the Court demonstrated willingness to broadly interpret environmental authority associated with particular federal powers.[79]

Kennett offers an incisive synthesis of these competing views.[80] He argues that the Supreme Court in fact envisioned two types of environmental authority associated with individual heads of power: comprehensive and restrictive. 'Comprehensive environmental authority' arises when one order of government has jurisdiction over an activity. That authority may be explicit, as in the case of shipping, or implied, as in the case of operation of interprovincial railways, which is implied by jurisdiction over interprovincial works and undertakings. With respect to comprehensive environmental authority, while the Court paid lip service to the traditional requirement that federal actions must be linked 'in pith and substance' to a particular head of power, it nonetheless adopted a surprisingly generous standard for what constitutes sufficient relevance in arguing that 'it is sufficient that the legislative body legislate on that subject. The practical purpose that inspires the legislation and the implications that body must consider in making its decision are another thing.'[81]

While adopting a generous view of federal jurisdiction associated with 'comprehensive' jurisdiction, the Court was more cautious in interpreting 'restrictive' jurisdiction, which Kennett characterizes as arising when an activity not falling directly within a government's jurisdiction nonetheless has environmental implications for an area of jurisdiction that is within that government's competence. In that case, the environmental jurisdiction is necessarily indirect and limited to consideration of impacts on areas of valid jurisdiction. Thus, since dam building, unlike shipping, is not an activity that falls constitutionally to the federal government, the federal government can only consider a range of environmental impacts of a dam that are relevant to areas of federal jurisdiction, such as fisheries, Aboriginal lands, and navigation. This aspect of the *Oldman* decision is consistent with earlier judicial interpretations of federal environmental authority associated with the fisheries power.[82]

The *Oldman* decision thus adopts a generous interpretation of federal (and provincial) environmental jurisdiction in the sense that it concedes that direct jurisdiction over a particular activity brings with it extensive authority to regulate environmental aspects of that activity. (That generosity subsequently was given additional emphasis by the Supreme Court's interpretation of environmental authority associated with the trade and commerce power in the *Grand Council of Crees* decision.) On the other hand, the *Oldman* decision adheres to past decisions in arguing that if jurisdiction is only indirect (i.e., the activity itself does not fall within a government's jurisdiction), the courts will be vigilant in ensuring that a government considers only the environmental impacts of that activity relevant to its own jurisdiction. Interestingly, the same head of power, whether sectoral or global, may give rise to both comprehensive and restricted environmental jurisdiction.[83] For instance, associated with the 'sea coast and inland fisheries' power, the federal government would have comprehensive authority to regulate environmental implications of fishing, but only restrictive authority to regulate activities that have an impact on fish and fish habitat.

It is ironic that although Alberta's factum quoted liberally from Justice LaForest's dissent in the *Crown Zellerbach* case, it was LaForest who delivered the majority decision in the *Oldman Dam* case, which readily dismissed the province's arguments. In some respects the Court once again offered a more expansive interpretation of the federal government's powers than did the federal government itself. The federal government's own factum did not stress federal authority to perform environmental assessments under the 'Peace, Order, and good Government' power. In contrast, both the Manitoba government and the respondent Friends of the *Oldman* River Society envisioned broad federal authority under the residual power, the latter arguing that 'it is neither possible nor desirable to constrain an environmental impact analysis within a "division of powers" strait jacket.'[84] Although the Court did not dwell on the issue, its comment in passing that 'in any event, [the Guidelines Order] falls within the purely residuary aspect of the 'Peace, Order and good Government' power'[85] may have been the most chilling statement in the entire decision from the dissenting provinces' perspective.

It warrants emphasis that the expansion of the federal role in environmental assessment in the *Rafferty-Alameda* and *Oldman Dam* cases was not the result of a federal power grab. Rather, at the behest of environmental groups, the courts thrust jurisdiction upon a reluctant federal government. The federal government's unwillingness to use even uncontested powers, such as fisheries and navigation, to exert leverage over provincial environmental protection efforts was underscored by the fact that it took a court decision to force the federal government to comply with its own environmental assessment guidelines.[86] Indeed, Canadians were given a rare opportunity to see a federal minister at a loss for words because he was granted more extensive powers vis-à-vis the provinces than he had sought.[87]

The Supreme Court has yet to rule on whether the fact that toxic substances migrate through the environment and food chain justifies federal involvement under either 'Peace, Order, and good Government' or the criminal law power. An opportunity to do so may arise in the near future. In 1991, a Quebec trial court ruled that a federal regulation to control PCBs, issued under the emergency provisions of the 1988 Canadian Environmental Protection Act, was not justified by either federal power.[88] The defendant, Hydro Quebec, was joined by the Quebec government in challenging the constitutionality of the federal statute. Citing *Crown Zellerbach*, the Court ruled that the problem of toxic substances entering the environment does not have sufficient 'singleness, distinctiveness, and indivisibility' to evoke the national concern doctrine. The Court also concluded that the statute's broad definition of toxicity, which encompasses both threats to public health and threats to the environment, does not maintain a sufficiently close connection to the criminal law power. The decision was upheld on appeal by the federal government to the Superior Court and the Quebec Court of Appeal.[89] The Supreme Court is scheduled to hear the case in late 1996.

Limitations of Federal Jurisdiction over the Environment
The constitution limits federal involvement in environmental protection in several respects. First, like the provinces, the federal government may face future limitations as a result of the Charter. Second, the federal government may have to contend with interjurisdictional immunity. However, the courts have tended to grant the federal government greater immunity from provincial legislation than vice versa.[90] Extensive provincial proprietary powers present a third barrier to federal involvement in the field of environmental protection. However, although the courts traditionally have been reluctant to allow federal legislative powers to interfere with provincial proprietary powers, a number of Supreme Court decisions since the 1970s suggest that the Court has relaxed its defence of provincial resources in recent years.

Fourth, while federal environmental jurisdiction associated with navigation, fisheries, and businesses subject to federal control is undisputed, it is limited to the particular subject in question. With the possible exception of the fisheries power, these sectoral heads of power cannot individually offer the basis for far-reaching environmental protection policies. However, the *Oldman Dam* decision demonstrated that sectoral powers nevertheless can be significant because they give the federal government the capacity to exert leverage over provincial environmental protection strategies. The federal government can strengthen weak provincial policies by refusing to grant licenses to water resource developments it deems unacceptable. On the other hand, the federal government can frustrate provincial environmental protection efforts by failing to regulate in an area, such as a harbour, which is under its exclusive control.

Fifth, the federal government could be constrained by the range of policy instruments available to it. It is unclear whether the federal government would be allowed to use its taxation power as a regulatory tool. Moreover, to the extent that the federal government and the courts rely solely on the criminal law as a basis for federal legislation, regulatory options may be limited.

However, the most important constraint on federal powers is uncertainty. The courts *might* find broad federal jurisdiction within the criminal law, trade and commerce, and 'Peace, Order, and good Government' powers, but few of the relevant issues have been resolved in the courts. It is understandable that the uncertain limits of federal powers would give federal decisionmakers pause. Nonetheless, several factors lend support to those who favour a strong federal role.

It is striking that on several occasions, the courts have appeared more than willing to grant the federal government substantial jurisdiction over environmental matters. In the *Crown Zellerbach* case, a majority of the Supreme Court accepted marine pollution as a matter of 'national concern' with surprisingly little discussion and apparently few reservations.[91] In *Interprovincial Co-operatives*, a plurality of the Court was willing to grant the federal government significantly greater authority than it had sought. And, in a series of cases concerning the federal government's role in environmental impact assessments, culminating in the *Oldman Dam* decision, the courts effectively thrust authority upon a reluctant federal government. In the *Oldman Dam* case the Court again adopted a more expansive interpretation of federal environmental jurisdiction than did the federal government itself.

Trends in scientific understanding of environmental matters also lend compelling support to the federal role under 'Peace, Order, and good Government.' Toxins from industrial processes have been detected in remote corners of the globe, attesting to the mobility of pollutants and the coherence of the ecosystem. The emergence of global environmental problems like the greenhouse effect and destruction of the ozone layer provides further evidence that environmental protection is not merely a local or provincial concern.

Conclusion

It is not surprising that the division of powers over such a large and complex subject as environmental protection entails considerable overlap. What is striking is the extent to which the limits of federal authority remain ill-defined more than twenty years after the first wave of environmentalism. The courts cannot be blamed for this persistent uncertainty – they have had remarkably few opportunities to clarify the extent of federal powers. In fact, when questions of jurisdiction have arisen, the courts have been quite generous in granting the federal government jurisdiction over environmental matters.

Constitutional uncertainty persists primarily because the federal government has taken a narrow view of its own powers. As Thompson notes, 'despite strong public pressure concerning individual environmental issues, the federal government has steadfastly refused to extend its jurisdiction to include environmental matters that are essentially contained within provincial boundaries even where there have been extra-provincial spillovers.'[92] The federal government has rarely tested the limits of its constitutional powers with respect to the environment. Prior to the recent EARP litigation, in which environmental groups successfully forced the federal government to exercise its environmental authority, even heads of power that afforded clear, albeit indirect or sectorally limited, federal involvement in environmental protection were not exercised to their fullest extent. And, although the federal government occasionally has been willing to take chances by passing legislation based on its global powers, it has shown little inclination to implement the more controversial provisions of those statutes.[93] As a result, opportunities for judicial clarification have not emerged. Rather than losing a battle for environmental jurisdiction in the courts, the federal government has conceded its jurisdiction without a fight.

The extent of constitutional uncertainty undoubtedly has contributed to federal hesitance. However, the fact that the federal government's willingness to assert jurisdiction has varied over time suggests that other factors are also significant. The influence of federal reluctance to confront the provinces, relative to shifts in electoral incentives in explaining federal reluctance, are explored in Chapters 4 to 6, which analyze the political context of the most significant federal environmental statutes adopted between 1969 and 1995.

4
The Emergence of Federal Involvement, 1969-72

The next three chapters trace the evolution of the federal government's role in environmental protection, and of federal-provincial relations concerning the environment over a period of two and a half decades, from 1969 to 1995. This chapter reviews the emergence of federal involvement between 1969 and 1972.

Public interest in the environment surged in the late 1960s. Consequently, federal politicians, who had long argued that pollution control was a provincial responsibility, began to take a broader view of their own jurisdiction. As a result, the federal government passed nine environmental statutes during this period, in addition to creating a Department of the Environment to administer them.[1] Thereafter, the salience of environmental issues declined, as did the level of federal involvement. Chapter 5 documents the federal retreat between 1973 and 1985, when responsibility for environmental protection shifted back to the provinces and the promise of the first generation of federal environmental statutes remained largely unfulfilled. Chapter 6 then traces the re-emergence of federal involvement as public interest again peaked during the late 1980s.

Each of the three chapters begins with an analysis of public opinion concerning the environment, followed by a review of the federal government's willingness to exercise its environmental jurisdiction, and discussion of federal-provincial relations during the period. Although Chapters 5 and 6 analyze federal assertions of jurisdiction at four levels – constitutional, legislative, regulatory, and enforcement – this chapter addresses only the legislative and constitutional levels, since there was little or no federal environmental legislation to implement prior to 1972.

The First Wave of Public Concern

In the preceding chapter, an argument was advanced about the nature of public attitudes toward the environment and the implications of those attitudes for public policy. It is thus of particular interest to examine the empirical evidence offered by public opinion surveys concerning environmental issues.

Public consciousness of pollution problems in the Western hemisphere grew throughout the 1960s, prompted by a series of high profile events, including discovery of the impact of DDT on wildlife and oil spills off the coast of England in 1967 and Santa Barbara in 1969. By 1970, Canadians were confronted by environmental problems closer to home, when the Arrow tanker ran aground in Chedabucto Bay (Nova Scotia) and mercury contamination of waterways prompted extensive fishing bans. These events occurred at the end of a period of sustained economic growth, and faced a generation that had grown up amid relative affluence.[2] The combined result was a dramatic surge at the end of the decade in the levels of public awareness and concern about pollution.

'Public opinion' concerning the environment is neither a straightforward concept nor a simple thing to measure. In particular, trends in public concern for the environment elicited by open- and closed-ended questions can suggest very different conclusions. Closed-ended questions, such as those which ask respondents to rank the severity of various environmental problems, measure the degree of public concern. Open-ended questions, such as 'what is the most important problem facing government today?' measure the salience of environmental issues. It bears emphasis that the two types of questions merely provide different measures of the same public's attitudes, with closed-ended questions indicating the extent of latent concern available to be mobilized, and open-ended questions indicating the extent to which such concern is already 'top of mind.'

Given the consensual character of environmental values – virtually everyone professes to be in favour of a clean environment – it is not surprising that a relatively high degree of concern for the environment can coexist with relatively low salience of environmental issues. An analogy to child abuse is illustrative. Although most people would be expected to favour strong policies against child abuse when expressly asked how they feel about the issue, child abuse is not among the political problems foremost on most people's minds. Most voters do not seek information on a candidate's position on child abuse prevention, nor lend much weight to the issue in the ballot booth. It is thus conceivable that a high degree of public concern and support for policy change can coexist with relatively low issue salience and inattention to what governments are actually doing.

As noted in this and the following chapters, environmental issues often have evoked a relatively high degree of concern in public opinion surveys, yet ranked quite low in terms of issue salience. This finding is consistent with the Olsonian portrayal in Chapter 2 of members of the public as rational actors. Because most people's interests in environmental quality are diffuse, the issue would not tend to be foremost in their minds. Rather, one would expect issues that have a much more immediate impact on individuals' lives, such as the cost of living, to be higher priorities. However, if reminded by a closed-ended question where their interests lie, members of the public would be expected to express strong support for environmental protection.

It is difficult, unfortunately, to reconstruct a detailed picture of long-term trends in Canadians' attitudes concerning the environment because there has been little sustained examination of the subject in public opinion surveys. Indeed, the frequency of questions concerning the environment in opinion polls may well be one of the best available indicators of the issue's salience. There are no Canadian data on the emergence of the pollution issue prior to 1970, but by the time the environment rose to prominence in the media, questions began to appear in opinion polls in time to document the issue's decline.

Gallup Canada first asked a series of closed-ended questions probing public attitudes about the severity of pollution in March 1970. That survey revealed an extraordinarily high level of awareness, with 91 per cent of respondents expressing at least some familiarity with the issue. Of those surveyed, 63 per cent considered pollution to be a 'very serious' problem.[3] Although the level of public awareness remained high and even increased over time, the degree of concern expressed by respondents answering this closed-ended question declined very gradually throughout the 1970s and early 1980s, before resurging in the late 1980s, as illustrated by Figure 4.1.

With respect to issue salience, more consistent data is available. Gallup Canada has asked variations of the open-ended question, 'what do you think is the most important problem facing the country today?' throughout the period of interest.[4] In the mid-1960s through December 1969, pollution was not even reported among the responses to this question. Rather, Canadians' top priorities in 1968 were inflation and the economy (24 per cent of respondents), and unemployment and labour unrest (22 per cent of respondents).[5] Unfortunately, Gallup did not ask the 'most important problem' question during the critical period

Figure 4.1

Trends in public concern for the environment

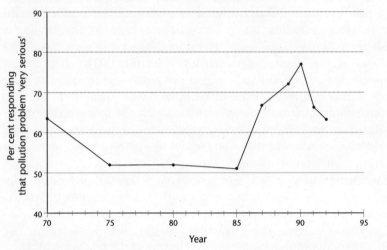

Figure 4.2

Trends in salience of environmental issues

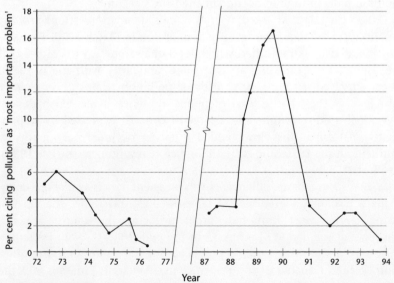

Source: Gallup Canada.
Note: Gallup did not report the per cent of respondents citing pollution as the nation's 'most important problem' between 1976 and 1987.
Source: Gallup Canada.

Figure 4.3

Rank of pollution among most important problems facing Canada

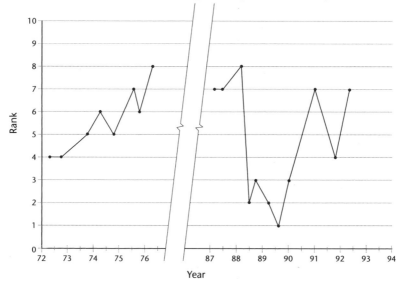

Year

Note: Gallup did not report the per cent of respondents citing pollution as the nation's 'most important problem' between 1976 and 1987.
Source: Gallup Canada

between 1969 and mid-1970, when media coverage and comparable US trends (both discussed below) suggest that the salience of the pollution issue likely peaked. However, Gallup did document the decline from 1972 onward. In April 1972, pollution was the fourth most frequently identified 'most important problem,' cited by 5 per cent of respondents.[6] As illustrated by Figures 4.2 and 4.3, the salience of the issue declined by April 1976 to an eighth place ranking, when only 0.6 per cent of the public cited it as the country's most important problem.[7] Thereafter, neither pollution or the environment were even mentioned by Gallup in relation to the 'most important problem' question until 1985.

As the pollution issue faded, economic concerns returned to the top of the public agenda. Indeed, the decline in the salience of pollution was a mirror image of the emergence of inflation as a political issue. Between September 1972 and October 1974, when public attention to the environment subsided, the proportion of Gallup respondents citing inflation as the country's most important problem rose from 37 to 82 per cent.[8]

Not surprisingly, closed-ended questions about voters' top priorities yield trends midway between the open-ended 'most important problem' question and the closed-ended questions concerning severity of environmental problems. When respondents are reminded about the environment by a list of suggested responses, they are more likely to identify it as a priority. Thus, Market Facts found that the fraction of respondents selecting water pollution as the most important problem facing the country from a list of choices fell from 18 per cent in August 1970, to 10 per cent in October 1971, and 9 per cent in June 1973.[9] It is noteworthy that the comparable figure in 1973 from Gallup's open-ended 'most important problem' question was only 4 per cent.

The environment also fared better when respondents were given an opportunity to identify more than one top priority. Gallup has occasionally included a question asking respondents to identify the three problems they considered most urgent from a list of problems. In December 1970, pollution was the single most frequently identified problem, selected by 65 per cent of respondents as one of the top three problems, followed by unemployment at 62 per cent and poverty at 35 per cent. The same question was asked in September 1976 and August 1982. By 1976, pollution was chosen by 35 per cent of respondents and had fallen to fifth place, behind inflation (65 per cent), unemployment (52 per cent), government spending (42 per cent), and crime (41 per cent). It was still in fifth place in 1982, but was selected then by only 22 per cent of those surveyed, following unemployment (79 per cent), inflation (75 per cent), government spending (59 per cent), and crime (35 per cent).[10]

In the latter two surveys respondents were asked, as a follow-up question, to indicate which of their three choices they felt was the most important problem. Pollution still ranked fifth in both years, chosen by 9.9 and 4.7 per cent in 1976 and 1982, respectively. However, again it is noteworthy that the percentage of those surveyed that identified pollution as their highest priority was significantly higher than indicated by responses to the same question when no list of choices was provided. During this period, pollution/environment was even not mentioned often enough to be coded among the responses to the open-ended 'most important problem' question. This confirms that by the mid-1970s, although there was a high level of latent public concern for the environment – elicited by closed-ended questions that reminded respondents of the existence of environmental problems – the issue simply was not 'top of mind' for most Canadians.

Although responses to questions about the 'most important problem(s)' facing the country and the degree of concern for environmental problems followed similar trends, both peaking around 1970 and declining thereafter, the trends in issue salience were much more pronounced. These observations can be readily reconciled. Degree of concern as elicited by closed-ended questions represents an absolute indicator of concern, while salience represents a relative measure, since the open-ended 'most important problem' question implicitly asks respondents to rank their most serious concerns. It is thus not surprising that the two measures would tend to move in the same direction, nor that trends in salience would be more pronounced. One might be quite concerned about several issues at once, yet relatively small shifts in degree of concern about one problem relative to the others could nonetheless produce dramatic shifts in one's choice of the single most important problem.

The trends in Canadian public opinion concerning the environment in the late 1960s through the early 1970s are supported by two other indicators: comparable trends in US public opinion, and trends in media coverage of environmental issues. Woodrow argues that increased Canadian concern was in part provoked by the 'demonstration effect' of slightly earlier US attention to the issue.[11] Survey research in the United States indicates that both the degree and salience of public concern for the environment surged in the late 1960s with such suddenness that it has been referred to by one scholar as a 'miracle of public opinion,' which 'sprang from nowhere to major proportions in a few short years.'[12] The fraction of Americans indicating that pollution was 'very or somewhat serious' in response to closed-ended questions rose from 28 to 69 per cent in the case of air pollution and 35 to 74 per cent in the case of water pollution between 1965 to 1970.[13] Unfortunately, national pollsters did not continue asking these same questions into the 1970s. However, based on state-level studies, Dunlap concludes that 'although the available evidence on trends in public concern for environmental quality in the early 1970s is sparse, it consistently indicates a significant decline in environmental awareness and concern among the [American] public in the early 1970s.'[14]

As in Canada, the salience of the pollution issue in the US rose and fell rapidly around 1970. Nationally, the per cent of respondents identifying the environment as the 'most important problem' facing the United States rose from 2 per cent in 1968 to 17 per cent in 1970, then declined to 10 per cent by 1972, and to the point were it was not even mentioned by Gallup after 1974. At the same time, Americans indicated declining willingness to trade-off economic growth for environmental protection. As in Canada, when respondents were allowed to choose three problems from a list of ten, the environment fared somewhat better. It ranked ninth of ten problems in 1965, when it was chosen as one of three top problems by 17 per cent of respondents, rose to second in 1970, when it was chosen by 53 per cent of respondents, and fell to sixth in 1980, when it was chosen by 24 per cent.[15]

In both Canada and the United States there was a dramatic increase in media coverage of pollution issues in the late 1960s. Major Canadian newspapers' coverage began to increase dramatically in 1968, peaked in 1970, and then fell off as sharply as it had emerged.[16] For instance, the *Globe and Mail* reported less than 100 stories concerning pollution in 1968, approximately 700 in 1970, and only about 400 in 1971.[17] Woodrow reports similar trends in periodical coverage; the *Canadian Periodical Index* cited roughly twenty articles on pollution in 1968, 140 in 1970, then only forty in 1971.[18]

Not surprisingly, in the late 1960s, politicians discovered the environment at the same time as their constituents. The surge in both media and public attention was reflected in debate in the House of Commons. The proportion of questions in Question Period that concerned environmental matters increased from 0.9 per cent in 1968, to 2.8 per cent in 1969, and 6.3 per cent in 1970, only to decline back to 1.1 per cent by 1973.[19]

The first wave of environmental interest also gave rise to an organized environmental movement in Canada. Environmental groups such as Greenpeace and Pollution Probe were established in the early 1970s, while older groups, such as the Sierra Club and the Canadian Wildlife Federation, shifted their focus from conservation to pollution control. However, as Woodrow argues, the nascent environmental groups of the day were as yet ill-prepared to play a significant role in shaping the government response.[20]

Collectively, the data presented in this section suggest that the public concern for the environment and the salience of environmental issues both increased in the late 1960s. Although the available evidence cannot support conclusions about the causal relationship between elite opinion, media coverage, and public opinion, it is clear that political elites, the press, and the public all turned their attention to the environment around 1970. Thereafter, although the degree of public concern subsided only gradually, the salience of the pollution issue declined quite dramatically, mirroring the suddenness with which it had emerged. When the economy took a turn for the worse early in the 1970s, pollution was promptly displaced on the national agenda by economic concerns. While the level of awareness of environmental problems remained quite high, public attention quickly shifted from the environment back to 'bread and butter' issues of inflation and the economy. The question of how to interpret the coincidence of a high degree of concern and low salience of environmental issues is considered in greater depth in Chapter 5.

Attitudes Toward Federal Jurisdiction

The first 'green wave' witnessed a dramatic change in attitudes toward federal jurisdiction concerning the environment. Prior to the late 1960s, the subject of pollution arose in the House of Commons only sporadically, usually in connection with local water pollution problems. Federal cabinet ministers resisted occasional calls from the Opposition for a federal response to such problems by arguing that 'the conservation of natural resources within the provinces is primarily a provincial responsibility.'[21] Muntz notes that 'Hansard contains no end of official rationalizations containing either specific reference or veiled allusions to constitutional restraints upon federal action.'[22] Along a similar vein, Woodrow argues that federal cabinet ministers 'constantly trotted out the same basic argument that pollution was primarily a provincial responsibility and that the federal government must be careful not to infringe upon provincial jurisdiction.'[23]

The government's reticence initially persisted as the Opposition began to press for federal action to combat pollution in the late 1960s. The Opposition's calls for a more aggressive federal role found support from recent academic publications that asserted that the federal government had broader jurisdiction than it acknowledged.[24] However, in response, the acting minister of Energy, Mines, and Resources, Otto Lang, continued to maintain that 'water pollution control and abatement is primarily a provincial responsibility.'[25] The prime minister himself suggested that the problem was the constitution in stating, 'this challenge of pollution of our rivers, and lakes, or our farmlands and forests, and of the very air we breathe, cannot be met effectively in our federal state without some constitution reforms or clarification.'[26] One cabinet minister reportedly summed up the government's initial response: 'I've said it before – it's not our baby.'[27]

Under sustained pressure from the Opposition and an increasingly concerned public, however, the government soon underwent a change of heart with regard to its jurisdiction. The throne speech of October 1969 vowed aggressive action to control pollution, and the 28th Parliament passed no less than five major pollution control statutes: the Canada Water Act, the Amendments to the Fisheries Act, the Clean Air Act, the Northern Inland Waters Act, and the Arctic Waters Pollution Prevention Act. In keeping with the focus on the federal government's role within 'federal Canada,' only the first three of these statutes are discussed in this chapter. Although numerous examples can be offered of persistent constitutional timidity, each of the first generation statutes nevertheless staked out new and untested federal jurisdiction, including uncertain powers over the environment based on the criminal law power and 'Peace, Order, and good Government.'

Other political actors offered their own views of the extent of federal jurisdiction. Provincial government perspectives are reviewed in a subsequent section of this chapter. Polluting industries generally were wary of federal involvement. In particular, the pulp and paper industry, which was identified as the first target for federal controls, strongly opposed national environmental standards in favour of exclusive provincial responsibility.[28] In contrast, newly established environmental groups called for a strong federal role, but typically were 'not much concerned about matters of jurisdiction.'[29]

The weak voice of the environmental movement was amplified, however, by the parliamentary opposition, which harshly criticized the government for its lack of leadership and excessive deference to the provinces. As one critic argued:

> The various departments of government find it convenient to ignore many of the major causes of pollution. They get around the problem by saying, 'We can do nothing, because if we act we shall upset the provincial governments.' Their attitude is that many pollution problems fall under provincial jurisdiction and have nothing to do with the federal government. I say that it is the duty of this government, which has hidden behind the gimmick of constitutional issues in order not to accept responsibility for pollution control, to iron out constitutional problems in this field.[30]

Opposition environmental critics showed little patience for constitutional excuses, alternating between refusing to acknowledge any constitutional limitations and demanding constitutional change to overcome such limitations.

Interestingly, despite the high profile of the pollution issue during this period, it did not emerge as a significant electoral issue. This can be explained by the fact that the issue rose to prominence quite suddenly after the 1968 election, and had already been eclipsed by economic issues by the time of the 1972 election.[31]

Testing Federal Jurisdiction at the Legislative Level

The Canada Water Act
The Canada Water Act, passed in 1970, was the first legislative assertion of broad federal powers over the environment. The flagship of the package of

environmental statutes introduced during the 28th Parliament was unveiled with great fanfare in August 1969 by Otto Lang, who declared that 'the Government is determined, as a matter of national urgency, to implement anti-pollution programs and measures to prevent pollution from reaching crisis proportions on a national, or regional scale.'[32] Lang promised that the bill would 'put an end to the buck-passing between overlapping agencies and jurisdictions.'[33]

A 'national water policy' had been under development within Energy, Mines, and Resources since the mid-1960s. In explaining why earlier proposals to draft the legislation failed to come to fruition, Parlour concludes that 'perhaps the most significant factor ... was the predominance of bureaucratic conservatism and the constraints imposed by the federal interpretation of its own constitutional and jurisdictional authority in this area. The lack of executive initiative was reinforced by an almost total lack of interest in a more assertive federal role within the legislative branch, the Cabinet and the central control agencies.'[34] However, the emergence of public concern for the environment at the end of the decade prompted cabinet to abandon its constitutional conservatism, and gave the much-delayed bill greater urgency.

The Canada Water Bill was written by the 'bright boys' in the Water Sector, a youthful division that had been created when the Department of Energy, Mines, and Resources was established in 1965.[35] They drafted an economist's dream bill, reflecting state-of-the-art academic thinking on resource management. Although originally envisioned as comprehensive water resource management legislation, which only implicitly addressed water quality, explicit pollution control provisions were grafted onto the bill at cabinet's insistence in May 1969, after the pollution issue gained public prominence.[36]

From the outset, the Canada Water Act was predicated on a model of cooperative federalism, reflecting the preferences of Jean-Luc Pépin, who was minister of Energy, Mines, and Resources during the early stages of development of the bill.[37] The minister's cooperative approach resonated with the academic enthusiasm of the drafters, who were unwilling to succumb to the constraints of the division of powers in their pursuit of efficient solutions. 'Optimal resource management' would require pooling of both federal and provincial powers. As a result, Part I of the act proposed the joint development by federal and provincial governments of comprehensive water resource management plans. However, the bill did allow for the possibility that provincial cooperation would not be forthcoming. Part 1 also authorized unilateral federal development of water resource management plans should efforts to cooperate with the provinces fail in any 'federal waters' (e.g., those in the territories or national parks), and in interjurisdictional waters where there was a 'significant national interest.'

Part II of the act took a similar cooperative approach to water quality management. The environment minister was authorized to enter into agreements with the provinces to establish joint federal-provincial water quality management agencies in waters where water quality management had become a matter of 'urgent national concern.' As originally envisioned, these joint agencies would establish water quality standards for individual river basins, rather than set uniform national standards, on the grounds that variation in the value of water resources and the costs of control in different settings demanded regionally varied standards. As in Part I, the federal government was authorized to act unilaterally at any time in 'federal waters,' but in interjurisdictional waters only if prior efforts to reach an agreement with a province failed.

Part III, which authorized federal regulations to limit phosphates in detergents, was added by the government after second reading in the House of Commons, in response to recommendations of an International Joint Commission report on eutrophication of the Great Lakes. Before adding the provision, the federal government first sought and obtained support for these nutrients provisions from all ten provincial governments.[38]

The act's use of phrases like 'urgent national concern' and 'significant national interest' clearly reveal the federal government's intent to rely on 'Peace, Order, and good Government' for the first time to protect the environment. The assertion of unilateral federal powers was particularly controversial. The constitutionality of the Canada Water Act was challenged by several legal scholars (though defended by others) as well as two provincial governments.[39] Interestingly, although the courts might have been expected to find that particular instances of federal action did not constitute 'significant national interests' or 'urgent national concerns,' it would have been difficult for them to rule the legislation itself ultra vires, since it so clearly evoked the court's own national concern doctrine.[40]

Opponents of the act's assertion of unilateral federal powers tended to overlook its concurrent timidity. The Canada Water Act not only authorized a cooperative federal-provincial approach, it made it a precondition of federal action. Moreover, on closer examination, even the declaration of unilateral federal powers was hesitant. Saunders concludes that 'Part I is predicated – whether for legal or political reasons – on a very cautious view of the constitutional limits of federal authority over water.'[41] He notes that, in a 'surfeit of caution,' the act authorizes the federal government to develop water resource management plans in interjurisdictional waters, yet not to implement them. The federal government thus tied its own hands even in Canada-US or interprovincial waters.

Part II was much stronger, since it authorized not only planning but unilateral federal implementation of water quality management plans in interjurisdictional waters. Moreover, 'interjurisdictional waters' were broadly defined to include any water bodies within a province that have a significant impact on water quality outside the province. However, unilateral federal involvement still was authorized only in federal or interjurisdictional waters. The statute did not attempt to rely on the criminal law power to authorize federal control of any water pollution that threatens public health.

The federal opposition parties complained that the assertion of federal authority in the Canada Water Act was not strong enough. They were particularly critical of the absence of national standards and of the cooperative approach, which they argued reflected a lack of federal leadership. One of the government's critics argued, 'if the government had the will to do so, it could really clamp down on water pollution across the country with the authority it has ... This is constitutional pollution ... We have the situation that in respect of many fiscal matters, either federal or provincial, the federal and provincial governments say that they cannot do this or that because of the constitution.'[42]

Government spokespersons responded with assurances of their willingness to take action unilaterally if necessary. However, the tone of government statements concerning federal jurisdiction remained conciliatory. The minister, J.J. Greene, emphasized that overlapping federal and provincial authority with respect to water resources necessitated a cooperative approach, and argued that 'it is not less bold to agree to joint actions with the provinces; it is not less bold to be realistic with regard to the constitution, imperfect though we may feel it is.'[43]

The Fisheries Act

In 1969, Minister of Fisheries Jack Davis proposed an alternative federal strategy for water pollution control for his own department. Since 1868, the federal Fisheries Act had incorporated a provision prohibiting the discharge of 'a deleterious substance of any type in water frequented by fish.' Ironically, the weakness of the provision was that it was too strong. A strict reading of the blanket prohibition of discharges would have shut down virtually every industry (and toilet!) in the country. The executive had complete discretion to enforce the provision only as it saw fit; however, such an approach would have demanded time-consuming negotiation of effluent requirements with individual polluters on a case-by-case basis.

The intent of the 1970 Fisheries Act Amendments was to authorize a more generic regulatory approach. The amendments added new provisions authorizing national effluent regulations and exempting sources covered by such regulations from the blanket prohibition of discharges. Fines for non-compliance also were significantly increased. According to Parlour, the approach taken in the Fisheries Act Amendments reflected the personal influence of Jack Davis:

> The Minister was an arch-pragmatist who had little patience for erudite academic arguments about alternative control strategies and no time at all for the socio-economic bases for these arguments. An engineer by training and an individual with very strong ideas about what the public wanted, he was instrumental in making many of the key decisions which determined the ultimate form of the water pollution control legislation put forward by his department.[44]

There were three key elements of Davis's approach, each of which was in direct conflict with the approach taken by Energy, Mines, and Resources in the Canada Water Act. First, Davis argued that the federal government should rely on its uncontested fisheries power as the basis for a water pollution control strategy, rather than taking a chance on 'Peace, Order, and good Government.'[45] The minister made little effort to disguise the fact that the federal government planned to exercise its jurisdiction over fisheries to pursue pollution control indirectly, testifying that the 'main thrust of the Bill ... is protection of the aquatic environment against pollution.'[46] Davis thus advocated reliance on fish as the 'first line of defence' against pollution.[47] In addition to a lower degree of constitutional risk, Davis argued that another important advantage of the fisheries power was that 'it's a direct federal vehicle. We do not have to go through the provinces.'[48] The minister openly disapproved of the Canada Water Act's reliance on cooperative federalism in emphasizing that reliance on federal fisheries jurisdiction would not be vulnerable to the 'tender mercies of jointly-manned [sic] federal-provincial committees of civil servants.'[49]

The second element of the strategy was the emphasis on uniform national standards to prevent 'pollution havens.' In his speeches, the minister stressed the need for the federal government to treat all polluters equally to counteract the temptation faced by individual provinces to set lax standards in order to attract investment or protect local industry.[50] Davis proposed that similar industrial facilities should be required to adopt comparable control measures, thus controlling their effluents equally 'at the factory fence' without regard to the varying assimilative capacities of local receiving waters.[51] Consistent with the approach emerging during the same period in the US, effluent standards were to be developed for different industrial sectors based on the availability of affordable control technology, rather than the needs of the receiving environment.

The concept of uniform effluent standards had been rejected by the proponents of the Canada Water Act on the grounds of economic efficiency. They argued first that two identical plants would have markedly different environmental and health impacts if one were situated on a small river in a populated area and the other on a large water body. More stringent and costly standards could be more easily justified in the former case than the latter. Moreover, the costs of meeting the same effluent quality standard could vary among plants. It would be more cost effective to demand greater reductions from polluters who could install controls at a lower cost and to demand less from those who faced higher marginal costs. In contrast to the Fisheries Act approach, the philosophy of the Canada Water Act allowed for both of these factors to be taken into account in setting local, rather than national, water quality standards and discharge fees.

The final element of Davis's strategy was 'reasonableness.' The threat posed to industry by national effluent standards was softened by promises of gradual implementation. The minister testified that 'we want to work with industry, not against it.'[52] Although immediate compliance would be demanded of facilities constructed after the issuance of new federal regulations, compliance schedules for existing plants were to be negotiated on a case-by-case basis, taking into account the economic circumstances of individual polluters. The harsh consequences of uniform national standards thus would be mitigated by gradually phasing them in.

Although competition between the two departments within cabinet and in the Interdepartmental Committee on Water was fierce – one minister described it as a 'jungle-like atmosphere'[53] – Davis won considerable support by taking his case to the public. The opposition parties, media, and the public were more receptive to promises of tough national standards than arcane academic arguments about 'optimal resource management.' The protracted struggle within cabinet eventually was resolved by proceeding with both bills, despite the contradiction between them. The government sought to rationalize its indecision by describing the Fisheries Act Amendments as a short-term complement to the longer-term strategy of the Canada Water Act. The Fisheries Act Amendments and the Canada Water Act, two pieces of legislation reflecting fundamentally inconsistent approaches to pollution control, both received royal assent on 26 June

1970. Woodrow reflects that 'what may be perhaps most striking about this double-barrelled case study in policy development lies in the seeming failure of government to take the difficult decision of choosing clearly' between two radically different approaches.[54]

The Clean Air Act

In 1970, the Liberal government was under pressure from the Opposition to follow the lead of the United States and United Kingdom in creating a Department of the Environment. The government initially resisted, resurrecting the argument of inadequate constitutional jurisdiction. The prime minister argued that 'it would be impossible to [establish an environment department] ... because many aspects of the pollution problem do not come under federal jurisdiction.'[55]

However, the government soon relented, promising in the October 1970 throne speech to establish an environment department. Environment Canada was created by Order in Council on 26 November 1970, and subsequently affirmed in June 1971 by proclamation of the Government Organization Act. The prime minister chose Jack Davis as the first minister of the new department, which combined the portfolios of Environment and Fisheries, Davis's former portfolio. Responsibility for environmental protection fell to the newly formed Environmental Protection Service within Environment Canada.

The new department immediately assumed responsibility for air pollution control legislation already under development by the Department of National Health and Welfare. The resulting Clean Air Act, passed in 1971, combined elements of the Fisheries Act's reliance on uniform national regulations with the Canada Water Act's preference for federal-provincial cooperation.

The act authorized the federal government to issue regulations establishing 'National Ambient Air Quality Objectives.' In introducing the legislation, the new environment minister once again stressed the importance of 'national standards' to prevent 'pollution havens.'[56] However, in the case of the Clean Air Act, the commitment to the national air quality objectives was largely symbolic. Environment Canada was not given adequate authority to ensure that those objectives actually would be met.[57] The minister was authorized to issue emission standards to achieve the objectives in a given province only if the provincial government invited federal involvement by formally adopting the federal air quality objectives. The act thus allowed the federal government to claim credit for establishing uniform national goals, while avoiding offending the provinces' and polluters' sensitivities by leaving open the question of how or even whether those goals would be achieved.[58]

The Clean Air Act did provide for enforceable national emission regulations in the case of sources that present a 'significant danger to the health of persons.' The emphasis on public health belied the federal government's intent to rely primarily on its criminal law power, rather than 'Peace, Order, and good Government.' The parliamentary opposition pressed for an even stronger federal role predicated on the presumption that air is an inherently 'national concern' because it does not respect provincial borders. The federal government did rely on 'Peace, Order, and good Government,' however, in making an assertion of federal authority to implement international treaties. The Clean Air Act authorized the issuance of national emission standards if there was danger of violation of an international treaty.

Like the Fisheries Act, and unlike the Canada Water Act, this legislation met with little opposition from the provinces. Davis reported that the provinces 'almost uniformly welcome(d)' the bill.[59] The opposition parties also voted in favour of the bill. In fact, the act drew surprisingly few reactions from any corner. The committee reviewing the bill received only one submission from either industry or environmental groups.[60]

Alhéritière describes the Clean Air Act as a 'carrot and stick' approach: the provinces were offered a carrot of cooperation, but threatened with the stick of federal unilateralism.[61] However, in reality, the threat of federal action was neither forceful nor credible. The act clearly envisioned a federal role that supplemented rather than supplanted provincial efforts.[62] The minister himself stressed that unilateral federal involvement in pollution control was not foreseen.[63] Nemetz suggests that, rather than competing with the provinces in air pollution control, the federal government chose to provide a 'de facto staff function' for them by providing environmental monitoring and establishing unenforceable emissions 'guidelines.'[64]

Federal-Provincial Relations Concerning the Environment

In the late 1960s and early 1970s, provincial governments also were scrambling to satisfy public demands for pollution control. During this period, all ten provinces passed environmental protection statutes, with some preceding the federal government's initiatives (most notably, British Columbia and Ontario), and others trailing.[65] Provincial reactions to the federal government's proposals also varied. Although there was quiet support for federal legislation among the smaller provinces, the four largest provinces openly resented what they perceived as unnecessary federal intrusion in an area of provincial jurisdiction. As a result, federal-provincial relations concerning environmental protection during this period were characterized by tension and conflict.

Federal-provincial relations in the new policy field were facilitated by the availability of a forum for intergovernmental bargaining – the Canadian Council of Resource Ministers (CCRM). CCRM was established by the eleven federal and provincial governments after the 1961 Resources for Tomorrow Conference, and it subsequently had sponsored a national conference on Pollution and Our Environment in 1966. The provinces and the federal government participated in CCRM as equals, with the chair rotating among them annually. Although the council's name implied that all resources were covered, from the start the emphasis was on management of renewable resources other than fisheries, excluding the highly contentious non-renewable resources such as oil, natural gas, and minerals. The new emphasis on pollution control thus required only a minor shift in focus.

The pollution issue was a prominent part of the agenda of the 1969 premiers' conference. At that meeting, nine of the ten provinces (Newfoundland did not attend) passed a resolution directing CCRM to develop proposals 'to accelerate the formulation of uniform minimum standards and a common approach towards the solution of that problem.'[66] At the premiers' conference the following year, the same provinces considered CCRM's response. The council recommended that each government create a single agency or department responsible for environmental protection, and that a new intergovernmental council be formed with one representative from each of those federal and provincial departments. The premiers, many of whom had yet to establish environment departments, chose instead to rely on the existing forum provided by CCRM, and directed the council to revise its mandate accordingly.[67] Thereafter, the name of the council was changed to the Canadian Council of Resource and Environment Ministers (CCREM).

Several authors have stressed the jurisdictional jealousies that emerged in this period, particularly the provincial opposition to the Canada Water Act.[68] Certainly the four largest provinces – Ontario, Quebec, British Columbia, and Alberta – all registered objections to federal proposals, ranging from reservations about the consistency of federal and provincial programs to outright rejection of any federal involvement. However, the extent of provincial support for federal involvement has been underestimated. The Atlantic provinces as well as Manitoba and Saskatchewan, together constituting the majority of the provinces, generally were supportive of federal involvement. As discussed below, some even advocated constitutional amendments to strengthen federal jurisdiction over the environment. And even the champions of provincial jurisdiction were not averse to demanding federal funding to aid the provinces and industry in their pollution control efforts, or to blaming the federal government for failing to resolve high profile pollution problems.[69]

It is noteworthy that the defensive provinces resisted federal involvement for very different reasons. Provinces that felt they already were active in pollution control – Ontario, British Columbia, and on occasion Alberta – tended to perceive the federal government as a 'johnny-come-lately' who only discovered the environment when it appeared on the front page.[70] Quebec typically placed much greater emphasis on the threat to provincial jurisdiction per se, although the province often was joined in its constitutional arguments by British Columbia.

Although they differed in their reactions to particular federal proposals, it is significant that all provinces stressed the need for minimum national standards. Provincial politicians were acutely aware of the dilemma of trying to satisfy public demands for environmental protection without placing local industry at a competitive disadvantage. The Alberta minister was particularly candid in acknowledging the difficulty of clamping down on industry if other provinces did not do the same.[71] Although the provinces were in agreement on the need for national standards, not all agreed that such standards should be incorporated in federal law. Quebec and BC lobbied for national standards to be devised through CCREM, where the federal government represented just one voice among eleven.[72]

Politicians in all provinces clearly were concerned about the prospect of being undercut by other jurisdictions, and as a result were able to reach consensus on the need for 'minimum national standards.' However, the inclusion of the word 'minimum' suggests that it may not have been as easy for the provinces to reach agreement on just what those standards should be. There are two very different reasons why provincial politicians would insist on minimum standards. Provincial governments that perceived themselves as environmental leaders, while supportive of strict national standards that would force other provinces to catch up, insisted on 'minimum' standards so that they would not be precluded from adopting more stringent standards on their own if they desired. Less aggressive provinces called for minimum standards to ensure that they would not be forced to meet the standards of the most stringent provinces. There was thus potential for conflict among the provinces over just how minimal national standards should be.

Provincial Responses to Federal Legislation

The Canada Water Act was the source of much of the intergovernmental tension during this period. Although the act was predicated on a vision of federal-provincial cooperation, the threat of unilateralism was a lightning rod for provincial opposition. The federal government first informed the provinces of its plans for the act in 1967, when senior Energy, Mines, and Resources officials visited each province with a proposal for cooperative water resource management. Ontario subsequently sponsored a meeting of provincial governments to discuss the federal proposal,[73] and by the next CCRM meeting, BC and Alberta had joined Ontario and Quebec in voicing objections to the act. The acting federal minister, Otto Lang, personally visited each province immediately after releasing the government's proposal in August 1969. And, at the request of the provincial premiers, the Canada Water Act was discussed again at a First Ministers Conference in February 1970.

The federal proposal faced strong opposition from Ontario, Alberta, Quebec, and British Columbia, though only the latter two challenged the constitutionality of the act.[74] Although the four dissenting provinces constituted a minority of the provinces, they did represent a majority of the population. Two provinces, Prince Edward Island and Newfoundland, made no public comment on the act, while the remaining four, New Brunswick, Nova Scotia, Saskatchewan, and Manitoba, supported the federal initiative.[75]

Ontario, and to a lesser extent BC and Alberta, argued that they already had strong environmental programs in place which could be jeopardized by conflict between federal and provincial approaches. Beyond wounded pride, these provinces feared the constraints that federal strategies could pose on provincial programs. Although the Canada Water Act was predicated on federal-provincial cooperation, the provinces nevertheless were invited to participate on the federal government's terms. The act's reliance on regionally varied effluent fees was inconsistent with the more straightforward regulatory approach already embraced by those provinces, and with their desire for uniform national discharge standards.

Resentment appears to have been particularly acute among provincial bureaucrats. The staff of the Ontario Water Resources Commission (OWRC) were among the strongest defenders of provincial jurisdiction, even while their political masters were relatively conciliatory (at least in public). When the federal proposal first was released in August 1969, both the Ontario Energy and Resources minister George Kerr and Premier John Robarts distanced themselves from their outspoken bureaucrats, publicly welcoming the federal act and expressing a commitment to cooperate with Ottawa, although both also made it clear that the province would not cede any of its authority in the field. OWRC persisted in its opposition to the Canada Water Act, however, obtaining an opinion from the office of the provincial attorney general that argued that the act was unconstitutional, and 'an invasion of provincial legislative authority in the guise of criminal law.'[76] Although the premier stressed that the OWRC report was not the government position, the province did continue to be a strong critic of the federal proposal behind the closed doors of executive federalism.

In contrast to Ontario, Quebec and British Columbia were less conciliatory. Those provinces registered their objections primarily on constitutional grounds, emphasizing what they perceived to be federal encroachment on provincial jurisdiction over natural resources. The BC minister of resources, Ray Williston, described the proposed Canada Water Act as yet 'another Ottawa intrusion into the provincial field.' He confirmed that the province would cooperate with the federal government, but only in the manner one would 'when someone points a revolver at your head.'[77] The premier of Quebec, Jean-Jacques Bertrand, also offered a strong defense of provincial resources jurisdiction at the February 1970 First Ministers Conference: 'the federal government is seeking authority to act unilaterally ... without provincial agreement and even against their will [sic], when it deems this to be in the "national interest" ... Quebec insists on control over its waters and no federal government will ever "nationalise" them without triggering unyielding opposition from the Quebec government.'[78]

In response, the federal government offered reassurances that it did not anticipate ever using its unilateral powers.[79] Moreover, the government assured the provinces that even cooperative, joint water quality management only was foreseen in a limited number of cases. Otto Lang declared that 'where a provincial authority is doing the job, there is no thought of interference.'[80] Accordingly, the bill was amended to clarify that the water quality standards authorized by Part II of the act would be jointly devised, and to authorize delegation of responsibility for implementation to existing provincial agencies. Finally, in respect for provincial concerns, proclamation of the Canada Water Act was delayed until after the September 1970 constitutional conference.

The resistance offered by the four largest provinces clearly had an impact. The federal government played down the threat of unilateralism and retreated from its proposals for joint water quality management. However, although the government was willing to make minor amendments in response to the more defensive provinces, it did not allow the bill to die on the order paper, nor did it remove the offending provisions authorizing unilateral action. The federal government could not be seen as retreating in the face of unprecedented levels of public concern and persistent demands from the Opposition for federal leadership on the pollution issue. The government could not fail to make at least the symbolic gesture of passing water pollution control legislation.

In contrast to the Canada Water Act, the Fisheries Act Amendments and the Clean Air Act met little opposition from the provinces or, for that matter, from the opposition parties or interest groups. The Fisheries Act Amendments were perfectly consistent with provincial demands for minimum national standards. Even those provinces that would have preferred that national standards be developed through CCREM probably felt there was little constitutional basis to challenge the federal government's reliance on its fisheries power.[81]

The provinces were also generally supportive of the Clean Air Act, which offered the promise of federal administrative support without the threat of interference. Interestingly, the federal environment minister's remarks suggest that small and large provinces had different reasons for welcoming federal involvement in air pollution control:

> The smaller provinces – several of the Maritime Provinces, Newfoundland and so on – are all saying: 'Go ahead, take the lead, and we will relate our legislation to yours; we will make it complementary; we would like Ottawa to proceed as quickly as possible; we would like to have your ideas of standards and so on. You develop the standards: by and large we will adopt them, and so on.'
>
> Several provinces, particularly Ontario – which is much further advanced than some of the other provinces in setting its own standards, administering them and so on – are more inclined to say that it is about time the other provinces caught up, that it is about time we had some national standards requiring the others to conform, requiring industry in other provinces to live up to the standards that they are insisting upon in industry in their provinces.[82]

The Constitutional Negotiations

The first wave of environmental concern coincided with a period of intense interest in constitutional renewal. In light of the prominence of environmental issues at the time, and of the debate over the limits of environmental jurisdiction, the low profile of the environment in constitutional discussions is noteworthy. In part, this may reflect the sense that pollution was a new issue; some participants in constitutional negotiations felt that it would be premature to make changes to the constitution before it was known how well governments could manage within the existing division of powers.[83] It is also true that the federal government assigned reform of the division of powers a relatively low priority.[84] However, it is noteworthy that the federal government, which had the most to gain given the degree of uncertainty with respect to its environmental powers, did not seek to take advantage of public support for federal leadership by pressing for reforms to clarify or strengthen federal jurisdiction. The federal government did not make aggressive demands, nor 'go public' to mobilize support for constitutional proposals concerning the environment. In fact, some provinces advocated reforms to strengthen federal authority that went well beyond the federal government's own proposals.

In 1970, the Constitutional Review Secretariat of the Privy Council Office undertook a study of the environment and the constitution. Jim MacNeill, a senior official from Energy, Mines, and Resources who had been closely involved with the development of the Canada Water Act, was seconded to the Privy Council Office to oversee the project. MacNeill's report, issued early in 1971, heavily influenced the position taken by the federal government in constitutional discussions.

The report differentiated between federal and provincial jurisdiction based on the spatial dimensions of the particular pollution problem at issue.[85] It suggested that matters involving only local impacts should be the responsibility of the provincial governments, while the federal government should have authority if interprovincial or international impacts were involved. Even then, MacNeill envisioned a purely supplementary role for the federal government, such that federal involvement would be authorized only if the affected provinces could not resolve an interjurisdictional environmental problem on their own.

MacNeill's report and subsequent proposals advanced by the federal government in constitutional negotiations acknowledged only the physical scale of pollution problems. There was no recognition of the political constraints faced by provinces in light of their economic interdependence. In fact, it is surprising that the federal proposals failed to acknowledge the 'pollution haven' issue, given the emphasis placed on it by the federal Minister of the Environment and even by the provinces. In fact, MacNeill's report did not mention 'national standards,' even to reject them. Indeed, in intergovernmental negotiations, the only suggestions that the federal government should have explicit authority to set national standards came from the provinces, including some of the more jurisdictionally sensitive ones.

The issue of responsibility for environmental protection was discussed at several federal-provincial constitutional conferences in 1970 and 1971. At the September 1970 constitutional conference, the federal government advanced a discussion paper consistent with MacNeill's proposal. It advocated that the federal government should have authority to act if an environmental problem had interprovincial or international impacts, but only if the relevant provinces failed to do so.[86] The federal discussion paper also stressed the need for supplemental federal regulations to control pollution from products traded interprovincially or internationally, such as automobiles.

At the same meeting, the Ontario and British Columbia governments presented their own statements on the environment. Both expressed reluctance to open up the division of powers with respect to the environment, and defended the flexibility of existing constitutional arrangements. However, Ontario adopted a relatively generous view of existing federal authority and recommended that the federal government should be 'fully and formally' responsible for international environmental problems and authorized to resolve interprovincial problems where the affected provinces invite federal involvement. In contrast, BC offered a more limited view of federal authority with respect to international spillovers, and did not even mention a federal role in the event of interprovincial spillovers.[87]

Other provinces were more supportive of the federal government, even stressing potential aspects of the federal role that the federal government itself did not mention. For instance, Nova Scotia suggested that many pollution problems could be dealt with under the federal criminal law power. And Manitoba proposed reforms to establish unlimited federal paramountcy with respect to air pollution.[88] The divergence of provincial views is reflected by the 'statement of Conclusions' from the conference, which noted only that 'some governments' accepted a federal role, left undefined, with respect to interjurisdictional pollution.[89]

At the next constitutional conference, in February 1971, the federal government offered a more detailed working paper on 'Constitutional Powers to Control Pollution.' The working paper proposed concurrent powers, with the federal government being paramount in the case of interjurisdictional pollution, and the provinces paramount in other cases. The federal working paper again adopted the territorially based approach of MacNeill's report, and neglected to even mention the question of national standards.

The federal proposal met resistance from several premiers. Ontario again argued that constitutional reforms were unnecessary, while British Columbia and Quebec sought stronger provincial powers than proposed by the federal government.[90] In the absence of consensus, the subject of the division of powers over the environment was set aside. As a result, no proposals concerning the environment or pollution were included in the consensus package, known as the Victoria Charter, which emerged from the subsequent conference in Victoria.

After the failure of the Victoria Charter in June 1971, a joint committee of the Senate and House of Commons held hearings on the constitution, which revealed the extent of public support for a stronger federal role in environmental protection.[91] In addition to public support, the government of Saskatchewan proposed to the committee a constitutional amendment to establish explicit concurrency over environmental protection, subject to federal paramountcy. The province advocated strong federal jurisdiction to authorize the federal government to set national effluent standards, even in the case of environmental problems contained within provincial borders, in order to prevent provinces from competing to attract industry.[92]

The joint committee's 1972 report was more aggressive than earlier federal proposals. The report recommended formal concurrency with respect to air and water pollution, subject to federal paramountcy. It stressed the need for national standards to prevent pollution havens.[93] The report had little impact, however. After the failure of the Victoria Charter, there was no significant activity on the constitution for several years. And, by the time the question of constitutional reform re-emerged in the late 1970s, environmental issues were all but invisible.

Conclusion

During this brief period of heightened salience of environmental issues, the federal government did assert extensive jurisdiction in the environmental field by passing statutes such as the Canada Water Act, the Clean Air Act, and the amendments to the Fisheries Act, as well as establishing a permanent federal administrative presence in the field of environmental protection. However, the federal role envisioned by the Canada Water Act and the Clean Air Act was limited in important ways. As foreseen by those statutes, the federal government would supplement, rather than compete with or supplant provincial pollution control efforts. Moreover, the federal government showed restraint in not pressing its relatively modest proposals for constitutional reforms concerning the environment.

The degree of residual federal deference to the provinces at first seems surprising given the strength of public support for federal involvement during this period, opposition demands for federal leadership, as well as support from a majority of the provinces. Indeed, on the question of national standards, the provinces often envisioned a stronger federal role than did the federal government itself. In part, the federal government may have resisted stronger assertions of jurisdiction because it feared provoking conflicts with the four largest provinces, particularly in light of its mission of constitutional patriation.

On the other hand, federal decisionmakers may have recognized that the mere act of passing legislation would suffice to satisfy public demand, particularly in the absence of sophisticated environmental groups. In that respect, the Clean Air Act can be seen as a masterpiece of symbolic politics, which offered the promise of national standards without committing the federal government to the onerous responsibility of achieving them. As noted in Chapter 2, the concentrated costs and diffuse benefits of environmental protection lead one to anticipate government reluctance as the norm. In that sense, the emergence of any environmental protection legislation at all is the anomaly to be explained. During brief periods of heightened salience of environmental issues, governments may take a greater interest in environmental protection, but one would not expect a complete and inevitable about-face.

What was the impact of federalism on policy outputs during this first wave of environmentalism? The existence of widespread public demand for government action to control pollution raises the prospect that intergovernmental competition to claim credit could emerge and lead to stricter environmental standards. It is true that both levels of government were active in passing environmental statutes during this period. That fact alone does not confirm that they were competing with each other, however, since both had independent incentives to respond to public demands. At least one province was candid about its strategic motives; British Columbia introduced legislation to stake out its claim to jurisdiction over water in response to the Canada Water Act.[94] Other provinces simply attempted to deflect federal claims of credit by stressing that they already had pollution control legislation. However, in the end, there was no evidence of jurisdictions trying to outdo each other with respect to the actual content of the new environmental statutes, nor competing over effluent standards, most of which had yet to be established. Any intergovernmental competition for public approval that did occur during this period was confined to the symbolic act of passing legislation.

5
The Federal Retreat, 1972-85

After 1970, the salience of the pollution issue subsided almost as quickly as it had emerged. It is not entirely surprising that legislative activity declined in the early 1970s, since the recently enacted statutes offered a wide array of new tools to combat pollution. The task at hand was to implement them. However, the promise of the first wave of environmental legislation was not fulfilled. Federal and provincial governments confronted the formidable challenge of implementing their ambitious environmental protection programs in a very different political environment than that which gave rise to the new statutes. The result was that few regulations were issued, and those that were were unevenly enforced at best.

Federal and provincial governments alike retreated from the ambitious goals they had set for themselves in the early 1970s. At the same time, however, the balance of federal and provincial roles in environmental protection shifted back toward the provinces. In effect, the federal government took advantage of overlapping jurisdiction to evade the blame-laden tasks of regulation and enforcement. As demands for a stronger federal role subsided, federal politicians reverted to depicting their constitutional jurisdiction as limited and subsidiary to provincial authority.

The federal retreat occurred in two stages. In the first, the federal government declined to implement the more controversial provisions of its new environmental statutes and left enforcement of other provisions to the provinces. In the second stage of retreat, the federal government withdrew completely from the commitment to establish national standards, nominally assuming a role of 'advocate' rather than regulator.

The cooperative intergovernmental relations concerning the environment that prevailed during this period are noteworthy given the conflict-ridden intergovernmental relations in other policy fields at the same time, including energy, the economy, and constitutional reform.[1] However, in light of federal deference to the provinces in the field of environmental protection, the cooperative character of federal-provincial relations during this period is not surprising. Rather than provoking conflict by competing with the provinces, the federal government provided non-threatening technical and administrative support to the provinces.

This chapter first presents an overview of trends in public opinion, followed by an overview of the evolution of the federal government's perception of its environmental jurisdiction. The subsequent sections consider how those attitudes were reflected at four levels of activity: constitutional reform, legislation, regulation, and enforcement. The final section reviews federal-provincial relations during this period, which includes a case study of intergovernmental relations concerning acid rain.

The Decline in Salience

As noted in the previous chapter, when the economy took a turn for the worse in the early 1970s, the salience of environmental issues declined precipitously. Pollution was promptly displaced on the national agenda by inflation and unemployment. As illustrated by Figure 4.2, the salience of the environment as a political issue declined to the point where, after August 1975, it was not even reported among responses to Gallup's open-ended 'most important problem' question again until the late 1980s. Between September 1972 and October 1974, as the salience of the pollution issue faded from view, the percentage of Gallup respondents identifying 'the economy, inflation, high prices' as their 'most important problem' increased from 37 to 82 per cent.[2] Similar trends of declining salience of environmental issues were observed in Australia and the United States.[3]

While the environment disappeared among responses to the open ended 'most important problem' question, levels of public concern for the environment elicited by closed-ended questions remained quite high. The percentage of those surveyed who felt that pollution was 'very serious' declined much more gradually, from 63 per cent in 1970 to a low of 51 per cent in 1985.[4] When respondents were asked in 1970 to select the top three problems facing the country from a list of items, pollution was the most frequently identified problem, chosen by 65 per cent of respondents. Although it had fallen to fifth place by 1976, pollution was still identified as one of the top three problems facing the country by a full third of those surveyed.[5] The contrast between the precipitous decline in salience and the more gradual decline in the degree of concern for the environment indicates that although there was substantial latent support for environmental protection, it simply was no longer 'top of mind' for most Canadians.

The reasons for the rapid decline in the salience of environmental issues undoubtedly are complex. One explanation that can be rejected is that environmental problems were resolved. There was no sudden improvement in environmental quality in the early 1970s that might explain the trend in public opinion. More plausibly, the decline in salience was a response to declining media attention to the environment after 1970.[6] At a more basic level, both the public and media appear to have succumbed to the 'issue-attention cycle' predicted by Downs.[7] However, Dunlap has revised Downs's thesis somewhat, arguing that rather than losing interest in the environment after confronting the costs of environmental protection, the public was reassured by the flurry of government announcements in the late 1960s and early 1970s, well before the costs of protecting the environment were ever incurred.[8] The fact that the environment was displaced at the top of the political agenda in the early 1970s by economic concerns may be another contributing factor. In research on policy cycles in the United States, Durr has found that citizens' expectations about the state of the economy strongly influenced the public's support for liberal government programs.[9]

As noted in Chapter 4, issue salience and degree of concern can be viewed merely as two different measures of the same public attitudes, one relative and one absolute. Relatively small shifts in level of concern could yield more pronounced swings in a respondent's relative priorities, and thus in the reported single 'most important problem.' While reconcilable in theory, however, the two measures send quite different signals about trends in public interest in environmental issues. Did public concern for the environment remain relatively stable, or plummet dramatically?

The question of how to interpret the combination of low salience and high level of public concern for the environment that prevailed between the early 1970s and late 1980s has been the subject of debate among US public opinion analysts for many years.[10] While some have emphasized the significance of the high degree of concern for the environment elicited by public opinion polls throughout the 1970s and 1980s, others have placed greater emphasis on the low salience of environmental issues during this period. This book falls squarely in the latter camp, finding support from Zaller's recent work on the importance of salience in public opinion more generally.[11]

At issue here is not the consistency of individuals' responses to survey questions, but how politicians perceive and respond to their constituents' attitudes. I argue here that to the extent that politicians are poll watchers,

they would perceive the 'most important problem' question as an indication of the public's priorities. Since governments and voters alike tend to
focus on a limited number of issues at any one time, it follows that questions soliciting voters' top priorities would provide the most relevant
measure of the impact of public opinion on the legislative agenda. While
public concern for the environment may be relatively stable, the public's
top priorities are less stable, reflecting the importance of changes at the
margin.[12] Furthermore, to the extent that politicians respond to direct
political pressure, in addition to public opinion polls, the salience of an
issue is again likely to be most significant. One would expect voters to be
much more inclined to lobby politicians directly by making phone calls
and indirectly by donating money to pressure groups if an issue is a top
priority for them.

Finally, it is noteworthy that it was economic concerns, which were
widely perceived to be antithetical to environmental protection, that displaced pollution from the top of the political agenda in the 1970s. In
1970, pollution ranked first among respondents' 'top three' problems,
ahead of unemployment and poverty, but by 1976, it had been overtaken
by inflation, unemployment, and government spending, among other
issues. Between the early 1970s and mid-1980s, politicians may have faced
public preferences for both jobs and environmental protection, but the
intensity of the former clearly was much greater.[13] Thus, when they perceived trade-offs between jobs and environmental regulation, politicians
would be expected to err on the side of the public's higher priority – jobs.

One might ask, however, what if politicians were aware of polls conducted during this period that included closed-ended environment-related
questions. Even the most conscientious of poll watchers would have
encountered such questions only every few years during this period, in
contrast to quarterly 'most important problem' questions. However,
responses to closed-ended questions throughout the 1970s and 1980s did
continue to indicate a high degree of public concern for the environment.
Such concern might have been interpreted by politicians in two ways: as
a deep well of public support available to be mobilized by astute political
entrepreneurship (particularly by opposition members who may be better
able to avoid confronting trade-offs between environmental protection
and higher priority economic objectives), or as a potential for backlash to
be avoided in the pursuit of other, more salient policy objectives.

In keeping with the latter, Dunlap describes the combination of high
levels of concern and low salience of environmental issues as a 'permissive
consensus.'[14] The public may not have actively demanded more environmental protection, but it was not willing to condone less. Thus, in

analyzing Americans' attitudes toward the environment during this period, Dunlap concludes that as long as voters were reassured that environmental problems were being adequately addressed, they displayed little interest in the issue. However, when they were alerted to a policy reversal, as by the Reagan Administration's highly publicized effort to roll back environmental regulations in the early 1980s, the salience of environmental issues began to re-emerge in that country. Dunlap emphasizes that, in the end, voters re-elected President Reagan by a solid margin despite their apparent disapproval of his environmental policies, presumably because they favoured his views on other, higher priority issues.

Ultimately, the question of which measure of public opinion is most significant in terms of its impact on public policy is an empirical one. To the extent that politicians primarily react to the public's priorities, one would expect salience to be most important. However, to the extent that politicians actively seek to mobilize public opinion, the degree of concern elicited by closed-ended questions concerning the environment is relevant. The evidence presented in this chapter suggests that salience was in fact more influential. As the salience of environmental issues declined, so did the federal government's degree of commitment to environmental protection. Indeed, the lack of effort by politicians – including the opposition parties – to mobilize latent public concern for the environment during this period is quite striking.

The evidence presented in this chapter also suggests that parliamentary institutions facilitate governments' ability to strategically retreat from environmental commitments without reviving public interest. In the US, the permissive consensus that prevailed in the environmental field in the 1970s was disturbed in the early 1980s by a very public battle between Congress and the Reagan Administration, which alerted the public to the president's proposed policy reversals. In contrast, the degree of discretion afforded the executive in parliamentary government, combined with the extent of agenda and information control exercised by a majority party in the legislature, can allow governments to renege on earlier commitments without provoking an outcry from the public or even the parliamentary opposition.

Toward the end of this period, environmental issues began to re-emerge in the media, led by the prominence of acid rain and hazardous wastes in the early 1980s.[15] However, these new concerns were felt most acutely in central Canada, particularly Ontario. In particular, acid rain is most significant in eastern Canada, and hazardous wastes also are of greatest concern in the industrialized heartland, where Love Canal, the detection of dioxins in Great Lakes fish, and the Mississauga train derailment generated considerable concern.[16] In contrast, the number of environmental citations in the British Columbia News Index declined fairly steadily from 1970 through 1985.[17] In any case, the public was preoccupied by the onset of a severe recession in the early 1980s. Thus, there was no national groundswell of public demand for environmental protection in the early 1980s to prompt a resurgence of the federal role. Nonetheless, the prominence of the acid rain issue did boost Environment Canada's visibility and credibility, setting the stage for a resurgence of the federal role in environmental protection later in the decade.

Attitudes Toward Federal Jurisdiction

Politicians were well aware of the decline in public interest in environmental issues. According to a former deputy administrator of the US Environmental Protection Agency, every member of Congress could palpably feel the decline in salience by 1974.[18] In Canada, a massive planning exercise undertaken by the Privy Council Office after the 1972 election confirmed declining public attention to pollution.[19] In the early 1970s, the prime minister referred to pollution less frequently in his speeches, and also began increasingly to stress the need to balance economic and environmental objectives.[20] Doern and Conway also confirm that the prime minister's enthusiasm for environmental protection began to wane in response to emerging economic problems as early as 1970.[21]

Faced with declining demand for pollution control and with significant economic and political costs of implementing its new environmental statutes, the federal government beat a hasty retreat from its earlier assertions of jurisdiction over the environment. By 1972, the federal environment minister once again was emphasizing the preeminence of provincial jurisdiction over pollution control.[22] In 1973, an Environment Canada official testified, 'we start with the premise that the provinces have the responsibility and authority to control pollution within their boundaries.'[23] That same year, less than three years after passage of the much vaunted Canada Water Act and the Fisheries Act Amendments, a technical newsletter observed that Ottawa had 'almost vacated the field' of water pollution control.[24] Government spokespersons began to downplay the potential for comprehensive authority under 'Peace, Order, and good Government' and the criminal law power.[25] The federal proposal for a constitutional amendment to establish formal concurrency in the environmental field was quietly dropped, and was not resurrected during constitutional discussions later in the decade. And, there was no discussion of the environment in federal throne speeches between the mid-1970s and mid-1980s, save for one brief reference to fuel-efficiency standards.[26]

The federal government clearly did not attempt to generate litigation that would force the courts to define the limits of its jurisdiction. Moreover, the government did not even take advantage of passive opportunities that arose. When an Ontario court ruled that a provincial environmental statute was ultra vires on the grounds that environmental protection was a 'national concern' and thus the exclusive responsibility of the federal government, the federal environment minister stated, 'if there is any vacuum to be filled, I hope [the provincial minister] will have some suggestions as to how the province can fill it.'[27]

A second opportunity arose in the *Interprovincial Co-operatives* case (discussed in Chapter 3), in which the defendant challenged the Manitoba government's authority to regulate acts of pollution committed beyond its borders. If the federal government had wanted control of environmental matters in interprovincial rivers, it could have intervened in support of the defendant or simply declined to intervene at all. Instead, the federal government intervened in support of the province. Although the federal factum did assert that the federal government could find authority to legislate with respect to interprovincial pollution by framing its legislation in terms of the protection of fisheries, it is striking that the federal government did not even allude to federal authority over interprovincial waters based on 'Peace, Order and good Government.'[28]

Reminiscent of the situation before 1970, federal ministers sought to deflect the opposition parties' attempts to attribute blame for the occasional pollution problems that did capture public attention by claiming that such problems fell within provincial jurisdiction. Thus, federal spokespersons resisted calls for action to address continuing mercury pollution in Ontario of the interprovincial English-Wabigoon river system. They argued that the Canada Water Act 'is not normally used to deal with this type of problem and is not considered appropriate in this case,' although it would appear to be precisely the sort of interjurisdictional environmental hazard used to justify the legislation only a few years earlier.[29] The prime minister's office responded to one citizen's letter concerning the same matter by offering only that 'the initiative will come from the Ontario government which has jurisdiction in this area.' Interestingly, the Ontario premier passed the buck right back, arguing that the decision whether or not to close the fishery in the polluted river system was a federal responsibility.[30]

In some cases, government representatives argued not that they were constrained by inadequate constitutional authority, but that administrative efficiency demanded that the federal government not exercise its jurisdiction to the fullest. The federal government gradually assumed a role of providing technical support for the provinces' own pollution control efforts. In this first stage of the federal withdrawal, the federal government remained involved in setting national discharge standards, but left the task of implementing them to the provinces, reportedly at cabinet's insistence.[31]

In keeping with this approach, a 1975 Environment Canada publication depicted the federal role in enforcement as strictly supplemental:

> In the control of effluents and emissions, provinces in their own right have enforcement responsibilities, and Environment Canada will look to them to lead in enforcing rules and regulations satisfactory to both governments ... But the federal government must act directly, where it has jurisdiction, if the provinces are unable or fail to provide adequate protection. With cooperation and experience, direct federal action will be the exception.[32]

An internal Environment Canada planning manual put the point even more strongly: 'wherever possible and appropriate, reliance must be placed on the systems of other departments, agencies and governments which have responsibilities related to renewable resources or the natural environment.'[33]

Although a handful of enforceable federal regulations were issued, much of the federal government effort in the 1970s was directed toward working with the provinces to develop unenforceable national guidelines, with the hope that the provinces would rely on them when issuing their own enforceable regulations or permits. The federal government thus sought to facilitate intergovernmental consensus on national standards. Yet, it is striking that the federal government chose to encourage national consistency by supporting provincial regulatory efforts, rather than proceeding unilaterally to impose its own standards. The prevailing characterization of federal efforts to coax the provinces to adopt consistent standards as 'leadership' suggests an effort to put a brave face on a withering federal role.

The second stage of the federal retreat, which began in 1979, was provoked by several factors. The shift in federal environmental policy was part of a broader federal effort to improve the state of federal-provincial relations after the energy-related conflicts of the mid-1970s. The desire to restore intergovernmental harmony was underscored by both the threat to national unity posed by a separatist government in Quebec and by plans to rekindle federal-provincial negotiations to patriate the constitution. Moreover, as discussed below, even in the area of environmental protection, federal-provincial relations were uneasy in light of provincial opposition to the government's 1977 Fisheries Act Amendments. At the 1978 Premiers Conference, the provinces had identified the environment as one of several areas where federal-provincial duplication of effort should be reduced.

The federal government complied. A 1978 letter from the prime minister to the Fisheries and Environment minister indicates that the federal government was considering significant devolution of federal authority in the field: 'I have asked Mr Marchand [the federal minister of state for the environment] to work with the Federal-Provincial Relations Office to elaborate more specifically what responsibilities of his new Department should be delegated to the provinces and *whether there is an argument for the complete transfer of any of those responsib*ilities to the provinces.'[34] Under pressure from the Privy Council Office, Environment Canada drafted an internal White Paper that sought to clarify Environment Canada's role. Doern and Conway attribute the fact that the White Paper was never published to 'political cold feet as to just what to do about the environment and, in part, to the fact that an election year was pending, during which environmental issues were unlikely to be central.'[35] However, the redefinition of Environment Canada's role nonetheless proceeded in the absence of a formal discussion paper. In 1979, the federal environment minister announced a renewed federal commitment to eliminating federal-provincial duplication in the environmental field.[36] Another federal minister underlined the intention of the government 'to rely to the maximum extent possible on the provinces for the administration of environmental programs.'[37]

The 'advocacy approach' that emerged involved an almost complete retreat from regulation, and thus from the commitment to national standards. One Environment Canada report describes the advocacy approach as 'a shift in emphasis from [the Environmental Protection Service's] mandatory role to a more conciliatory role of persuasion.'[38] By 1983-4, the department's annual report noted that 'regulatory powers are used sparingly as a last resort.'[39]

Although the advocacy approach was intended to appease the provinces, to Environment Canada's surprise, the new approach provoked a negative reaction both from the provinces and regulated industries. The provinces were wary of the spectre of the federal government 'taking sides' and mobilizing public demand for provincial action. Brown and Coté report that the new approach also generated resistance from federal civil servants, who were reluctant to stick their necks out in the absence of political and public support.[40]

As the federal government retreated from its regulatory role, Environment Canada officials attempted to carve out a niche for the federal government by specializing in acid rain and toxic substances.[41] The department established a Toxic Chemicals Management Program in 1980, and its efforts on acid rain also assumed an increasingly high profile in the early 1980s. However, Conway notes that civil servants' efforts to revive the federal role ultimately were frustrated by limited legislative and financial resources.[42]

When the Conservatives returned to government in 1984, there was certainly no immediate effort to strengthen federal involvement in the environmental field. The new environment minister, Suzanne Blais-Grenier, followed the example of her predecessors from both parties in depicting the federal role in environmental protection as strictly supplementary.[43] Although it had long since ceased to be of any significance, the advocacy approach finally was laid to rest in 1986, after the Nielson Task Force, appointed by the newly elected Conservative government to conduct program reviews across the federal government, was critical that the implication of partisanship undermined Environment Canada's credibility.[44]

During this period, the perspective of the parliamentary opposition parties, like that of the government, paralleled the decline in salience of the environment. Even in the face of a Liberal minority government between 1972 and 1974, the Opposition did not attempt to rekindle the pollution issue, choosing instead to respond to public opinion by pressing the government on more prominent issues of the day.[45] The nature of opposition members' arguments concerning high-profile environmental problems that did occasionally emerged changed markedly over the course of the decade, from demanding a strong federal role to demanding greater deference to the provinces. When the Environmental Contaminants Act was before the House in 1975, there were fewer opposition demands for federal leadership than in 1970. And by 1977, when proposed amendments to the Fisheries Act were under review, members of the Opposition actually criticized the government for inadequate respect for provincial jurisdiction.

The Opposition's tone reversed again, however, with the emergence of the acid rain issue. Reminiscent of 1970, members of the Opposition called for a stronger federal role, arguing that 'we cannot wait for jurisdictional duels to take place at the peril of our environment.'[46] Both the Liberal and Conservative parties demanded a stronger federal role while in opposition, yet both cited constitutional constraints and the need to cooperate with the provinces while in government.[47]

The Constitutional Function

With the preceding discussion as a backdrop, the next four sections review the federal retreat in greater detail, considering in turn the constitutional, legislative, regulatory, and enforcement functions. Federal-provincial constitutional discussions were reactivated in the late 1970s, culminating in the Constitution Act of 1982. Questions of environmental jurisdiction were even less visible than during the constitutional discussions in 1971. However, after years of federal-provincial conflict concerning oil and gas revenues, the Western provinces did place great emphasis on ownership and control of natural resources, which indirectly touched on the issue of environmental jurisdiction. The result was the inclusion of Section 92A, which gave the provinces exclusive jurisdiction over exploration, development, conservation, and management of non-renewable natural resources, as well as over forestry and sites for the generation of electricity. It is noteworthy, however, that Section 92A does not address responsibility for other renewable resources, such as water and air.

Several provinces were also eager to redefine the fisheries power in the constitution. Although it did not occur in the end, the federal government reportedly was quite receptive to calls for a transfer of federal authority over inland fisheries.[48] In light of the federal government's heavy reliance on the fisheries power to support its pollution control efforts, the federal position concerning inland fisheries jurisdiction suggests little effort was made to defend federal environmental authority.

In the end, however, what is most striking about the constitutional negotiations concerning natural resources is the invisibility of environmental concerns. The primary focus was authority to direct and profit from the exploitation of resources, rather than to protect them. That fact is particularly noteworthy in light of the persistent uncertainty surrounding environmental jurisdiction. Indeed, since the previous round of constitutional negotiations, the Supreme Court had only added to the confusion with the *Interprovincial Co-operatives* decision. Yet, while the legal questions remained clouded, the political question had been resolved. The federal government had demonstrated its willingness to concede provincial dominance in the field.

The Legislative Function

Although federal legislative activity declined sharply after 1971, there was sufficient momentum in the early 1970s to carry through two additional statutes already under development: the Ocean Dumping Control Act and the Environmental Contaminants Act. This delayed activity is consistent with Peters and Hogwood's observation that there is often a lag between a decline in public attention to an issue and the decline in administrative activity on that issue.[49] Beyond the passage of the two new statutes, the only significant legislative activity during this period was the amendment of the Fisheries Act in 1977 and the Clean Air Act in 1980.[50] A new Canada Environment Act was proposed, but did not get very far. This section considers each of these statutes in turn.

New Legislation

The Ocean Dumping Control Act was passed in 1975 to fulfil Canada's commitment to implement the 1972 London Convention on ocean dumping. The assertion of federal authority to implement an international treaty concerning marine pollution was far from daring, since the Supreme Court previously had affirmed extensive federal powers with respect to offshore resources. At the time, the federal environment minister reported that the provinces were 'enthusiastic' about the Ocean Dumping Control Act.[51] The degree of provincial support is somewhat surprising in light of the fact that the act went further than called for by the International Convention by extending federal control of ocean dumping to provincial marine waters, such as the Georgia Strait in British Columbia. It is unclear why the federal government sought that additional authority. However, at the time authority with respect to inland marine waters, such as the Georgia Strait, and ownership of potentially significant offshore resources therein, were still contested by the federal and provincial governments.[52] Thus, the extension of the act to inland marine waters may have been intended more to reinforce federal claims of resource ownership than to assert authority to protect those resources.

The Environmental Contaminants Act, proclaimed in 1976, was the last item of business from the flurry of legislative activity of the early 1970s. It was originally proposed in 1972 by the federal Task Force on Environmental Contaminants Legislation, which was confident that the federal government's residual and criminal law powers would support such legislation.[53] Rather than indicating renewed federal interest in the environment in the mid-1970s, however, the delayed passage of the act can be seen as an indication of just how low the environment had fallen among federal legislative priorities.[54]

The goal of the act was to ensure that toxic chemicals were evaluated and, if necessary, controlled. However, like the Clean Air Act, the Environmental Contaminants Act envisioned a strictly supplementary role for the federal government. Federal regulations were authorized only if the federal environment and health ministers were satisfied, after mandatory consultation with the provinces and other federal departments, that the hazards posed by a particular substance would not be adequately addressed by provincial or other federal laws. Although concern about the extent of federal deference to the provinces was expressed by one environmental group and at least one member of the Opposition during hearings on the proposed act,[55] the tone of the parliamentary debate had changed significantly since 1970. In contrast to the heated debates over the Canada Water Act, the relative strength of federal and provincial roles was a non-issue in 1975.

The act required that chemical manufacturers report to the federal government any information in their possession concerning health hazards. However, because they were not required to systematically collect such information, their reports were of little use. International efforts to standardize testing requirements for new chemicals, embodied in a 1980 agreement among OECD countries, provided the impetus to revise the act.[56] However, although plans to revise the act were announced as early as 1980, no amendments were made until 1988, after public interest in the environment had revived. The Environmental Contaminants Act was then replaced by the Canadian Environmental Protection Act (CEPA), which is discussed in Chapter 6.

Amendments to the Fisheries Act
In 1977, the federal government introduced amendments to the Fisheries Act to address various problems encountered during implementation of the 1970 amendments. However, times clearly had changed since the 1970 amendments, which met little resistance from the opposition parties, the provinces, or industry. In contrast, the 1977 amendments met a vigorous campaign of opposition from industry and seven of the provinces.

The most substantial and controversial change to the Fisheries Act was the addition of a new provision prohibiting destruction of fish habitat. The act also was amended to expand the definition of 'fish' to include fish eggs, to increase penalties for non-compliance, and to require reporting of accidental spills. Another minor but important change authorized the fisheries minister to designate federal or provincial officials to promulgate enforceable compliance schedules for individual polluters. Ironically, in light of provincial objections to the stringency of the package of amendments, the intent of that provision was to shield polluters from private citizens' aggressive enforcement efforts by exempting the negotiated agreements reached by polluters and government officials from the more stringent absolute prohibition on discharges found in the act.[57]

The proposed amendments generated immediate opposition from most of the provinces and from regulated industries, both of which argued that the legislation conferred almost unlimited powers upon the federal government. On the face of it, it is surprising that the government would introduce such controversial legislation in the absence of clear public demand. However, the extent of provincial opposition simply was not foreseen. The amendments were originally proposed by federal bureaucrats, who saw them as minor but necessary adjustments to strengthen implementation of the act. In particular, the controversial habitat provisions, which were developed by the Department of Fisheries and Oceans, had been favourably received by provincial fisheries officials prior to introduction. Since provincial fisheries officers administer the federal legislation in most provinces, they welcomed amendments that would, in effect, strengthen their own authority. However, the federal government had not discussed the full package of proposals with provincial environment departments, whose opinions of the bill differed greatly from that of their colleagues in Fisheries.[58]

Although the government continued to support the bill after provincial opposition emerged, its tone was markedly less strident than during the early 1970s. The government certainly did not use the occasion to claim federal leadership in pollution control. While in 1970 Jack Davis made little effort to disguise the federal government's intent to use its fisheries power to control water pollution indirectly, in 1977, his successor, Roméo LeBlanc, offered reassurances that the Fisheries Act really was intended only to protect fisheries, not as a back door approach to pollution control.[59]

Provincial opposition coalesced at a CCREM meeting in June 1977. Thereafter, representatives from the environment departments of four provinces – Nova Scotia, Ontario, British Columbia, and Alberta – appeared on behalf of their governments before the parliamentary committee reviewing the bill. Four others (New Brunswick, Newfoundland, Saskatchewan, and Prince Edward Island) submitted briefs to the committee.[60] Only Prince Edward Island supported the legislation, while the governments of Manitoba and Quebec were silent on the issue.[61]

The argument most commonly raised by the provinces was that the federal proposal would lead to unnecessary duplication of provincial environmental protection efforts. The provinces predicted public confusion, unnecessary cost to taxpayers, and a threat to provincial environmental programs should a court rule that the federal government occupied the field. The creation of provincial environmental departments since 1970 had broadened the basis for bureaucratic resentment of federal interference. While only Ontario and BC could claim credible environmental protection programs earlier in the decade, by 1977 they were joined in their criticisms by even the smallest provinces.

The second argument raised by the provinces was that the bill was an unwarranted federal intrusion into provincial jurisdiction over natural resources. The Ontario government joined Alberta in openly questioning the constitutionality of the bill, a step it had not taken in 1970 despite its reservations concerning the Canada Water Act. Nova Scotia, New Brunswick, and Saskatchewan, all of which supported the Canada Water Act in 1970, also now objected to the proposed amendments on constitutional grounds. Saskatchewan, which went so far as to advocate a constitutional amendment to strengthen federal authority in 1971, now spoke of 'an unwarranted intrusion into provincial affairs and jurisdiction.'[62] It is noteworthy that the only province to support the bill, Prince Edward Island, is the one with the least extensive (and least profitable) Crown resources.

Finally, several provinces made veiled references to the possibility that the federal government would be overly zealous in protecting the environment, an argument that would have been unthinkable in the environmentally conscious atmosphere of 1970. Submissions to the parliamentary committee indicate that several provinces opposed the bill, not because they sought unchallenged authority to protect the environment, but because they wanted the flexibility not to do so. Provincial representatives raised the spectre of arbitrary federal closures of vital industries. Nova Scotia's representative argued that Environment Canada 'often does not take account of all the economic realities of a particular industry, or of the overall interests of the community the industry supports, or of the province, in its decisionmaking respecting pollution control,' a concern echoed by Newfoundland's spokesperson.[63] Similarly, the Alberta government representative stated that 'the province through its department of business development and tourism is often able to assist industrial clients with their concerns and relations with provincial environmental protection agencies. Most times these matters can be resolved within this process to everyone's satisfaction. A further federal review procedure and authority regulating industrial development in the province would be unacceptable.'[64] Even Ontario alluded to 'unreasonable' federal requirements for industries and municipalities.[65]

There was a substantial degree of convergence between the views of the provinces and those of industries regulated under the act. As in 1971, the pulp and paper industry was particularly outspoken. The Canadian Pulp and Paper Association (CPPA) strongly advocated a 'single window' approach, arguing that 'the orderly and efficient conduct of environmental management requires co-operative and joint action through a single agency in any given region.'[66] The industry clearly preferred that that single agency be a provincial one; CPPA openly sought to defend provincial jurisdiction from federal intrusion. In contrast, advocates of regulation, ostensibly representing the public, appeared nonplussed by the inevitable public confusion predicted by the provinces and industry.[67]

The position of the opposition parties on the proposed amendments was particularly interesting. Between 1968 and 1972 the Opposition had repeatedly demanded that the government take a stronger stand with respect to federal jurisdiction. By 1977, however, the opposition parties criticized the government for inadequate consultation with the provinces, and challenged the extension of federal powers as unnecessary interference in provincial jurisdiction.[68] One member of the Opposition even likened the proposed amendments to 'a deliberate plan to break up Canada, a deliberate plan to confront the provinces with policies and powers that should be vested in the provinces.'[69]

In response to these arguments, the government reiterated its intent to rely on provincial implementation whenever possible.[70] Although only minor amendments were made before the bill was passed by the Liberal majority in Parliament, the real response of the government can be seen in the subsequent administration of the act. According to Doern and Conway, after being burned on the Fisheries Act amendments, the federal minister, Roméo LeBlanc, 'did not want anything to do with the [Environmental Protection Service],' thus Environment Canada 'did not do anything on regulation for almost a decade.'[71] As promised, the government did not use the new tools provided by the act to extend the federal role in environmental protection. In fact, the much needed provision to authorize enforceable compliance schedules was never used, despite pleas from Environment Canada's regional offices. The federal retreat from regulation embodied in the previously discussed advocacy approach also can be seen as a response in large part to the provinces' objections to the 1977 amendments.

The Canada Environment Act and Clean Air Act Amendments
In addition to provincial hostility, Environment Canada was beset during this period by interdepartmental competition. Since the creation of the department, the relationship between the Fisheries Service and the Environmental Protection Service (EPS) had been uneasy at best. In 1971, the two had reached an accommodation concerning their respective roles under the Fisheries Act, with the Fisheries Service assuming responsibility for physical threats to habitat, and EPS assuming responsibility for chem-

ical pollutants.[72] However, conflict persisted largely because the Fisheries Service frequently took a more aggressive approach to prosecution of offenses than EPS.

In 1978, the fisheries and environment functions finally were separated into two departments. The dilemma for Environment Canada was that the new fisheries minister assumed formal responsibility for the Fisheries Act, EPS' most important tool. The prime minister refused a request by the new environment minister for a formal transfer of responsibility for the pollution control provisions of the Fisheries Act to Environment Canada, but did order that the informal accommodation between EPS and the Fisheries Service reached in 1971 remain in place pending a permanent solution.[73]

In light of its uncertain statutory authority, Environment Canada proposed an overhaul of federal environmental legislation to give the department its own statutory mandate with respect to water pollution control. Work began on an 'Omnibus Environmental Amendment Act' or 'Canada Environment Act' to replace the pollution provisions of the Fisheries Act. The effort coincided with plans to revise the Environmental Contaminants Act to conform with Canada's commitment to the OECD.

Plans for the Canada Environment Act were shelved, however, in 1982. The precise reasons for abandonment of the proposed legislation are unclear. One legal advisor to the department reflected that there was less willingness to take a chance on 'Peace, Order, and good Government' in the early 1980s than later in the decade, when CEPA was finally proposed.[74] Also, at the time the government was preoccupied with intergovernmental conflicts on the constitutional and energy fronts, and there was a conscious effort to mend federal-provincial fences in the environmental field. Finally, in light of the low public profile of environmental issues, there simply was no promise of electoral reward to justify picking another fight with the provinces over environmental jurisdiction.

The final legislative action during this period was amendment of the Clean Air Act in 1980 in response to the problem of acid rain. The amendment authorized federal action to prevent damage in another country caused by domestic air pollution (as long as the other country's legislation provided reciprocal protection). The fact that such action was authorized even in the absence of an international treaty represented a significant extension of the earlier international provisions of the act. However, it was made abundantly clear by the environment minister that the extension of authority was never intended to support federal action.[75] Rather, the intent was to satisfy a comparable reciprocity requirement in the US Clean Air Act, in order to force US action. The minister explained that 'this is a message which we in this House are sending to the administration, Congress, and people of the United States.'[76]

With the support of the Opposition, the bill was rushed through all three readings in a single day, to allow the outgoing Carter administration to initiate action (subsequently overturned by the US courts) before the arrival of President-elect Reagan's less sympathetic appointees. It is noteworthy that at the same time one of the few controversial provisions of the 1971 act was quietly weakened. Section 20 of the Clean Air Act originally authorized the federal environment minister to issue emission standards if a province took the relatively minor step of adopting national ambient air quality objectives. The amendment clarified the government's intention that all efforts should be made first to resolve air quality problems through provincial laws.

The Regulatory Function

Regulatory statutes passed by parliamentary governments typically authorize the executive to perform a broad variety of actions, rather than demanding that particular actions be taken. As a result, when the first generation of federal environmental statutes was passed around 1970, many difficult decisions were merely postponed. However, when the time came to move beyond symbolic promises and impose the very real costs of pollution abatement, public attention and thus political will had waned.

Several factors hampered Environment Canada's ability to implement the new statutes. First, in the early 1970s, just as the new environment department needed an infusion of resources to meet the challenge of implementation, the federal government became preoccupied with budgetary restraint. Environment Canada's share of federal resources actually declined by a third between 1974 and 1979-80, from 1.6 per cent of the federal budget to 1.1 per cent.[77] The department was further decimated by the Mulroney government's budget cuts in 1984. Under the stewardship of the Conservatives' first environment minister, Suzanne Blais-Grenier, federal spending on environmental protection was cut by 14 per cent in one year alone.[78]

Another problem was the fact that the position of environment minister remained a junior portfolio, thus preventing an effective champion of the environment from emerging within cabinet. Although the first federal environment minister, Jack Davis, maintained a relatively high profile until his defeat in the 1974 election, he was followed by a rapid succession of junior ministers. Twelve different ministers held the environment portfolio in the thirteen-year period between 1972 and 1985.[79]

Environment Canada also was constrained by continuing resistance from the provinces and from other federal departments. Tensions between the Department of Fisheries and Oceans and Environment Canada persisted after the two were separated in 1978. Armed with the recommendations of the Pearse Commission on the West Coast fisheries, which concluded that the continuing division of responsibilities for the Fisheries Act impeded effective habitat management, the Department of Fisheries and Oceans sought in 1983 to wrest control of the pollution control provisions of the Fisheries Act, the Ocean Dumping Control Act, and related staff resources from Environment Canada.[80] Although the two departments eventually reached a truce of sorts in 1985 in the form of a Memorandum of Understanding, in the meantime, Environment Canada was required to deflect scarce resources to fight interdepartmental battles.

The department also was constrained by the limits of its own statutory mandate. As noted in the previous chapter, the first generation of federal environmental statutes often reflected continuing hesitance, authorizing only supplementary federal actions. Moreover, authority for many environmental matters was left to line departments, like Transport, Agriculture, and Indian and Northern Affairs, which were considerably less committed to environmental protection than Environment Canada.

Finally, one cannot underestimate the significance of voluntary bureaucratic hesitance. The challenge of imposing substantial costs on polluters typically was left to civil servants who were confronted with resistance from both regulated firms and provincial civil servants. Limited in resources and political support, they had few incentives to rock the boat by aggressively implementing federal statutes.[81]

Implementation of Statutes

The first action taken under the Clean Air Act was the promulgation of National Ambient Air Quality Objectives in January 1973, based on the recommendations of a committee of federal and provincial air quality experts. The act also provided for the issuance of enforceable national emission regulations if there was 'significant danger to the health of persons.' Only four such regulations ever were issued, the last in 1979. The government was more active in developing hortatory emission guidelines under the act, which it did for seven industries.[82] The federal government also supported provincial air pollution control programs by operating a national air quality monitoring network.

The federal government never exercised its authority under the Clean Air Act to establish limits for emissions from federal activities. The Federal Facilities Program, designed to put the federal government's own house in order, was eliminated in 1975.[83] Nor were the international provisions of the act ever invoked. In fact, Environment Canada's administrative capabilities in the area of air pollution control gradually were eroded until the Air Pollution Control Directorate was dissolved in 1984-5. The Clean Air Act Annual Report for that year describes the federal role as one of performing research and developing guidelines, failing even to acknowledge Environment Canada's regulatory authority under the act.[84] A similar picture emerges concerning implementation of the Environmental Contaminants Act. Only five substances or classes of substances were regulated in the act's thirteen-year life.

Environment Canada was more aggressive in implementing the Fisheries Act, however. Even then, regulations ultimately were issued for only six industries, though twenty such regulations had been planned by 1977.[85] In comparison, over fifty broad industrial categories were regulated during this same period under the US Clean Water Act. Moreover, it is noteworthy that, with the exception of regulations concerning chlor-alkali industrial plants, the Fisheries Act regulations applied only to plants constructed after the date of issuance of the regulations. One Environment Canada official estimated in 1991 that less than 100 facilities among over 10,000 significant industrial dischargers were covered by federal regulations under the Fisheries Act.[86]

With the announcement of Environment Canada's new advocacy approach in 1979, standard setting under the Fisheries Act ground to a halt. Two proposed regulations that were well advanced were put on hold, pending work on the proposed Omnibus Environmental Amendment Act.[87] However, when that legislation never materialized, regulatory activity under the Fisheries Act did not resume. Indeed, the last new regulation issued under the act was passed in 1979, to exempt a mine in British Columbia from the earlier federal regulation concerning discharges from mines. Since then, no new regulations under the Fisheries Act have been issued, and not until 1992 were any of the existing regulations amended.

The Canada Water Act fared even worse. Part I was used to justify federal programs to monitor water resources that existed before the act was passed in 1970, as well as federal participation in several federal-provincial studies of river basins in the 1970s. However, the ambitious goal of comprehensive water resource management never came to pass. Nor were the water quality provisions of Part II implemented; no joint water quality management agencies ever were established. Only Part III, which called for regulation of phosphates in detergents, was fully implemented. Although the act remains on the books (with the exception of Part III, now incorporated in CEPA), there is little prospect that it will ever be used.

Several authors have offered explanations for the failure of the innovative approach of the Canada Water Act. Woodrow emphasizes the personal influence of Jack Davis. The fact that the champion of the Fisheries Act Amendments became the first federal environment minister undoubtedly contributed to the demise of the competing approach of the Canada Water Act. The minister took little interest in the ongoing water basin planning studies, and continued to favour the command and control regulatory approach of the Fisheries Act. Under Davis's leadership, the Canada Water Act provisions for joint federal-provincial water quality management agencies were 'gradually but deliberately put on the shelf.'[88]

Others have emphasized provincial resistance to the act as the reason for federal hesitance.[89] To a large degree, the Canada Water Act was predicated on a politically naive belief that the power of ideas would prevail over jurisdictional jealousies. However, British Columbia, Ontario, and Quebec continued to resist the act, and until the mid-1970s refused to participate in bilateral committees that were proposed for each province, by which time it was clear that the committees were quite harmless.[90]

Thompson stresses federal reluctance to rely on constitutionally uncertain powers.[91] Yet, as Thompson himself observes, the federal government made little effort to get involved even in interprovincial and international waters, where the constitutional basis of its authority was more assured. Thompson also argues that the threat of federal unilateralism spurred action by the provinces, thus limiting the need for federal involvement. However, the fact remains that few provinces actively implemented their new statutes, and still the federal government deferred to them.

Two important factors that contributed to the demise of the Canada Water Act have been overlooked. First, the timidity of the act itself has been underestimated. Federal hesitance in 1970 resulted in an act that laid out a path to implementation fraught with obstacles. The fact that Part I did not authorize federal implementation of water resource management plans rendered Environment Canada 'essentially dependent on the willingness of the provinces to participate.'[92] With respect to water quality management, rather than making a once-and-for-all assertion of federal powers, any exercise of unilateral federal powers demanded a location-specific declaration, which would have been politically difficult each and every time. The cautious form of the statute rendered implementation vulnerable to provincial unwillingness to cooperate, and to lack of federal resolve to wield the instrument of unilateralism.

Finally, and perhaps most importantly, the government confronted the daunting task of implementation in a climate of apparent public indifference. Federal politicians were not willing to take a constitutional risk or to provoke conflict with the provinces because they had no obvious electoral incentive to do so. In the end, rather than being the blunt instrument of federal unilateralism that its critics claimed, the Canada Water Act endures as a symbol of federal timidity.

The Enforcement Function

Just as statutory authority to issue regulations does not require that regulations be issued, the issuance of regulations does not require that they be enforced. Traditionally, the executive in parliamentary governments has enjoyed almost unlimited discretion with respect to enforcement. Canadian regulators have exercised that discretion by promoting compliance via informal negotiations with polluters, rather than strictly enforcing the 'black letter law' by routinely prosecuting non-compliance.[93] In 1980, Thompson reported that 'bargaining is the essence of the environmental regulatory process as it is practised in Canada.'[94] Bargaining between government and industry has been the norm from the development of regulations through to enforcement at the individual plant level. Regulatory standards as well as schedules for individual polluters to come into compliance typically have been negotiated behind closed doors in a tripartite process involving federal and provincial officials and representatives of the polluting industry.[95]

As a result, as Huestis observes, 'one striking feature of the Canadian environmental protection process is the fact that litigation is not a major part of the process.'[96] Indeed, up to 1988, there were only ten prosecutions under the Canada Water Act, Environmental Contaminants Act, Clean Air Act, and Ocean Dumping Control Act combined.[97] Legal action under the Fisheries Act has been more common in the case of accidental spills, but prosecutions of continuing discharges under the act have been rare.[98]

The paucity of lawsuits alone cannot be accepted as proof of failure to enforce environmental regulations, since the approach of negotiated compliance would be expected to yield few prosecutions. However, the effectiveness of the cooperative approach, in terms of actual compliance rates, has been quite dismal. For instance, sixteen years after the issuance of the pulp and paper regulations for new mills and guidelines for existing mills, 70 per cent of Canadian pulp mills still failed to comply with federal standards that were considered economically feasible in 1971.[99] Even allowing for gradual implementation, federal officials had promised that full compliance would be achieved within ten years.

Webb attributes this disappointing record of compliance to flaws in the legislation itself and the associated regulations.[100] He argues that the Fisheries Act penalties for non-compliance do not present a sufficient deterrent, and that the act's reliance on a criminal standard of liability placed an unreasonably onerous burden of proof on federal prosecutors. In addition, the fact that most federal regulations do not apply to existing industries has meant that federal officials have had to bargain with polluters without the supporting threat of a firm deadline for compliance.

These constraints were felt most keenly by Environment Canada's regional offices, which were responsible for negotiating compliance with individual polluters. Because bargaining for enforcement is even less visible than the development of regulations, regional officials were indeed caught 'between a rock and a hard place.'[101] On one side, they faced unwavering resistance from polluters, and on the other, they were constrained by flaws in the statute and regulations. The exclusion of environmental groups from the process left public servants particularly vulnerable to regulated interests. Indeed, over time, regulators often developed sympathy for the plight of regulated firms, with whom they had established long-standing relationships.

However, the flaws of the regulatory system provide only a partial explanation for the poor record of compliance. One cannot ignore the fact that the federal government had the capacity to remedy those flaws. Yet, no effort was made to pursue the quite straightforward solution of revising the Fisheries Act regulations to impose a uniform deadline for compliance for existing facilities. Nor was there any inclination to invoke the 1977 amendments to give the regions authority to negotiate enforceable compliance schedules, despite the pleas of Environment Canada's regional officials.

Although they professed to support the 'polluter pays policy,' federal politicians showed a distinct preference to motivate polluters with the carrot rather than the stick. Regulated industries were offered a variety of subsidies to encourage compliance, including tax exemptions, loans, grants, and technology transfers. For instance, the pulp and paper industry in eastern Canada received $542 million in subsidies for modernization, on the condition that mills fully comply with all federal and provincial environmental standards after modernization.[102] Although the subsidies did have some positive impact, the rate of compliance among mills that received subsidies remained abysmal, despite government grants averaging $10 million per mill.[103] Although subsidies clearly were not sufficient to purchase full compliance, the federal government showed little inclination to wield the stick of prosecution to force polluters to accept the remaining costs of pollution abatement.

Delegation of Enforcement
The federal government retreated from enforcement largely by shifting the responsibility to the provinces. A clear division of responsibilities emerged

during this period, with the federal government relying on the provinces to take the lead in enforcing federal regulations.[104] The origins of the delegation of enforcement lay in the federal government's reliance on the Fisheries Act to control water pollution. Early in the century, administrative arrangements evolved between the federal government and six provinces (all but the Atlantic provinces), delegating responsibility for administration of the federal Fisheries Act to the provinces.[105] However, it was not immediately obvious that administration of the new pollution control provisions of the act was covered by earlier federal-provincial fisheries agreements. In any case, given the informality of existing arrangements, there was no legal impediment to the federal government reasserting responsibility for any provision of the act at any time. Despite that fact, since about the mid-1970s, Environment Canada has operated under the assumption that the primary responsibility for enforcement of the Fisheries Act regulations rested with the provinces.[106]

It is pertinent to ask whether delegation of administration to the provinces was intended all along, or whether the federal government retreated from a commitment to enforce its own regulations only after public support waned. A search of ministerial correspondence provided no clear answer to this question.[107] The minister did not comment during legislative debates on the Fisheries Act on the question of which level of government would be responsible for enforcement. On one hand, a representative of the Department of Justice noted during the committee hearings that the provinces presently were responsible for enforcement of the act, and that the federal government probably would not step in unless the provinces failed to do the job.[108] On the other hand, three persons who participated on the committee that devised the first set of federal regulations under the Fisheries Act, a federal government representative, a provincial government representative, and a representative of the pulp and paper industry, each recalled working under the assumption that the federal government would enforce its own regulations.[109] The conflicting evidence suggests that the whole question of enforcement was given little thought in the rush to draft the legislation and issue the first regulations.

However, as the new environment department turned to the task of enforcing its new statutes with limited resources, the prospect of relying on the provinces undoubtedly became increasingly attractive. As early as September 1971, Davis remarked at a conference that provincial pollution control agencies probably would be the ones that polluters would deal with most often, and that he hoped they would incorporate federal standards in their own permits.[110] Environment Canada subsequently commissioned a study to clarify the status of delegation arrangements under the Fisheries Act.[111] By 1972, Davis clearly was sold on delegation when he stated, 'it is our intention ... to develop standards which the provinces will adopt, standards which the provinces will in fact copy, and which they will enforce.'[112]

Although doubts may have remained about the status of administrative arrangements under the Fisheries Act, the informal delegation of enforcement was strengthened and extended to other statutes in any case by a series of federal-provincial accords signed in the mid-1970s. Encouraged by the promise of a 1971 Canada-Ontario agreement on Great Lakes water quality, the federal government pursued bilateral accords with the other provinces as well. The basic approach was agreed to by federal and provincial Ministers at a 1973 CCREM meeting, and by 1975 all provinces but Quebec, British Columbia, and Newfoundland had signed similar accords with the federal government. Although negotiations continued off and on for several years, those three provinces never did sign accords.

In the accords, the federal and provincial governments expressed a commitment to cooperate in the area of environmental protection by sharing data, expertise, and the costs of monitoring environmental quality.[113] More importantly, the accords reflect a shared understanding of the roles of the federal and provincial government in environmental regulation. The accords identify several roles for the federal government, including controlling discharges from federal facilities, establishing ambient environmental quality objectives and, in consultation with the provinces, developing 'national baseline effluent and emission requirements and guidelines.' In turn, the provinces agreed 'to establish and enforce requirements at least as stringent as the agreed national baseline requirements.'[114] In effect, the federal government agreed not to enforce its own standards unless requested to do so by a province or unless the province failed to fulfil its promise to meet national standards.

The accords were originally signed for a five-year term in 1975, and several were extended in 1980, 1981, and 1982. The accords with New Brunswick, Nova Scotia, Prince Edward Island, and Manitoba at one time were considered by the federal government to have been extended indefinitely in 1982.[115] The Saskatchewan and Alberta accords expired in 1980 and 1987, respectively.[116] The Ontario accord appears to have expired as well, although, in any case, the focus of the federal-provincial relationship in that province has always been the more detailed Canada-Ontario Agreement Concerning Great Lakes Water Quality.

The result of the accords was to effect what has become known as the 'one window' approach. Ideally, polluters would be required to deal with only one set of requirements and one level of government – the provinces. However, in practice there was considerable variation in the relationships between federal and provincial environmental officials, ranging from federal-provincial partnership in the Atlantic provinces, to systematic consultation in British Columbia and ad hoc consultation in Ontario, to virtually no federal involvement in Saskatchewan, Quebec, and Alberta.[117]

In justifying the one window approach, EPS and provincial officials invariably emphasized public impatience with unnecessary duplication. Yet it was not 'the public' that was concerned. The public at large was oblivious to administrative arrangements for environmental enforcement, and the environmental groups that testified concerning the 1977 Fisheries Act amendments were quite supportive of overlapping federal and provincial roles. It was regulated industries, rather than the beneficiaries of regulation, that strongly opposed independent action by the two levels of government, not only because of the additional administrative costs of having to satisfy two sovereigns, but because they feared the potential for 'leap-frogging,' where each level of government would try to outdo the other by issuing more stringent standards.[118] One federal official recalled that at the time the accords were developed, 'the industry was screaming "who's in charge?"'

Provincial governments pursued the one window approach for their own reasons. The provinces' testimony concerning the 1977 Fisheries Act amendment suggests that they were motivated by a desire to defend provincial jurisdiction over natural resources, and to defend local industry from the prospect of overzealous federal enforcement. However, personal pride clearly was a powerful motivation as well. When asked why the provinces would seek the added responsibility and administrative expense of administering the federal government's laws, provincial officials and politicians interviewed invariably replied, 'we're already doing the job,' or 'we can do a better job.'[119]

The question remains why the federal government was willing to delegate its enforcement responsibility. Enforcement is staff-intensive, and the new Department of the Environment was constrained by limited resources. Moreover, Huestis asserts that EPS bureaucrats welcomed delegation to the provinces at least in part to escape constant pressure from the federal Fisheries Service.[120] Fisheries officials disapproved of any negotiated compliance agreements that tolerated residual threats to fish or fish habitat and, as a result, they occasionally laid charges under the Fisheries Act over the objections of EPS. A senior Environment Canada official explains: 'our fisheries colleagues are very concerned that the fishery be protected, we are concerned that industry be dealt with against a reasonable background of legitimate interest for that industry's activities and also our desire to work through the province, when you put all that together you find us very often in the middle and it can be very difficult in the middle.'[121]

In theory, the delegation of responsibility for enforcement to the provinces was conditional. The federal government threatened to reclaim its enforcement role should the provinces fail to enforce national standards within a reasonable time. However, in practice, despite a record of widespread and persistent non-compliance with federal standards, the federal government only rarely intervened. Not only did the provinces fail to enforce their own permits, but those permits often did not satisfy federal requirements. A comparison of provincial permits for pulp and paper mills with federal regulations in five provinces, comprising roughly 90 per cent of mills nationally, revealed that in 1987 only 40 per cent of provincial permits matched federal standards.[122] Moreover, even where the accords expired or were never signed, the provinces were given priority in enforcement.[123] The federal government was particularly reluctant to take enforcement action in Quebec, despite abysmal rates of compliance with federal regulations in that province.[124]

The federal-provincial accords had the intended effect of reducing intergovernmental conflict and duplication. However, the accords fell far short of the objective of achieving national consistency in environmental standards and enforcement. A number of authors have been extremely critical of the federal retreat from enforcement. Huestis describes the federal policy as 'a virtual abdication of responsibility,'[125] while Estrin concludes that 'such accords ... can be viewed as providing little more than an excuse for Ottawa to close its eyes to inaction at the provincial level.'[126] The flaw of the approach lay not in the objective of reconciling delivery of environmental programs, but in the almost complete absence of federal oversight.

Compared to the relatively visible activities of passing legislation and even issuing regulations, the day-to-day details of enforcement evade public scrutiny. Thus, enforcement offered little promise of credit for federal politicians or bureaucrats, yet much enmity. In the absence of public pressure for enforcement, EPS evaded pressure from the Fisheries Service, the provinces, and regulated industries by conceding the lead enforcement role to the provinces. The history of the accords calls into question whether the federal government's intent really was administrative efficiency, or merely escape from costly and politically unpleasant responsibilities.

Federal-Provincial Relations

According to Woodrow, 'the early 1970s seemed to witness federal-provincial relations with regard to pollution control and environmental management turn its face from confrontation to co-existence.'[127] The turf battles that accompanied the passage of the Canada Water Act soon subsided as the federal government assumed a supporting role of providing research and technical expertise to the provinces and facilitating consensus on national standards.

When the pollution issue fell from the limelight, the Canadian Council of Resource and Environment Ministers (CCREM) found itself struggling for its existence. In 1973, the federal and provincial ministers voted to significantly reduce the size of the secretariat, which had grown to support a significant public education program.[128]

CCREM was relatively inactive in the late 1970s. Regular publications ceased, and there are few records to indicate what the council accomplished during that period. However, the emergence of the acid rain issue in the early 1980s led to a partial rejuvenation of the council. The remainder of this section examines federal-provincial relations concerning international environmental matters, with particular attention to acid rain, before closing by considering the institutional role of CCREM in Canadian environmental policy-making.

Federal-Provincial Relations in International Affairs

Although the federal government was active in international environmental affairs throughout this period, federal leadership abroad was not matched by actions at home.[129] The federal government did not attempt to use international commitments as leverage to extend its role in environmental protection. Rather than asserting federal authority concerning transboundary pollution under the 'Peace, Order, and good Government' power, the federal government relied on the provinces to meet Canada's international obligations. The federal government secured provincial cooperation by consulting the provinces during international negotiations and, when necessary, purchasing provincial assent with federal subsidies to local industry or municipalities.

The federal government has been particularly active with respect to US-Canada boundary waters via the bilateral International Joint Commission (IJC), which was established by the Boundary Waters Treaty of 1909. Based on recommendations of the IJC, the Great Lakes Water Quality Agreement was signed by the two countries in 1972, and updated in 1978 and 1985. Prior to signing the agreement, the federal government and Ontario reached a bilateral agreement on Great Lakes water quality, which established a mechanism for fulfilling Canada's international commitments through provincial legislation. According to Munton, 'when the words are stripped away, the "deal" was essentially federal money for provincial cooperation.'[130] The federal government provided $167 million in subsidies for construction of municipal sewage treatment facilities and infrastructure.

The federal government took a similar approach a decade later with respect to the transboundary problem of acid rain. Many of the federal-provincial negotiations concerning acid rain took place under the auspices of CCREM. In 1982, the federal and provincial ministers agreed to a 25 per cent unilateral reduction of sulphur dioxide emissions, to be increased to 50 per cent only if the US agreed to reduce its own emissions proportionately. However, in 1984, under pressure from the federal government, Ontario, and Quebec, the federal and provincial ministers forged a commitment to a unilateral 50 per cent reduction in Canadian sulphur dioxide emissions.[131] The ministers agreed to 'go it alone,' with the hope that with its own house in order, Canada might stand a better chance of convincing the US to follow suit. Although the original agreement was reached under a federal Liberal government, by the time the details were finalized in 1985, the Conservatives had assumed office.[132]

Like the Great Lakes Water Quality Agreement before it, the acid rain strategy relied on provincial regulations supported by federal subsidies. A federal commitment to provide $150 million to subsidize pollution abatement by smelters was a critical element of the federal-provincial agreement.[133] Subsequently, bilateral agreements were signed between the federal government and the seven eastern provinces, the last in 1988.

Despite often divergent provincial perspectives and the potential for federal-provincial conflict, relations between the federal and provincial environment ministers on the issue of acid rain were remarkably harmonious. Three reasons can be offered. First, cooperation was easier to achieve because the federal and provincial governments faced a common enemy. Most of the acid rain that falls in Canada originates in the United States and thus domestic controls in the US were essential to mitigate the effects of acid rain in Canada. The fact that federal and provincial governments shared the goal of forcing the recalcitrant US government to reduce its emissions made cooperation easier. Even the separatist Quebec premier, René Lévesque, called for the federal government to establish national policies to combat acid rain.[134] The Canadian public directed its anger toward the US (with more than a little encouragement from Canadian political leaders), consequently there was no need for federal and provincial politicians to deflect electoral blame by pointing fingers at each other.

Because the federal government was able to claim credit with voters for dealing with the high profile problem of acid rain without alienating either the provinces or polluting industries, Liberal and Conservative governments alike deferred to the provinces.[135] As a result, federal-provincial consensus on acid rain was not threatened by turf wars. Even Quebec officials, normally highly sensitive to any hint of federal intrusion in provincial jurisdiction, acknowledge that the federal government never threatened unilateralism in federal-provincial discussions on acid rain.[136] The federal environment minister during the 1984 negotiations, Charles Caccia, later reflected, 'there was never any discussion of jurisdiction. We never needed to threaten [the provinces]. I don't know if I would have anyway. They could have said "go ahead."'[137]

The second explanation for federal-provincial harmony is that the federal subsidies made it possible for federal and provincial politicians to share credit for controlling acid rain. Provincial officials were candid in admitting that the 1984 deal rested on the federal promise of financial aid to polluters.[138] The former federal minister, Charles Caccia, recalls: 'They said "give us the money and we'll do it."'[139] Reliance on subsidies raised from diffuse taxes enabled the federal government to befriend the provinces and smelters without alienating those who ultimately would pay the price for that friendship.

Finally, federal and provincial ministers sought strength in numbers at a time when their departments' standing in their respective cabinets was tenuous at best. As a senior provincial official explained, 'it was helpful to be able to go to Cabinet and say "this is a national program. All the provinces have agreed."'[140]

Evaluation of CCREM

Much has been made of the capacity of the institutional forum of CCREM to promote intergovernmental cooperation during this period. Indeed, the success of federal-provincial relations in the environmental field in the 1970s and early 1980s has led some authors to propose CCREM as a model for intergovernmental relations in other policy fields.[141] Those authors emphasize several assets of CCREM.

First, the permanence of the CCREM has facilitated the emergence of relationships built on trust. It has been argued that as participants came to trust each other, it is easier to move beyond jurisdictional questions to more substantive issues. Although the rapid turnover of environment ministers at both the federal and provincial levels during the 1970s tended to preclude stable relationships at the political level, public servants at all levels developed solid working relationships with their counterparts in other governments through longstanding CCREM committees.

Second, CCREM supporters emphasize the unique structure of the council; the federal and provincial governments participate as equals with the chair rotating among them. The fact that the federal government was just one of eleven voices on the council, and that the independent secretariat reported to the council, rather than any one government, further facilitated trust between the federal government and the provinces. A former chair of CCREM also emphasized the privacy of the council, asserting, 'if CCREM tomorrow was a public thing, it would die ... You can sort out your dirty linen behind closed doors.'[142]

Others emphasize the extensive contact between scientists and engineers in CCREM committees. They argue that technical specialists are more likely to find common ground in light of their shared professional norms and focus on substantive questions.[143] Finally, the unusual claim has been offered that CCREM's lack of authority actually was an asset.[144] Since the council had no authority to impose the will of the majority on the minority, it was forced to operate via consensus.

There is reason to question whether CCREM in fact earned the many accolades it received. Many of the council's fans appear to have accepted intergovernmental cooperation as an end in itself. While the consensual decision-making practices of CCREM assure at least the appearance of harmony, they do not necessarily guarantee progress toward environmental protection. Given the impenetrability of CCREM, it is difficult to know how often the consensus that emerged merely reflected agreement on the lowest common denominator or avoidance of contentious issues. Moreover, it is not clear what was accomplished behind the facade of cooperation. With the exception of the acid rain accords, which urgency likely would have necessitated anyway, records of CCREM's accomplishments during the 1970s and early 1980s are remarkably thin.

Indeed, federal and provincial ministers and officials who sought to rejuvenate the council in the late 1980s offered much less favourable assessments of its performance. CCREM of the 1970s and early 1980s was described as 'useless,' 'ceremonial,' 'a talk shop,' and 'a backwater.'[145] Even one of the ministers who participated in the acid rain negotiations noted that 'the meetings were generally friendly, but in the end they were useless, because CCREM was a powerless organization.'[146]

The council's supporters have attributed too much importance to the nature of the institution itself. During this period, the federal government retreated from its aggressive jurisdictional claims, yet still offered to provide the provinces with valuable services, such as environmental monitoring and technical support. The absence of federal-provincial conflict thus can be seen more as a reflection of the fact that there was little to fight about, than an indication of the institution's capacity to resolve conflict.

Conclusion

The 1970s witnessed the federal government gradually extricating itself from the environmental responsibilities it had assumed earlier in the decade. Rather than competing with the provinces, the federal government increasingly assumed a supporting role. In the government's own words,

> The federal approach to environmental matters by the late 1970's, unlike the U.S. Environmental Protection Agency which kept pursuing an aggressive regulatory approach, gradually started to move away from its strong initial regulatory stance to favour more effort in guideline establishment for implementation at the provincial level, supplying general environmental information and building a leadership role in such issues as acid rain.[147]

Even a representative of the national pulp and paper industry, one of the few industries actively regulated by Environment Canada, reflected on this period as 'a great hiatus where the federal government really did nothing.'[148] By 1985, the federal government's own Nielson Task Force was puzzled as to why Environment Canada had made such limited use of its legislative authority.[149]

In explaining the federal government's reluctance, several commentators have emphasized the extent of provincial opposition to federal involvement in environmental protection.[150] However, it is noteworthy that at the same time as the federal government was retreating from its regulatory role in environmental protection, federal politicians showed little compunction in provoking various provinces by introducing the National Energy Program and attempting to patriate the constitution unilaterally. The contrast in the positions taken by the federal government before the Supreme Court in the *Interprovincial Co-operatives* and *Central Canada Potash* cases is illustrative. While the federal government intervened to support provincial jurisdiction over interprovincial pollution in the former, it took the unusual step of joining as a co-plaintiff to challenge provincial authority to collect natural resource revenues in the latter.

It also is significant that the federal government had not deferred to those same provinces in 1970, when it passed the contested Canada Water

Act. The crucial difference was that the salience of environmental issues had declined dramatically after 1970. While neither level of government faced palpable pressure to aggressively pursue environmental protection, the provinces did have institutional, financial, and personal incentives to defend their jurisdiction over natural resources. In contrast, federal politicians had no incentive to provoke conflict with either regulated firms or the provinces in the absence of public demand for environmental protection.

Federal public servants also had few incentives to take on hostile provinces and polluters in the absence of political and public support. Although many were personally committed to environmental protection, they were severely constrained by limited resources, flawed legislation, and lack of political support. As one regional official explained, 'you don't know if you've got backup from above, you know you don't have it in the regulations, so you're on your own against the industry.' On occasion, federal bureaucrats were constrained not just by benign neglect, but by active resistance. Another regional official reported that 'in negotiations, the industry would go to the Deputy Minister and signals would come back to back off.'[151]

The question remains whether the federal retreat was less a reflection of the decline in public interest in pollution control than a symptom of a transition from the symbolic stage of passing new legislation to the blame-laden stage of implementation. As the costs of environmental protection loom larger, regulated interests would be expected to oppose government policy with increasing vigour, even as the diffusely affected public would be expected to lose interest in the complex and often technical details of regulation and enforcement. Thus, one might argue that the federal government's retreat from its earlier commitments merely reflected politicians' general reluctance to implement environmental statutes, rather than the influence of trends in public opinion. However, government officials interviewed stressed time and again the climate of public indifference that prevailed in the late 1970s in explaining the lack of enforcement activity at the time. Moreover, as the next chapter demonstrates, when the salience of environmental issues re-emerged in the late 1980s, so did the level of federal enforcement activity.

Of course, the federal government's environmental policies were not immune to developments in other policy fields. Budgetary restraint in the early 1970s, federal-provincial conflicts over natural resource revenues in the mid-1970s, the national unity crisis that followed the election of the Parti Québécois government in Quebec in the late 1970s, and efforts to patriate the constitution in the early 1980s all affected Environment Canada's performance indirectly. Although the broader political context may have hastened the federal withdrawal, it is noteworthy that it was in the field of environmental protection that the federal government chose to sacrifice involvement to compensate for its aggressiveness in other areas.

The short-lived burst of federal concern for the environment around 1970 did have a lasting effect, however. A new federal department had been established, with a mission, if not always the wherewithal, to protect the environment. Federal 'leadership' efforts undoubtedly had some impact. Although provincial permits did not always match federal standards as promised, in some provinces they did. And even in those provinces that did not come up to federal standards, the alternative may have been no permits at all.

Federal officials probably also had some impact at the level of enforcement. Although enforcement was delegated to the provinces, Environment Canada's regional officials occasionally succeeded in pressuring provinces to tighten permit conditions or to prosecute persistent violations. On rare occasions, federal officials pursued enforcement action on their own, particularly in British Columbia.[152] Yet even Environment Canada officials in that province expressed frustration that they often were unable to convince the province to address their concerns, and 'we didn't have the horses to do the job ourselves.'[153]

Ultimately, federal officials' impact on provincial standards was limited by the provinces' willingness to accept federal input. It was as if the federal government volunteered to conduct an orchestra, without any guarantee that the musicians would play the same tune. When the musicians were willing to play the same music, the conductor provided a valuable service. But when they were intent on playing solo, all the baton-waving in the world would not produce a symphony.

6

The Second Wave: The Re-emergence of the Federal Role, 1985-95

The mid-1980s found Environment Canada's morale devastated by the newly elected Conservative government's first round of budget and personnel cuts. The new government had also laid to rest the advocacy approach, leaving the department with a mandate neither to regulate nor to encourage others to do so. However, public concern for the environment grew steadily, culminating in a dramatic surge in the late 1980s, and this prompted a revitalization of the federal role in environmental protection.

In many respects, this second 'green wave' was a replay of the first. In response to renewed public concern, both levels of government passed new environmental statutes and began to enforce their existing ones. Like the Canada Water Act before it, the Canadian Environmental Protection Act (CEPA) was proclaimed as the centrepiece of a new federal environmental strategy. And, the renewed federal presence in the environmental field provoked federal-provincial tensions reminiscent of the early 1970s.

An important difference between the first and second 'green waves,' however, was the role played by environmentalists. The early 1970s had witnessed the birth of hundreds of local voluntary environmental associations, which were ill-prepared to participate in the first round of environmental policy-making. By the late 1980s, however, many of those groups had matured to become professional organizations with substantial, if not extravagant, budgets.

Environmental groups' influence was reinforced by significant changes in the policy-making process. Schattschneider observes that the 'rules of the game' can shape policy outcomes by constraining or expanding the scope of conflict.[1] In the late 1980s, the scope of conflict in Canadian environmental policy was dramatically expanded when consultation mechanisms traditionally limited to federal and provincial governments and regulated industries were opened up to include environmental groups. Environmentalists thus were able to provide a voice for diffuse public concerns and, to some extent, to limit the federal government's ability to substitute symbolism for substance.

Even more significant, however, was environmentalists' success in using the courts to force the federal government to acknowledge its extensive environmental jurisdiction. A landmark court decision in 1989 had the effect of mandating that the federal government perform environmental impact assessments of proposed projects under a wide variety of circumstances. Thus, while the federal government was advancing rather tentatively on its own in response to public demand, environmental groups used the courts to give it a powerful push.

Although the passage of CEPA in 1988 had already disturbed the long-standing federal-provincial detente in environmental matters, the effect of the court decisions concerning environmental assessment was profound. Under the watchful eyes of environmentalists and the courts, the federal government no longer could restore intergovernmental harmony simply by retreating from the field. And as environmental groups across the country eagerly grasped the opportunity to sue the federal government to force environmental assessments of dozens of major projects, the tension between the federal role in environmental protection and provincial authority to promote economic development through exploitation of natural resources was brought sharply to the fore.

The early 1990s subsequently saw the federal government attempting to recapture control of its agenda from the courts, and federal and provincial governments working to restore administrative order in light of their new environmental mandates. The long-term implications of the re-emergence of federal involvement in environmental protection remain clouded. While aggressive new federal legislation and regulations seem to herald a new era of greater federal environmental activism, the record of non-implementation of the statutes of the early 1970s suggests that the new federal role must be viewed with considerable skepticism.

The Resurgence of Public Opinion

In terms of public opinion, the late 1980s were a replay of the late 1960s. There was a surge in both the degree of public concern for the environment and the salience of environmental issues, only to be followed by a rapid decline in salience and a less dramatic decline in public concern with the onset of a recession in the early 1990s.

In the second half of the 1980s, public fears were provoked by media reports of a seemingly endless series of ecological disasters, including

Bhopal, Chernobyl, and the Exxon Valdez oil spill. In addition, the discovery of a hole in the stratospheric ozone layer, detection of toxic substances in remote corners of the globe, and emerging evidence of global warming contributed to a growing perception that environmental issues are global in scope. Closer to home, Canadians read of a PCB spill in Kenora and the discovery of a toxic 'blob' in the St. Clair River in 1985, detection of dioxins in pulp mill effluents in 1987, a PCB warehouse fire at Saint-Basile-le-Grand in 1988, an oil spill off Vancouver Island in 1989, and toxic fires at tire dumps in Ontario and Quebec in 1990.

Brown reports that Environment Canada's own public opinion polls revealed an important shift in Canadians' attitudes concerning the environment as early as 1984.[2] Similarly, Doern and Conway report that the Prime Minister's Office was conscious of the rising prominence of the environment in public opinion polls conducted for the federal government by Decima as early as 1985.[3] In 1986, the government's Nielson Task Force apparently also was aware of high levels of public concern indicated by recent public opinion surveys.[4] A federal official involved with developing the Canadian Environmental Protection Act mid-decade recalled that it seemed like a new poll crossed his desk weekly.[5] By the late 1980s, heightened public concern for the environment was also reflected in national opinion polls. Gallup reported that the percentage of Canadians who perceived the dangers of pollution to be 'very serious,' which had declined between the early 1970s and mid-1980s to a low of 51 per cent, began to increase again in 1985, reaching an all-time high of 77 per cent by 1990. Thereafter, however, the percent of respondents perceiving environmental issues to be 'very serious' declined to 67 per cent by September 1991 and 63 per cent by April 1992.[6]

The growing salience of environmental issues was reflected in voters' responses to the open-ended question, 'what is the most important problem facing the country today?' As illustrated by Figures 4.1 and 4.2 in Chapter 4, Gallup did not even mention the environment in reporting responses to the question between 1975 and 1985. However, the percentage of respondents who identified the environment as their top priority increased dramatically during the late 1980s, and even surged briefly ahead of economic concerns. Gallup reported that the salience of the issue peaked in July 1989, when the environment was the top ranked problem, identified by 16.5 per cent of respondents, just ahead of unemployment at 16.4 per cent and inflation/high prices at 13.2 per cent.[7] Polling by Decima also confirmed that the environment had become the public's top priority by 1989, when it was cited by 16 per cent of respondents, ahead of the deficit, unemployment, and free trade.[8] Finally, Environics reported that the environment reached the top of the public's priorities during 1989, when 21 per cent of respondents identified the environment as the nation's most important problem in their polls.[9]

As in 1970, the surge in salience of environmental issues mirrored developments in the United States. The percentage of Americans identifying the environment as the most important problem facing their country began to increase in 1986, peaking at 21 per cent in 1990. It appears, however, that in the United States the rise in concern for the environment, as measured by closed-ended questions, began a few years earlier, when the Reagan Administration's controversial reversals of previous environmental positions apparently disrupted a fragile 'permissive consensus.'[10] A similar surge in the percentage of respondents identifying the environment as the nation's 'most important problem' also occurred in Australia in 1989 and 1990, where the environment issue peaked at 25 per cent.[11]

The salience of the environment as a political issue declined as suddenly as it had emerged, as it had two decades earlier. With the onset of a recession in the early 1990s, the public's attention returned to the economy. Thus, while the environment was the top ranked problem nationally, cited by 16.5 per cent of respondents as 'the most important problem' facing Canada in July 1989, it was identified by only 3.8 per cent in December 1990 (seventh place), and less than 1 per cent in January 1994.[12] Figure 6.1 compares the percentage of Gallup respondents identifying either the environment or unemployment as the country's 'most important problem' from 1985 to 1994. What emerges from this figure is a picture of economic and environmental issues jockeying for position at the top of the national agenda. The emergence of the environment as a political issue in the late 1980s was a mirror image of the decline in concern for unemployment; the peak in salience of environmental issues coincided precisely with the trough in the unemployment curve.[13]

Thereafter, with the onset of a recession, unemployment and the economy returned to the top of the national agenda, albeit with a more uneven trajectory reflecting competition for the pubic's attention with national unity in 1991 and 1992, and the deficit after 1993. The Gallup results are consistent with those of other Canadian polling firms. Angus Reid found that by late 1993, the environment was identified as Canada's most important problem by only 1 per cent of respondents, having fallen from a high of 33 per cent in 1989. According to Angus Reid, the top priorities in October 1993 were jobs (44 per cent), the deficit (20 per cent), and the economy (10 per cent).[14]

Thus far, public opinion concerning the environment in the 1990s echoes that of the 1970s, when environmental issues elicited a high degree

Figure 6.1

Relative salience of environmental and economic concerns

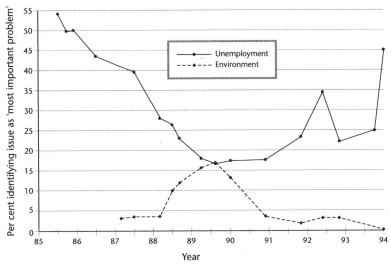

Source: Gallup Canada.

of public concern but relatively low salience relative to economic issues. Polls in recent years have indicated that Canadians either deny the existence of trade-offs between environmental protection and jobs or express willingness to sacrifice economic objectives in pursuit of environmental ones.[15] However, there appears to be a very real trade-off between the jobs and the environment when it comes to capturing the public's attention. As one environmentalist acknowledged, when 'people are worried about where their next mortgage payment is coming from,' the environment is a 'really tough sell.'[16]

The emergence of public attention to the environment around 1990 also prompted greater interest among pollsters. Of particular interest to this study are survey questions concerning Canadians' attitudes toward federal and provincial government responsibility for the environment. In 1991, Environics asked respondents which level of government should be held primarily responsible for the environment. Nationally, 43 per cent of respondents preferred to see either primary or exclusive federal jurisdiction, while only 28 per cent favoured the provinces.[17] The percentage that chose the federal government varied substantially, from a low of 31 per cent in Quebec to a high of 60 per cent in Saskatchewan. Quebec was the only province in which residents preferred provincial to federal jurisdiction, though by a surprisingly narrow 38 to 31 per cent margin.

At the height of the second 'green wave,' federal and provincial governments alike were cognizant of the widespread public support not just for government action, but for federal government action. One Environment Canada official reflected, 'I think what we're riding here is a tiger, a green tiger ... We have a grass-roots demand right across the country for federal intervention on resource management issues that have historically been the purview of the provinces.'[18]

Attitudes Toward Federal Jurisdiction

The Conservative government did not begin their term in government in 1984 as environmental crusaders. Under the government's first environment minister, Suzanne Blais-Grenier, Environment Canada's budget was slashed by 14 per cent in one year.[19] The resurgence of the federal role that followed can be seen as a response to four factors.

First, the new government had 'good policy' motives for renewed legislative activity. The government's Nielson Task Force recommended efforts to streamline the multiplicity of federal environmental statutes and reduce federal-provincial overlap.[20] Second, the federal government was propelled forward by developments in international environmental affairs, which assumed increasing prominence in the late 1980s with the emergence of the ozone layer and global warming issues. Third, the Conservatives clearly had not anticipated the adverse public reaction to their initial cuts to Environment Canada's budget. The government's own polls were indicating that the environment was one of the three issues which ranked highest in terms of public dissatisfaction (the other two being inflation and federal-provincial relations).[21] The government thus faced a pressing need to repair its image on environmental issues. Fourth, the government recognized an opportunity to capitalize on growing public concern for the environment.

When Suzanne Blais-Grenier was replaced as environment minister in 1985 by Tom McMillan, the new minister's first order of business was to repair both the department's morale and the government's reputation on the environment. McMillan thus reasserted the need for a strong federal role in environmental protection, and placed renewed emphasis on national standards. Despite the government's often stated preference for federal-provincial cooperation, the minister clearly envisioned a federal role that included federal unilateralism, thus going beyond the strictly supplementary role assumed in the past. According to McMillan, 'in the final analysis, the federal government has to act. Even though it may be an area of overlapping jurisdiction in some instances, we do have authority and the federal government intends to exercise it. We do not intend to do it by committee.'[22]

Initially, the government resorted to liberal use of its spending instrument to convince voters of its commitment to the environment. During the 1988 election campaign, the Conservatives announced commitments of $110 million for a St. Lawrence research centre, $75 million for cleanup of the Halifax harbour, and $6 million for a Winnipeg Centre for Sustainable Development, and reminded voters of an earlier $106 million commitment for a new national park in the Queen Charlotte Islands.

McMillan's successor after the 1988 election, Lucien Bouchard, continued to emphasize the need for a strong federal role, despite his own Quebec nationalism. Bouchard asserted:

> If there is a special role for the federal government, it is the development of national environmental protection standards and practices. The very nature of environmental problems demands this. Too often, the solutions adopted to control polluting emissions or hazardous waste, for instance, differ from province to province ... Ottawa must play a key role in the harmonization of standards and methods.[23]

The Green Plan

In the summer of 1989, Bouchard received cabinet approval to develop an ambitious five-year 'environmental agenda' for Canada. Unprecedented public demand for governmental action on the environment was a strong factor behind the initiative. Bouchard's own account of what became known as the Green Plan notes that the prime minister was particularly cognizant of trends in opinion polls.[24] One minister who participated in cabinet discussions of the Green Plan later reflected that the plan would never have been approved had it gone before cabinet one or two years later, after public attention to the environment had waned.[25] The troubled history of the Green Plan offers insight into the limits of the environment as a political issue.

As federal bureaucrats toiled in secrecy to devise the Green Plan, there was speculation that repeated delays in announcing the plan were the result of opposition within cabinet. The press reported that the strongest resistance came from the deputy prime minister, and the ministers of Finance, Industry, International Trade, and the Treasury Board.[26] The environment minister later recalled strong resistance from the Department of Finance as well as bureaucrats in other departments who feared a 'power grab' by Environment Canada.[27]

In a transparent attempt to capitalize on public concern to shore up the beleaguered initiative, the environment minister announced that public consultations would be held to guide the development of the Green Plan. The consultations got off to a bad start, however, when Lucien Bouchard resigned in protest over the government's proposals to salvage the Meech Lake Accord only days before the cross-country consultations were to begin. Moreover, the discussion paper released as the basis for the consultations was summarily dismissed by the Opposition, environmentalists, and academics for being weak and short on detail.[28] However, the government quickly appointed Robert de Cotret as Bouchard's successor, and forged on with a massive public consultation program, including forty-one information sessions attended by 6,000 people, two-day consultations in seventeen cities attended by 3,500 people, and a wrap-up session in Ottawa attended by approximately 400 'stakeholders,' all at a cost of roughly $7 million.[29]

As the public consultations progressed, the federal government simultaneously was consulting privately with the provinces, many of which were uneasy about the secretive federal plan. The government of Alberta was particularly troubled by rumours of a carbon tax to combat global warming. As the province with the highest per capita emissions of carbon dioxide, Alberta would be hardest hit by such a tax. The Alberta press highlighted the fact that the new federal deputy minister of the environment, Len Good, had played a key role in drafting the unpopular National Energy Program, and dubbed the yet-to-be-released Green Plan 'son of NEP.'[30]

The federal plan was finally released in December 1990. The government promised to spend an additional $3 billion on the environment over the next five years, although the time frame was soon extended to six years. While environmentalists' reactions were overwhelmingly negative, industry and the provinces' worst fears were unrealized. The Alberta business community, which had been especially hostile to the plan's development, openly praised the final product.[31] Provincial officials breathed a collective sigh of relief. An Ontario Ministry of Environment official recalled, 'our first reaction was "is that all there is?"' While an Alberta Federal and Intergovernmental Affairs official described the Green Plan as a 'paper tiger.'[32] In fact, the plan's repeated emphasis on the need for a federal-provincial 'partnership' was seen as a welcome invitation for the provinces to lobby for their share of the billions of new dollars the federal government had allocated to the environment.

The Green Plan listed 120 different targets and initiatives, which precludes discussion of each one.[33] In general, the plan can be viewed as a spending program. It comprised heavy emphasis on programs that win friends by providing local benefits, such as new national parks and research centres, and more innocuous spending commitments, such as environmental monitoring and education, that at least do not make enemies. There was significantly less emphasis on regulatory programs, which tend to alienate both the regulated and the provinces.[34] However, the Green Plan did include promises to cap sulphur dioxide emissions by 1994, extend the national acid rain control program to the western provinces, and stabilize emissions of carbon dioxide and other greenhouse gases by the year 2000. The Plan also reiterated the government's commitment under CEPA to assess forty-four priority substances by 1994, 'and to enact regulations for all those substances found to be toxic.'[35]

It is noteworthy that the Green Plan did not include specific financial commitments for individual initiatives. That omission not only avoided extending the cabinet battle over the plan, but also afforded a series of spending announcements at regular intervals to maintain the government's environmental profile. In the first year of implementing the Green Plan, Robert de Cotret and his successor, Jean Charest, announced seventeen individual initiatives projected to cost more than $1 billion.[36] The announcements, like the plan itself, were long on research and education, and short on regulation.

The difficulty with which the federal cabinet reached agreement on the Green Plan, despite unprecedented public concern for the environment, is noteworthy. Some have argued that the troubled history of the plan reflected the political naiveté of Lucien Bouchard. Bouchard's predecessor, Tom McMillan, reflected, 'if you go to Cabinet and say "you have to support this Holy Grail," everyone can pull a Holy Grail out of their pocket or purse ... Being Minister of the Environment isn't enough ... You need to cultivate the terrain, work the back rooms. It sounds sinister but that's the way politics works, and Lucien Bouchard just didn't have the experience.'[37]

However, perhaps more telling was the source of resistance within cabinet. Consistent with Mahon's depiction of state structures representing class interests, the strongest opposition came from ministers responsible for promoting economic development, who sought to defend business from the threat of over-zealous regulation.[38] The nature of the compromise that emerged from cabinet is also noteworthy. Despite tight budgetary restraints, the federal government resorted to its spending instrument in an attempt to garner credit from environmentally conscious voters and avoid the blame associated with regulation from the business community and the provinces. Federal politicians thus attempted once again to avoid the blame associated with imposing the costs of environmental protection.

There is reason to believe that federal politicians' reluctance was indicative of their doubts about the depth and permanence of the public's commitment to the environment. The government's own policy advisors on the Nielson Task Force had previously expressed such reservations:

> Considerable literature reviewed by the Study Team ... lays strong emphasis on recent opinion surveys, which consistently show overwhelming support for action on environmental concerns and regulations, even at the cost of job losses. At issue is whether these public opinion polls should be used as a solid basis for public policy, supporting an aggressive top-down federal approach to the environment.
>
> The Study Team has very severe reservations for the following reasons. First, despite the consistent results of such polls, governments have found it difficult to take action as strong as they would have preferred, particularly during the difficult economic recession of 1980-81. Second, with such popular support for environmental action, DOE should not have found it necessary to take such a strong 'advocacy' approach.[39]

Cabinet's resistance to the Green Plan may have reflected an instinctive belief that when it comes to bearing the costs of environmental protection, public concern is a mile wide and an inch deep.

Opposition and Interest Group Perspectives on Federal Jurisdiction

As in the early 1970s, during the second 'green wave' the opposition parties demanded ever stronger assertions of federal authority. They were impatient with claims of constitutional constraints, arguing that 'members on the government side have used constitutional excuses for government inaction.'[40] Also reminiscent of 1970, the Opposition placed particular emphasis on the need for national standards. Ironically, however, the situation was reversed, with the Liberals, who had resisted federal involvement in 1970 and later oversaw a gradual erosion of the federal role, now pressing for federal leadership. The Conservatives, who had ridiculed the Liberals' hesitance, now counselled respect for provincial jurisdiction.

Environmental groups were also supportive of a strong federal role.[41] Environmentalists clearly sought the reassurance of both federal and provincial involvement, so that if one government failed to protect the environment, the other could still do the job. One Alberta environmentalist explained that 'the environmental community sees the federal government as a big stick' which can motivate the provinces.[42] At the same time, environmentalists were wary of 'jurisdictional buck-passing,' and thus stressed the importance of federal oversight and accountability in intergovernmental agreements.[43]

With the possible exception of environmentalists in Ontario and Quebec, many environmentalists simply trusted the provinces less than the federal government, to the point of labelling them 'the environmental ogres of our time.'[44] One environmentalist explained, 'the provincial attitude is that "the resources are ours and it is up to us to decide whether to protect or despoil them."'[45] In addition to their suspicions of the provinces as resource owners, many environmentalists perceived provincial governments to be more vulnerable to threats of job losses and reductions in their tax base. One offered that 'the feds are just farther away from the cash register, so hopefully they're less motivated by economic gains and more able to take into account costs to the environment.'[46] Interestingly, that perspective was echoed by a provincial deputy minister who complained: 'it's easy for the federal government to be self-righteous because they don't bear the direct political impact of environmental standards like the provinces do. We pay the political price if a mill shuts down. So the provinces are more concerned about economic growth.'[47] The fear of provinces caving in to economic threats clearly underlay the environmental community's demands for stringent national standards.

The level of government industry lobbyists looked too varied. Consistent with the analysis of Mashaw and Rose-Ackerman, firms facing potentially inconsistent product standards in different provinces were inclined to favour the uniformity of federal jurisdiction. In contrast, firms facing process regulations tended to support provincial jurisdiction.[48] However, virtually all industries were in agreement in opposing simultaneous involvement by both levels of government. In addition to resisting the additional costs and uncertainty associated with overlapping regulations, business spokespersons were fearful of competition between federal and provincial politicians seeking to satisfy environmentally conscious voters. A representative of the mining industry complained that the federal government and the provinces were 'falling over one another' in attempting to regulate the industry.[49] When involvement of both levels of government seemed unavoidable, industry representatives invariably called for harmonization of federal and provincial standards and enforcement via a 'single window.'

The Constitutional Function

As in 1970, the heightened level of public and governmental concern for the environment coincided with a round of constitutional negotiations. After the failure, in 1990, of the Meech Lake Accord, which did not consider questions of environmental jurisdiction, the governing Liberal party of Quebec called for transfer to the provinces of exclusive jurisdiction over a number of policy fields, including the environment.[50] In response, in 1991, the federal government tabled its own package of constitutional proposals. The federal package paid little attention to the environment, with the exception of a symbolic statement expressing a 'commitment to the objective of sustainable development' in the proposed Canada clause.[51] However, several of the federal government's proposals had the potential to affect federal environmental authority indirectly, which drew a strong reaction from environmental groups.

Environmentalists attacked the federal proposal to entrench property rights in the constitution on the grounds that, because 'environmental protection and assessment, and land use planning laws, by their very nature, are designed to restrict the activities of property owners and users,' entrenched property rights would necessarily limit governments' authority to protect the environment.[52] Proposals to strengthen the economic union were criticized by environmentalists as well. They feared that movement in this direction would restrict individual provinces' ability to pass environmental laws if such laws could be cited as unfair trade barriers.[53] Environmentalists also were wary of the federal government's proposal to withdraw from several fields of provincial jurisdiction, including forestry and mining, since the federal proposals did not indicate whether withdrawal from environmental regulation of those areas also was foreseen. Finally, environmentalists were troubled by a proposal to amend the 'Peace, Order, and good Government' clause to transfer authority over 'new subjects' to the provinces. Although it appears that the federal government intended to retain both the national dimensions and national emergencies aspects of 'Peace, Order, and good Government,' environmentalists cautioned against tinkering with the clause in any way in light of its presumed significance as a source of federal environmental authority.

The debate over the federal government's constitutional proposals revealed the extent of environmental groups' support for a strong federal role. One environmentalist summed up her position on the constitution by arguing that 'the bottom line is that it is inadvisable for the federal government to give up any of its sources of jurisdiction.'[54] In response, the federal government denied that its proposals would have any impact on environmental jurisdiction. Minister for Constitutional Affairs Joe Clark insisted, 'if we were going to propose moving [responsibility for] the environment, we would have done so. We didn't propose it because we don't intend to do that.'[55]

On the surface, the package of proposals that finally emerged from federal-provincial bargaining paid no more attention to the environment than did the earlier federal proposals; although the one statement concerning the environment originally proposed for inclusion in the Canada clause was revised and repositioned in the social charter. The proposed curtailment of federal involvement in forestry and mining went forward, without any mention of continuing federal involvement in environmental regulation in those fields. However, in other respects, the final package satisfied environmentalists' criticisms. Entrenched property rights were omitted, as were the federal government's proposals concerning the common market, which were deferred to future discussions. Moreover, the suggested text for future discussion explicitly sought to exempt environmental legislation from being challenged as a trade barrier.

Although the package of proposals was rejected by voters in a national referendum, what is most interesting about the failed proposals from an environmental policy standpoint is the almost total absence of attention to questions of environmental jurisdiction. The federal government, faced with public pressure from one side and provincial pressure from the other, apparently opted for maintenance of the status quo. On one hand, there was no effort to strengthen or even clarify existing federal and provincial environmental jurisdiction. Environmentalists were critical that the federal government was passing up a 'golden opportunity' to seek explicit recognition of federal authority to set national standards and to implement international treaties.[56] However, it is doubtful that any extension of federal authority with respect to the environment would have received the requisite degree of provincial support. On the other hand, the proposals did not concede any federal environmental jurisdiction. Existing jurisdiction over the environment survived intact presumably because any reduction of federal jurisdiction would have been as unacceptable to the public as an extension would have been to the provinces.

The Legislative Function

In response to the second wave of environmental concern, federal and provincial governments alike passed a second generation of environmental statutes in the late 1980s. Reflecting on the renewed federal legislative activity concerning the environment, one justice department lawyer recalled, 'I was the centre of a growth industry, like Mickey Mouse in

Disney World.'[57] Doern and Conway's history of Environment Canada describes the rate of change during this period as 'almost convulsive.'[58]

The Canadian Environmental Protection Act

Like the Canada Water Act in 1970, the Canadian Environmental Protection Act (CEPA), proclaimed in June 1988, was offered as the centrepiece for federal environmental protection efforts.[59] With the new statute, the government sought to achieve two objectives. First, CEPA satisfied the Nielson Task Force's recommendation to rationalize federal environmental legislation by consolidating several statutes, including the Environmental Contaminants Act, the Ocean Dumping Control Act, and parts of the Canada Water Act and the Clean Air Act.[60] More importantly, CEPA significantly strengthened the federal government's role in toxic substance control, thus conspicuously ignoring another Nielson recommendation, to reduce federal-provincial overlap in the environmental field. Although efforts to revise the Environmental Contaminants Act had been in the works since at least 1980, with opinion polls indicating growing public concern for the environment it was an idea whose time had finally come.

In contrast to the first generation of environmental statutes, CEPA was the subject of extensive public consultations. Indeed, the consultations concerning CEPA became the prototype for a new approach of 'multistakeholder consultation,' in which 'stakeholders,' representing industry, environmental groups, and labour, among others, are encouraged to reach consensus on recommendations for government.[61]

The federal government took advantage of a consultation process initiated by the previous Liberal government in 1984. Although it was not the original intent of that process to advise the government on toxic substances legislation, participants were redirected to that end in 1985, when the Conservative government decided to pursue new legislation.[62] One working group issued a report in late 1986, which recommended a 'cradle to grave' approach to toxic substance control.[63] Government spokespersons embraced the concept, and routinely cited the report's influence on CEPA. In contrast, the government largely ignored the recommendations of a second working group, which had been asked to offer concrete suggestions for revising the Environmental Contaminants Act.[64] The government took the unusual step of tabling a draft bill in the House of Commons in December 1986, and subsequently sponsoring another set of consultations across the country, culminating in a workshop in Ottawa in March 1987, before formally submitting a revised version of the bill for first reading in June 1987.

As with the Green Plan, closed door negotiations with the provinces were conducted at the same time as the public consultations. Provincial resistance to the proposed legislation was strongest from Quebec, Ontario, Alberta, and British Columbia, the same provinces that had led opposition to the Canada Water Act. The arguments raised by the provinces were by now familiar. They argued that federal interference was unnecessary because the provinces were already doing the job. Interviews with provincial officials revealed that pragmatic concerns about unnecessary duplication were reinforced by a strong element of personal resentment. One provincial official recalled, 'it was as if the federal government discovered the environment in 1987.'[65] Although sensitive to any hint of federal paternalism, some provincial officials nevertheless were receptive to national standards; federal controls could ease their task of justifying regulatory requirements in their own provinces, as long as they could administer them via a 'single window.'[66] However, their colleagues in intergovernmental affairs departments were more inclined to defend provincial constitutional jurisdiction per se. As one provincial spokesperson argued, 'who has the primary responsibility for the protection and enhancement of the quality of air, land and water? I think the answer is very clear. It is the provinces.'[67]

Among the provinces, the Quebec government offered the strongest opposition to CEPA. By the fall of 1987, when other provinces had conceded the inevitability of federal legislation, the Quebec environment minister, Clifford Lincoln, continued to strongly oppose CEPA at the annual CCREM meeting. In response, a committee was struck comprised of representatives of the federal government, Quebec, British Columbia, Ontario, Alberta, and New Brunswick. Federal and provincial officials interviewed by the author indicated that, at Quebec's instigation, the committee proposed the concept of 'equivalency,' which would allow federal regulations to be revoked if the federal government and a province agreed that the province's own regulations were equivalent to federal standards. After second reading, the federal environment minister introduced a series of amendments to the government's CEPA bill in December 1987 – including one to incorporate an equivalency approach – which subsequently were adopted by the Conservative majority.

The Constitutional Basis of the Act

CEPA represented the strongest assertion of federal authority over the environment to date. Sensitive to the long-standing tension between the Department of Fisheries and Oceans and Environment Canada over the Fisheries Act, justice department lawyers saw it as their task to construct a constitutional mandate for Environment Canada.[68] They perceived broad but untapped federal authority under both the criminal law and 'Peace, Order, and good Government' powers. However, mindful of provincial opposition, they were careful to design a statute that they were confident could survive constitutional challenge.

The preamble of CEPA, which states that 'the presence of toxic substances in the environment is a matter of national concern,' clearly indicates the federal government's intent to premise its actions on 'Peace, Order, and good Government.' The preamble also stresses the inherently interjurisdictional nature of toxic substances and the need to fulfil international obligations, both of which evoke the residual power. The statute also relies heavily on the criminal law power in its emphasis on environmental threats to public health. In particular, the definition of a 'toxic substance' as one that may pose a threat to either public health or the environment was carefully crafted to invoke both the criminal law power and 'Peace, Order, and good Government.'

The cornerstone of the statute's approach to toxic substance control is a formal finding that a substance is 'toxic.' Once a substance is placed on the 'list of toxic substances,' the statute authorizes the government to undertake a wide variety of regulatory actions, including regulation of discharges into the air, water, and soil. That multimedia emphasis represents a controversial extension of federal jurisdiction to the area of waste disposal, which long had been considered strictly a provincial matter.[69]

It is noteworthy, however, that at the same time, the federal government gave up even the pretence of comprehensively managing air quality. CEPA retained only parts of the Clean Air Act, even though federal regulation of air pollution had been upheld in the *Canada Metal* case as a matter of national interest. The federal government also declined to assert federal authority with respect to interprovincial or international water pollution, although the government's advisors in the justice department felt there was sufficient constitutional authority to do so.[70]

CEPA followed the example of the first generation of federal environmental statutes in taking a consultative approach to the provinces. However, unlike its predecessors, the new statute began with a presumption of federal action and, for the first time, demonstrated federal willingness to exert leverage over the provinces to ensure conformance with national objectives.

On one hand, the international air pollution provisions of CEPA actually strengthened the requirements for consultation and deference to the provinces over the original wording of the Clean Air Act. CEPA also provided for the establishment of a federal-provincial committee to advise the federal government, and made consultation mandatory with respect to certain regulatory actions, including promulgation of discharge standards. Moreover, the equivalency provisions provided that cabinet can declare that federal regulations do not apply in a province where the federal provincial governments agree in writing that the province has adopted 'equivalent' regulations. CEPA also provided for federal-provincial administrative agreements, to authorize provincial enforcement of federal regulations.

On the other hand, the federal government was not initially required to consult the provinces with respect to regulatory actions predicated on its trade and commerce power, including standards for import, export, and product composition. (However, that section was subsequently amended in 1989 to make consultation mandatory for all regulations issued under Section 34.)[71] Moreover, although the equivalency provisions were harshly criticized by environmentalists and the opposition parties as excessively deferential to the provinces, equivalency had the potential to strengthen, rather than weaken, the federal role for two reasons.

First, the federal government effectively maintained control over its regulatory agenda by offering equivalency to the provinces at the conclusion of the regulatory decision-making process, rather than the outset. Under the predecessor Environmental Contaminants Act, the provinces were given an effective veto over the initial decision of whether or not to list a substance. In contrast, under CEPA, the provinces were not guaranteed any input to the decision to list, which at the time was considered tantamount to a decision to regulate.

Second, while CEPA acknowledges concurrent provincial authority, it no longer unconditionally concedes the lead role to the provinces. Under the Environmental Contaminants Act, if a provincial government indicated its intent to handle a problem, it was taken at its word. In contrast, CEPA establishes relatively strict conditions for equivalency, with the clear intent of promoting national standards. The statute also requires that the federal environment minister report on the status of equivalency agreements annually, providing yet another check on federal deference.

Ironically, provincial efforts to resist federal involvement in the environmental field may have resulted in a more intrusive statute. The equivalency approach introduces an element of hierarchy in the federal-provincial relationship, since any provinces seeking equivalency agreements will be held accountable to the federal government's conditions. As Duncan observes, 'the very provision thought to ensure provincial sovereignty over pollution sources has created a large opening for ongoing federal and ultimately extensive public scrutiny' of provincial policies.[72]

Opposition and Interest Group Perspectives

The parliamentary debate over CEPA echoed the debate over the Canada Water Act almost twenty years earlier. Liberal and NDP members of Parliament condemned the government for not being sufficiently assertive. The opposition parties criticized CEPA's requirements for mandatory consultation with the provinces as too deferential,[73] and argued that the proposed federal-provincial administrative agreements would result in 'checkerboard enforcement' of federal regulations.[74] However, the opposition critics reserved their strongest attacks for the equivalency provisions. Led by Charles Caccia, the Liberal environment critic, and his New Democrat counterpart, Lynn McDonald, the Opposition asserted that equivalency would undermine national standards and result in a 'patchwork' of inconsistent provincial regulations.[75] Not surprisingly, the Liberal opposition did not acknowledge the extent to which the previous Liberal government's deference to the provinces already had undermined enforcement of national standards.[76]

Regulated industries clearly were troubled by the possibility that expanded federal involvement in the environmental field would lead to inconsistent federal and provincial regulations.[77] In contrast, environmental groups complained that the proposed statute was 'apologetic rather than assertive.'[78] Echoing the Opposition, environmentalists argued that the equivalency approach would result in inconsistent standards and enforcement practices.[79] They also were worried that any acknowledgment of the sufficiency of provincial regulations could undermine the act's constitutional basis in the national concern doctrine, an argument that had, in fact, been raised by the government's own legal advisors.[80] Environmentalists' opposition to the bill was intensified by resentment of the fact that, just when it appeared that the public would be granted meaningful input into federal environmental policy, the federal and provincial governments followed the tried and true approach of striking a deal behind closed doors.[81]

In devising CEPA, the federal government thus found itself caught between the provinces, which opposed any federal intrusion in their jurisdiction, and environmentalists and the Opposition, who demanded ever more forceful assertions of federal authority. The environment minister himself maintained: 'I think the fact that we were being attacked at both ends was an indication that maybe we got pretty well right the balance between exercising federal authority in an area of increased political salience while respecting the fact that we did live in a federal state and there was legitimate jurisdiction resident in the provinces.'[82]

Although the government offered a concession to the provinces by way of the equivalency clause, the strength of the statute that emerged never-theless suggests that public demand had the upper hand. CEPA went beyond the first generation of federal environmental statutes in envision-ing an independent, rather than merely supplementary, federal role. The federal environment minister, Tom McMillan, maintained,

> I believe the federal government has a responsibility to act to the lim-its of its own jurisdiction in this and in other areas. While loathe to provoke inter-jurisdictional territorial warfare, the federal govern-ment recognizes it must take a strong role, both through direct action and through example. And that role must not be reduced to exercis-ing only what authority the provinces themselves choose not to wield.[83]

Perhaps more significantly, for the first time, the federal government demonstrated willingness to twist provincial arms in the pursuit of national standards.

Lucas aptly views CEPA as a turning point in federal environmental pol-icy.[84] However, while CEPA provides extensive statutory authority, it does not guarantee that the federal government will actually use it. The 1990s will reveal whether CEPA will sustain a stronger federal presence in envi-ronmental protection or succumb to the same fate as the Canada Water Act.

The Canadian Environmental Assessment Act

In 1987, with CEPA already in the works, the federal cabinet consented to a proposal to develop legislation that would replace the Environmental Assessment and Review Process (EARP) Guidelines Order. As with CEPA, consultations were held across the country, culminating in a national workshop in 1988. The government formally announced its intent to introduce environmental assessment legislation in the throne speech of April 1989. However, within the same month, the Federal Court decision in the *Rafferty-Alameda* case lent much greater urgency to efforts to devise federal environmental assessment legislation.

In that landmark 1989 decision, the courts gave the EARP regulation much greater force than the federal government ever intended and, in so doing, pitted environmental groups against the federal government and the federal government against the provinces. The combined effect of the

Rafferty-Alameda and subsequent *Oldman Dam* decisions was to force the federal government to acknowledge and exercise its considerable jurisdiction over the environment. Although the 1992 Supreme Court ruling in the *Oldman Dam* case subsequently restored some limits on the requirement for federal environmental reviews,[85] in the intervening three years the federal government was forced to operate under the assumption that it could be compelled to perform an environmental review of virtually any project that impinged on an area of federal jurisdiction.

In response to the court decisions, environmental groups across the country initiated dozens of lawsuits seeking to force the federal government to perform environmental assessments of a wide variety of activities, ranging from projects sponsored by private firms and the provinces to federal cabinet decisions. Although some of the cases met with success, many others failed. However, one of the main reasons they failed was that the initial court decisions spurred an increase in federal environmental assessment activity and consequently there were fewer cases to win. Although only thirty-five proposals were referred for public reviews by the federal government in the fifteen-year period from 1974 to 1989, there were twenty-four reviews in less than two years after the *Rafferty-Alameda* decision.[86]

It is important to note that the EARP Guidelines did not limit the federal government's discretion to approve any project; they merely required that federal decision-making be informed by an assessment of a project's environmental impacts. That being the case, why was the opportunity to force the federal government to perform environmental reviews so attractive to environmentalists? First, they had few legal alternatives. The appearance of the non-discretionary 'shall' in the EARP Guidelines Order was highly unusual among federal environmental statutes. Thus, environmentalists simply had no comparable legal avenues to challenge other federal statutes and regulations.

Second, as Schattschneider observes, the outcome of street fights are not determined by the strength of the combatants, but by their ability to elicit the support of the surrounding crowd.[87] Environmentalists used the very public environmental review process to expand the scope of conflict. Although federal decisionmakers formally were not obliged to accept the recommendations of EARP panels, it would have been difficult for them to ignore their own advisors in the face of unprecedented public concern for the environment. (However, politicians' ability to disregard their advisors undoubtedly increased as public attention to environmental issues declined.)

Although the EARP Guidelines Order long had created the potential for the federal government to interfere in a broad range of projects, including those pursued by the provinces, the government's narrow interpretation of its own regulation prior to *Rafferty-Alameda* had not engendered serious federal-provincial disagreements. However, both the federal and provincial governments were frustrated by the situation created by the *Rafferty-Alameda* and *Oldman* decisions. The federal government resented the loss of control of its agenda to environmental groups and the courts, while the provinces resented the uncertainty introduced by belated federal reviews of projects that they had already approved, many of which were already under construction.

The nature of the EARP decisions limited the ability of the two levels of government to resolve their differences through compromise. In granting citizens enforceable claims to federal actions, the courts effectively empowered private litigants to drive a wedge between the federal and provincial governments. As one provincial official bitterly complained, 'as it now stands, it's no longer a matter between us and them. It's up to third parties who walk in off the street and demand an environmental impact assessment.'[88]

The Legislative Response
The most straightforward solution to the problem would have been for the federal government simply to amend its EARP regulation to remove the 'shalls.' However, federal politicians clearly feared that such a move would be interpreted by the public, with encouragement from environmentalists and the Opposition, as a retreat from the goal of environmental protection. Despite provincial pressure for an interim amendment of the EARP Guidelines Order, the federal government chose instead to proceed with its proposal to introduce legislation to replace the regulation. The government finally introduced its Canadian Environmental Assessment Act in June 1990. The first bill died on the order paper, but was reintroduced in 1991, as soon as the new session of Parliament began. The new statute received royal assent in June 1992, and finally was proclaimed in January 1995. Not surprisingly, Quebec's Parti Québécois environment minister objected even more strongly than his Liberal predecessor, describing the bill as 'domineering, uncompromising, intolerant, totalitarian federalism.'[89]

The legislation undoubtedly differs from what would have emerged from the consultation process in early 1988, since the EARP litigation had established a new baseline for federal involvement in environmental assessment. The challenge for the government was to strike a balance between the practical imperative to recapture control of its agenda from the courts and the political imperative not to appear to be retreating in the eyes of an attentive public. Thus, although the federal government retreated from the EARP Guidelines Order in many respects, in others it retained and even strengthened the strong language of the Guidelines Order.[90]

On one hand, the Canadian Environmental Assessment Act protects the federal government from the unpredictability of court decisions on which projects fall within federal jurisdiction. It authorizes cabinet to issue regulations specifying which classes of projects or statutory decisions require environmental assessments and which will be exempted. The legislation also restores a degree of executive discretion through use of phrases such as 'where the Minister is of the opinion that' and 'that the responsible authority considers appropriate' to qualify seemingly inflexible requirements.[91]

On the other hand, the new legislation maintains the EARP Guidelines Order's requirement for mandatory environmental assessment if a project involves federal lands, federal grants or loan guarantees, or if the federal government is a proponent in whole or in part. In fact, it extends the EARP Guidelines Order in prohibiting federal departments or agencies from proceeding with projects or regulatory decisions where, after implementation of mitigation measures 'that the responsible authority considers appropriate,' 'the project is likely to cause significant adverse environmental effects that cannot be justified in the circumstances.' Although the primary responsibility to perform reviews is left to the proponent department, the Minister of the Environment is given a new oversight role in determining whether a full panel review is warranted.

With respect to the provinces, the legislation authorizes federal-provincial administrative agreements and joint assessments. However, the new statute has the potential to limit provincial discretion in certain respects. Of particular interest is a provision that authorizes the minister to order an environmental review of a project if she or he 'is of the opinion that the project may cause serious adverse environmental effects' in another province or country.

The Provincial Perspective

The provinces displayed an unprecedented degree of consensus in their opposition to the Canadian Environmental Assessment Act. The Alberta government, and in particular the Department of Federal and Intergovernmental Affairs (FIGA), led the charge and rallied the other provinces in opposition to the federal proposals. Alberta received strong support from Newfoundland, Saskatchewan (which was in the throes of the Rafferty-Alameda debate), and Quebec (which hoped to preclude federal involvement in the second phase of its James Bay hydro development). Ontario, Manitoba, and British Columbia also were wary of the federal proposals, but tended to be more receptive to cooperative approaches to environmental assessment. Even the Maritime provinces, which traditionally have been receptive to federal involvement in environmental protection, joined the other provinces in opposing the bill.

As with CEPA, the provinces declared that federal involvement was unnecessary, since they were already doing the job. Provincial bureaucrats and politicians alike complained of a federal 'cherry picking syndrome,' arguing that the federal government only sought involvement in the few prominent cases that capture the public's attention.

Second, it was significant that the most prominent EARP cases, those concerning the Rafferty-Alameda and Oldman dams and the James Bay hydroelectric development, challenged provinces' authority to develop their own Crown resources. The provinces particularly resented that the federal government could use relatively minor fields of jurisdiction, such as navigation, to justify all-encompassing environmental reviews. As the Alberta forestry minister stated, 'we fought hard for control of the resources in this province, and we're against the federal government coming into this process through the side door.'[92]

Finally, as one provincial official put it, 'the bottom line is not environmental protection here, but economic development.'[93] The potential invasiveness of federal environmental jurisdiction was brought home by environmental groups' efforts to use the EARP regulation to block dozens of major projects in virtually every province. The provinces' shared desire to control the pace and direction of economic development within their jurisdictions spurred them to present a common front in opposition to federal proposals.

The provinces apparently received encouragement from the business community, which was anxious about the climate of uncertainty surrounding new projects and resentful of duplication of federal and provincial reviews. Alberta officials claimed that Japanese investors had threatened not to invest in the province until jurisdictional questions were resolved.[94] However, at the same time, the business community's fears about duplication were actively reinforced by Alberta officials intent on defending provincial jurisdiction. One FIGA official explained: 'industry doesn't care who [performs the environmental assessment] as long as only one of us does. We spend a lot of time explaining to them that they don't want the feds making decisions about whether or not a plant in

Alberta can go ahead. We're the ones that are here. Do they want some-one in Ottawa deciding?'[95]

The provinces' perceptions of federal motives varied. Officials from Ontario, New Brunswick, Manitoba, and British Columbia adopted a rela-tively benign view that responsibility was thrust upon the federal government. As one official stated, 'it isn't like the feds thought they've killed the NEP, so how will we torment the West now?'[96] Quebec and Alberta officials were less generous, however. Indeed, the attitude of Alberta's intergovernmental affairs officials bordered on paranoia. One argued, 'some federal government in the future could say "I want to reori-ent economic activity in this country. There are too many pulp mills in Alberta – let's move some mills to Nova Scotia" or "Alberta is making too much money, so let's stop this project."'[97] Even the Alberta environment minister, Ralph Klein, publicly expressed concern that the federal govern-ment would use its expanded role in environmental assessment to redirect economic development from one province to another.[98]

After the provinces were shown partial drafts of the bill at a special meeting of the Canadian Council of Ministers of the Environment (CCME) in May 1990, the Alberta government led provincial efforts to propose amendments. Alberta's proposals received the support of the nine provinces present at the next CCME meeting in December 1990. (Quebec was no longer attending federal-provincial meetings after the failure of the Meech Lake Accord.) However, the federal environment minister clearly had learned a lesson from the lambasting his predecessor received in proposing the equivalency amendments to CEPA. Although the minister agreed to present the provinces' suggestions to cabinet, he refused to appear before the legislative committee considering the bill to offer them as formal amendments.

In place of the federal minister, British Columbia Minister of the Environment John Reynolds appeared before the committee as chair of CCME to propose amendments on behalf of the nine provinces and both territories. The provincial and territorial governments sought several sig-nificant amendments, including an equivalency provision. The provinces also sought to limit the scope of federal reviews to matters relevant to the particular source of constitutional authority supporting the review. This would prevent the federal government from using a relatively narrow source of authority, such as navigation, to justify an all-encompassing review.[99]

When the first bill died on the order paper, Alberta Minister of the Environment Ralph Klein appeared before the second parliamentary com-mittee as the new CCME chair to renew the provinces' requests, only to be rebuffed by government and opposition members alike. Although the government accepted the provinces' recommendation to make consultation with the provinces mandatory under certain conditions, it denied their more substantive proposals.

As the bill reached third reading, the Quebec government, which had not been a participant in the CCME discussions, launched a public attack on the bill, depicting it as a 'totalitarian' attempt by Ottawa to seize control of economic development in Quebec.[100] The province's criticisms came as no surprise to the federal cabinet, since the environment minister had received a series of letters and a final urgent telegram from his Quebec counterpart between December 1990 and March 1992, conveying the province's strong objections. When the bill cleared the House of Commons, the provincial government renewed its campaign in the Senate, urging Quebec senators to block the bill. Finally, when the bill cleared the Senate in June 1992, the Quebec environment minister vowed that the province would respond with 'judicial guerilla warfare.'[101]

As had been the case with CEPA, the federal government found itself walking a tightrope between the provinces and environmental groups. For environmentalists and the public, the government offered reassurances of a strong federal presence. As Environment Minister Lucien Bouchard stated unequivocally, 'we have jurisdiction. We have responsibilities and we will fulfil them.'[102] The government even responded to opposition and environmentalists demands by introducing amendments to reduce the extent of ministerial and cabinet discretion afforded by the bill. In contrast, the provinces fared even less well than they had in the earlier CEPA debate.

The federal government was considerably more conciliatory behind closed doors, however. Federal officials privately reassured the provinces that they were not planning to get involved in '99% of projects that arise.' One federal official explained that federal involvement was foreseen in only ten to twenty assessments per year, those that 'attract national attention and make it difficult for either level of government to be seen backing out of it.'[103] Although the glare of public scrutiny made it difficult for the federal government to publicly stray very far from the broad federal role defined by the courts, the new statute did restore some of the discretion that facilitated the federal retreat in the 1970s, and the federal government reassured the provinces privately that it did not intend to push its new statutory authority to its limits.

The Regulatory and Enforcement Functions

The late 1980s witnessed a renewal not only of federal legislative activity, but also of regulatory and enforcement activity reflecting the influence of two factors. First, the increased salience of environmental issues was accompanied by specific pressure for enforcement. During the late 1980s, the paucity of either federal or provincial prosecutions in the face of widespread non-compliance became a minor cause célèbre. Environment Canada's credibility was dealt a harsh blow in 1989 when, at the height of public attention to environmental issues, the press obtained a leaked departmental report which acknowledged that the vast majority of Canadian pulp mills still failed to comply with the 1971 regulations.[104] In response to public demand, federal and provincial officials alike resorted to prosecutions with greater frequency. There even were allegations of races between federal and provincial officials to lay charges.[105]

The second factor was that CEPA represented an important new tool for Environment Canada. CEPA provided federal officials with a new mandate to assess several dozen priority substances and, if necessary, to develop regulations to control each of them. At the same time, Environment Canada's regional officials were empowered by the fact that CEPA, unlike the Fisheries Act amendments, was not accompanied by a long-standing commitment to defer to the provinces with respect to enforcement. In that respect, the CEPA Enforcement and Compliance Policy, which was released at the same time as the draft legislation, was particularly significant.[106] The policy's promise that compliance with CEPA would be mandatory was nothing short of a 'radical shift in philosophy' from the traditional approach of gradual, negotiated compliance.[107]

Implementation of CEPA

Federal and provincial officials' efforts to reconcile their new roles in regulation and enforcement largely were played out through negotiations over the implementation of CEPA. In February 1989, the federal government published its list of forty-four 'priority substances' for evaluation under CEPA. The provinces viewed the list with particular apprehension in light of the federal government's commitment to evaluate and, if necessary, regulate each of those substances within five years.

The daunting task remained to define 'equivalency.' The federal government sponsored two workshops in 1988, at which federal and provincial officials sought to develop criteria for equivalency agreements. However, the meetings ended in an impasse, with provincial officials complaining of federal inflexibility. The effort was given renewed urgency when a fire at a PCB storage facility in Saint-Basile-le-Grand later that year renewed the threat of overlapping federal and provincial regulations. Federal and provincial officials quickly agreed to an interim approach to regulating PCB storage, and redoubled their efforts to define 'equivalency' once and for all.

In the spring of 1989, CCME established a Task Force on Federal-Provincial Partnerships for Environmental Protection comprised of senior federal and provincial officials. The task force's report, completed in January 1990, placed heavy emphasis on the concept of 'partnership,' with the implication of equality among partners.[108] The report offered draft administrative and equivalency agreements, described as 'work sharing' and 'work limiting' arrangements, respectively. Five criteria for equivalency were offered: equal standards, comparable rights of individuals to request an investigation of compliance and to receive a report, comparable penalties for non-compliance, comparable enforcement policies, and comparable measurement and testing procedures. The first two criteria are found in the act itself, while the other three were included at the insistence of the federal government.

Considerable disagreement remained, however, between the federal government and Quebec. The Quebec government argued unsuccessfully for CCME consensus standards as an alternative to federal regulations. Thereafter, Quebec announced that it would refuse to sign any equivalency agreement on the grounds that to do so would sanction federal intrusion in an area of provincial jurisdiction. Quebec's rejection of equivalency is ironic, since the province proposed the concept in the first place. However, Quebec officials emphasize that the statutory conditions on equivalency introduced by the federal government in late 1987 were not what they originally agreed to.

Quebec was not the only province wary of equivalency. Several others objected to the statutory requirement for investigations in response to citizen petitions. More importantly, many provinces objected to the fact that they would have to be held to account by the federal government in order to qualify for equivalency. As a BC official complained, 'the federal view is that the federal government will set the rules and *allow* the provinces to do the work, pay for it, and be held accountable to them.'[109]

Negotiations stalled in 1990 as both sides waited for the first set of federal regulations to be issued under CEPA. The provinces held out for more flexible criteria, betting that the federal government would retreat from its strict criteria when the extent of the resources required to implement its own regulations became apparent. Indeed, as discussed below, as the prospect of implementation of the first set of CEPA regulations edged closer, federal officials in Ottawa once again began to voice strong support for the 'single window' approach.

Federal-Provincial Relations
When the federal government's role in environmental protection re-emerged in the late 1980s, so too did federal-provincial tensions. Indeed, as described below, federal-provincial relations reached a new low in the *Rafferty-Alameda* case, with the federal environment minister and the Saskatchewan premier levelling accusations against each other in court.

Federal-provincial relations during the second wave of environmentalism differed from the first in two respects. First, the environment was no longer a new field in the late 1980s. The provinces had at least symbolically colonized their jurisdiction, and thus were all the more resentful of renewed federal interest. Second, the scope of conflict was much broader than in the 1970s. In the face of environmental groups' legal claims to federal assessments, federal and provincial governments no longer were able to resolve their disputes behind closed doors.

The scope of conflict expanded within governments as well. The environmental issue moved beyond the bounds of environment departments, first to intergovernmental affairs departments and other line departments, such as energy, and finally to the governmental level. As anticipated by Smiley, officials from provincial intergovernmental affairs departments tended to be less inclined to cooperate with the federal government than were their counterparts within the provincial environment ministries.[110] One official in the Alberta Department of Federal and Intergovernmental Affairs (FIGA) explained, 'their mandate is protection of the environment, ours is protection of provincial jurisdiction.'[111] Interestingly, in contrast, federal officials in the Federal-Provincial Relations Office were relatively conciliatory in the wake of the failure of the Meech Lake Accord, describing their role as one of 'avoiding provincial irritants.'[112]

The Canadian Council of Ministers of the Environment
As in 1970, the late 1980s witnessed a rejuvenation of the federal-provincial Council of Ministers. CCREM meetings were held more frequently, increasing from a single annual meeting to two or more meetings per year. The focus of the council moved from mere information exchange to development and oversight of substantive joint programs, including funding for cleanup of abandoned sites contaminated by hazardous wastes, a national strategy to reduce packaging waste, and a wide-reaching national plan to control urban smog.

The council's sharper focus during this period was facilitated by the departure in the mid-1980s of ministers responsible for several natural resource portfolios, including wildlife, forestry, and parks. These past members left to form their own councils. Reflecting the narrower emphasis of the remaining members of CCREM, the council was renamed the Canadian Council of Ministers of the Environment (CCME) in 1988. At the same time, the council was reorganized, relocated (to Winnipeg), and the number of staff was substantially increased.

As in 1970, the rejuvenation of the council was not merely a reflection of federal and provincial governments' desire to reconcile their new programs. It also reflected a conscious strategy by several provincial governments to preempt federal unilateralism. Reminiscent of 1970, Quebec and Alberta in particular strongly supported the development of CCME standards and national 'codes of practice' as an alternative to federal standards. Alberta officials, fearful of the 'temptation for provinces to jump ship and strike deals with the feds,'[113] pressed for multilateral arrangements, in which the provinces could present a common front.

The council responded to the passage of CEPA in two ways. It established the Task Force on Federal-Provincial Partnerships for Environmental Protection, discussed above, which drafted model bilateral agreements. A second task force drafted a multilateral Statement on Interjurisdictional Cooperation (STOIC), signed by all the federal, provincial, and territorial governments in March 1990.[114] On the surface, STOIC represents a relatively innocuous agreement to cooperate 'in the spirit of partnership.' The signatory governments expressed a commitment to several principles, including the sharing of information, timely consultation, and harmonization of environmental standards.

It is nonetheless striking that all provinces were willing to concede that 'both the federal and provincial governments have legislative authority enabling them to regulate matters relating to the environment.' Defensive provinces like Alberta and Quebec not only agreed to sign the statement, they were among its strongest proponents. After the passage of CEPA and the Supreme Court's *Crown Zellerbach* decision, federal involvement in the environmental field was accepted as inevitable. The provinces thus reverted to a second-best strategy of precluding federal unilateralism and immobilizing the federal government with consultations. As one of the architects of the statement explained, 'if some guy moves into your basement and you can't evict him, you at least try to keep him in the basement.'[115]

The emphasis on harmonization of standards in STOIC also reflected provincial concerns about potential interprovincial competition for investment. As in 1970, the provinces clearly were troubled by the prospect that they or their neighbours would be pressured to attract new investment and protect existing industries by lowering environmental standards. However, STOIC's call for harmonization left open the possibility of overcoming destructive competition through interprovincial cooperation, without the need for federal standards. One provincial official described the concept of harmonization as a 'watered-down' version of equivalency.[116]

Federal officials recall that the first drafts of the statement offered by the provinces were totally unacceptable from the federal government's perspective. Protracted negotiations followed over the wording of virtually every clause. Why did the federal government persevere? Most importantly, the federal government gained formal provincial recognition of its role in the environmental field. The federal government also welcomed the objective of harmonization of standards, which opened the door for provincial acceptance of federal standards.

It remains to be seen whether the cooperative or obstructive impulse in STOIC will prevail, however. The very existence of the statement signals acceptance by each level of government of the other's presence in the field, and a broad commitment to coordinate federal and provincial programs. On the other hand, the overriding objective of the statement for at least some provinces is to restrain the federal government. Thus, STOIC may prove more effective as a rhetorical weapon in federal-provincial disputes than as a benchmark for federal-provincial cooperation. As soon as the agreement was signed, provinces that objected to federal 'intrusions' began to cite the agreement to buttress their arguments. It is noteworthy, however, that the same provinces that complained of not being treated as full 'partners' in the development of federal programs are not so eager to involve the federal government in the development of their own environmental policies.

Federal-Provincial Relations in Environmental Assessment

Federal-provincial relations, already strained by CEPA, were dealt a further blow by court decisions concerning the EARP Guidelines Order. The following three case studies reveal how the courts' EARP decisions pitted the federal government against the provinces, and in so doing, generated intergovernmental disputes that spilled out from behind the closed doors of traditional intergovernmental negotiations into the front pages, and ultimately back into the courts. The cases illustrate the profound tension between federal authority to protect the environment and the provinces' authority to promote economic development through exploitation of their own natural resources.

The Rafferty-Alameda Dam

The Canadian public first heard of the proposed Rafferty-Alameda project in 1988, when a political aide to the federal environment minister resigned, alleging that the federal government had struck a deal with the province of Saskatchewan not to perform an environmental assessment of the dams. This accusation was denied by the federal environment minister, Tom McMillan.[117] Within months, two Canadian environmental groups went to court in an attempt to force a federal review.

The trial division of the federal court quashed the license granted by the federal government to the province and required that Environment Canada conduct an initial assessment, as required by the EARP Guidelines Order. The environment department then reissued the license after performing an initial assessment, and concluding that the impacts were not 'significant.' However, in a surprising departure from traditional judicial deference to executive discretion, the federal court rejected the minister's conclusion that the impacts were insignificant as clearly inconsistent with his own environment department's findings, and ordered the federal government to perform a full environmental review.[118]

It is significant that the court did not quash the license that had been reissued by the federal government to the province of Saskatchewan.[119] As a result, there was no legal impediment to continued construction of the dams. In January 1990, the federal government and the province reached an out-of-court agreement in which the province agreed to delay construction pending a full federal review of the project, in return for which the federal government agreed to pay the province $1 million per month for up to ten months. However, before the review could be completed, the provincial agency responsible for the project resumed construction, prompting the federal environmental assessment panel to resign in October.[120] The provincial agency reinforced its 'game of chicken' with a media and public relations campaign designed to pressure and embarrass the federal government.[121]

The federal environment minister, Robert de Cotret, initially declined to pursue an injunction to halt construction. However, he soon relented under pressure from environmentalists and the opposition parties. The province counter-sued for $10 million in damages, claiming that the federal government had breached an agreement reached in September in a private meeting between the premier and the federal environment minister, in which the latter consented to the province's completion of the dam.[122] In affidavits submitted to the Saskatchewan Court of Queen's Bench, the federal minister and his officials testified that there had only been an 'agreement to agree.'[123] Saskatchewan officials countered with condemning testimony that they had heard the federal environment minister affirm his intention to amend the federal-provincial agreement to allow construction to proceed, and declare that if the EARP panel resigned it would actually increase his options.[124] Although the conflicting testimony made it impossible to reconstruct just what was in fact agreed to, the allegations of secret deals nonetheless tarnished the reputation of the federal minister and raised questions about the depth of the federal government's commitment to its own environmental review process. The court subsequently denied the injunction on the grounds that it was not warranted to preserve a 'badly flawed' federal process.[125]

A second federal environmental assessment panel, appointed after the first's resignation, issued its report in September 1991.[126] Since construction was almost complete, the panel declined to draw conclusions about whether or not the project should proceed. However, it did identify several areas of concern and recommend mitigative measures.

The Al-Pac Pulp Mill

In December 1988, Alberta premier, Don Getty, announced construction of the largest single-line kraft pulp mill in the world. The $1.3 billion Alberta-Pacific (Al-Pac) mill was backed by a provincial government investment of $350 million, including construction of roads and a loan of $275 million, as well as a renewable long-term lease covering 10 per cent of the province.[127] The Al-Pac project was to be the cornerstone of a provincial government strategy to develop Alberta's northern forests. In the late 1980s, the province actively courted investment by pulp and paper companies, and succeeded in attracting proposals for seven new mills by offering forest companies a total of over $1 billion in loan guarantees, timber rights to roughly one-third of the province, and the second lowest stumpage rates in North America.[128]

However, the provincial government clearly had not anticipated the extent of public opposition to the projects on environmental grounds. The provincial NDP opposition called for a freeze on construction of new pulp mills pending comprehensive reviews of their environmental impacts, a demand supported by 300,000 Albertans who signed a petition to that effect. Most importantly, after the *Rafferty-Alameda* decision, environmentalists and Aboriginal groups opposed to the projects were able to use the threat of litigation to force the federal government to perform a full review of the Al-Pac project.

Prior to *Rafferty-Alameda*, the federal government had declined to play a significant role in environmental assessment in Alberta. The federal and provincial governments had signed a formal agreement that effectively left responsibility for most environmental assessments to the province.[129] However, when that agreement expired in May 1989, a month after the *Rafferty-Alameda* decision, the federal government informed the province that it could not renew the agreement while the EARP Guidelines Order remained in place; the court decision had made it clear that the federal government would be required to fulfil its own environmental responsibilities.

The Al-Pac project fell within federal jurisdiction by virtue of the potential impacts on fisheries, Aboriginal lands, and federal lands (Wood Buffalo National Park). After some initial sparring, the federal government and the province agreed to a joint environmental review panel. However, at Alberta's insistence, the panel's terms of reference did not include authority to review the impacts of forestry activity associated with the mill. In fact, Minister of Forestry, Lands and Wildlife LeRoy Fjordbotten, who had been the chief architect of the province's new forest development strategy, did not allow his department's officials to participate in the panel's hearings, even though their fish and wildlife expertise clearly fell within the panel's terms of reference.[130]

After the panel's hearings began, federal-provincial tensions were rekindled when the Regional Director of Environmental Protection for Environment Canada testified on behalf of Environment Canada and the federal Department of Fisheries and Oceans that Al-Pac's proposal was 'unacceptable.'[131] Alberta politicians reacted angrily, even though their own Ministry of the Environment had been highly critical of Al-Pac's environment impact assessment. The forestry minister called the federal testimony a 'sinister' attempt to impose 'unreasonable' standards on Alberta mills even while the federal government was subsidizing much dirtier mills in Quebec and Ontario.[132]

After a conversation with his federal counterpart, the Alberta environment minister, Ralph Klein, reported to the press that the unfortunate incident was all caused by a rogue federal bureaucrat, whose testimony did not reflect the federal government's position. However, the federal minister, Lucien Bouchard, subsequently called his own press conference to stand behind his official.[133] The episode was damaging not only to the federal-provincial relationship, but to the province's environmental image. Alberta officials, who already had proposed the most stringent standards for pulp mills in the country, greatly resented the federal government's new-found environmentalism. As one official complained, 'forty stinking mills in Quebec and they tell us the cleanest mill in the world shouldn't go ahead? Give us a break!'[134]

After completing its hearings, the joint environmental assessment panel released its report, which essentially concurred with the position taken by the federal officials in their testimony.[135] The panel expressed grave concerns about the potential for cumulative effects of several pulp mills that either already existed or were proposed for the Athabasca River. The panel recommended that additional studies, expected to require two or more years, be performed before making any final decisions on the Al-Pac project.

The Alberta government announced that it would fully accept the panel's recommendations,[136] and the proposed studies soon were undertaken jointly by the federal and provincial governments. However, within weeks, the premier was referring to the panel's report as 'unbalanced.'[137] The province hired a consulting firm to perform an alternate review of Al-Pac's proposal. However, even before the consultants could report, Al-Pac submitted a revised proposal to the province in May 1990, which entailed substantially reduced discharges of persistent toxins.

In July, the province announced the formation of a three-person 'scientific Review Panel,' which was charged with reviewing the technical feasibility of the company's new proposal. It is noteworthy that the terms of reference for the second panel carefully excluded the question of environmental impacts, although that was the basis for the first panel's rejection of the project. In keeping with the narrow terms of reference, the Scientific Review Panel refused to hear testimony or to accept submissions concerning the environmental impacts of the project. The panel required only three days of hearings to address the relatively narrow technical questions before it.

The second panel was not a joint federal-provincial undertaking, although one federal specialist on pulp mill technology was appointed to the panel by the province. Federal participation in the first round had been orchestrated primarily by Environment Canada's staff in the Western and Northern region. However, during the second round, negotiations were handled at the highest levels in Ottawa. Federal officials concluded that Al-Pac's revised proposal could be considered a 'mitigative measure,' as allowed for under the EARP Guidelines Order, and thus did not require another full environmental review. Environment Canada did not testify nor offer a written submission to the second panel, a striking contrast to the department's controversial participation in the first round. The Department of Fisheries and Oceans did seek to testify, but its statement, which was critical of the proposed mill's environmental impacts, was rejected as beyond the terms of reference of the panel.[138]

After receiving the Scientific Review Panel's report, which affirmed the technical feasibility of Al-Pac's revised design, the provincial cabinet voted in December 1990 to approve Al-Pac's proposal. In fact, the government offered the company an additional $100 million in financing as compensation for the cost of delays associated with the environmental review.[139] The federal environment and fisheries ministers wrote to their Alberta counterparts specifying the federal government's conditions for approval of the Al-Pac project, which the province agreed to meet in the project's license. The redesigned mill commenced operations in late 1993.

The James Bay Project

The federal government's expanded role in environmental assessment presented an even greater dilemma in the case of the proposed second phase of the Quebec government's James Bay hydro development. In light of the strength of the federal Conservative government's Quebec caucus, and of the national unity crisis that followed the demise of the Meech Lake Accord, the government was not eager to provoke a conflict with the Quebec government over the environment. However, after the *Rafferty-Alameda* decision, it had little choice. Moreover, Western politicians and pundits were watching to see that the federal government took as hard a line with Quebec as it had with Alberta and Saskatchewan in the Al-Pac and Rafferty-Alameda cases.

The second phase of the James Bay project, known as Grande-Baleine or Great Whale, long had been a pet project of the Quebec premier, Robert Bourassa.[140] As proposed, the project would involve flooding almost 400 square miles of land. One of the most serious environmental problems, which had been revealed by the first phase of the James Bay project, was that soil and decomposing vegetation that have been flooded release mercury, contaminating the fish that form a major component of the local native diet.[141]

Despite his sovereignist background, Lucien Bouchard took an aggressive stance on James Bay during his term as federal environment minister. The federal government had jurisdiction over the project by virtue of the potential impact on Indians and Indian lands, fisheries, interprovincial waterways, and migratory birds. In November 1989, Bouchard wrote to his Quebec counterpart, threatening to conduct a unilateral federal environmental review of the project if necessary.[142] The two levels of government subsequently engaged in protracted negotiations over the terms of a joint review.

A key sticking point was the province's insistence on a two-stage review, with the first stage considering only the impact of roads, airports, and marine terminals, to allow construction of those aspects of the project to proceed while a more lengthy second-stage review of the rest of the project was conducted. The proposal for a two-stage review was strongly opposed by environmentalists and the Cree who live in the vicinity of the proposed project. Both feared that after the province had already spent $600 million on infrastructure, it would not seriously consider cancellation of the project, whatever the outcome of the second phase of the review.

The federal and provincial governments reached a tentative agreement on the terms of a joint environmental review in June 1990.[143] However, in September, the Quebec environment minister, Pierre Paradis, reversed his earlier position and called for a single set of hearings.[144] A public dispute ensued between Paradis and the deputy premier, Lise Bacon, who as energy minister was responsible for the project and strongly advocated a two-stage review to avoid delays in construction. Bacon charged that, 'on the pretext of protecting the environment, the federal government has in fact given itself the possibility of intervening in the overall management of natural resources in Canada ... Tomorrow it could be forestry, it could be mines.'[145]

The tension between nationalism and environmentalism made for strange bedfellows. The federal government's chief negotiator with the province had been an unsuccessful candidate for the Parti Québécois in the last provincial election, while Quebec's chief negotiator was the prime minister's former chief of staff. The former federal environment minister, now leader of the separatist Bloc Québécois, Lucien Bouchard, continued to support a full federal review, arguing that, 'for the time being, Ottawa has powers and jurisdictions in the environment, and it might be that even some nationalists in Quebec must thank God for that, because Quebec is not taking care of the environment now.'[146]

Even the provincial environment minister sought backup from the federal government to bolster his own tenuous position in cabinet in favour of a single-stage review. Paradis even joined environmentalists in pressing the federal government to seek an injunction in the *Rafferty-Alameda* case, arguing that it was necessary to defend the principle that environmental reviews must be completed before construction begins.[147] The provincial minister was undercut by the federal government, however, when Bouchard's successor as environment minister, Robert de Cotret, announced that the federal government would accept a two-phase review.[148] Paradis subsequently reversed his own position and agreed to a two-phase review.[149] The provincial environment minister again turned to the federal government for support, however, in arguing for a federal review under the terms of the more forceful James Bay Agreement, rather than the EARP Guidelines Order.[150] However, the federal government again undercut the provincial minister by arguing that the federal government had no role under the former.[151]

After public opinion polls indicated strong support for a single review, even in Quebec, the federal minister, Robert de Cotret, stiffened his position somewhat and offered assurances that no federal permits would be granted until the government was satisfied that the project was environmentally sound.[152] His successor, Jean Charest, took an even stronger position, reversing de Cotret's earlier concession which supported a two-stage review.[153] In July 1991, Charest announced that the federal government would proceed unilaterally with a full environmental review.[154]

That announcement was made just a week before hearings were to begin to consider the Cree's request for a full federal review of the project under the more authoritative James Bay Agreement, rather than the EARP Guidelines Order as proposed by the federal government. At the hearing, the federal government's lawyers argued that a federal review under the terms of the agreement would be unconstitutional because the project fell within the exclusive jurisdiction of the provincial government. This prompted the Federal Court judge to chide the government for 'looking for a way to avoid [its] responsibilities.'[155] The Federal Court ruled in September that a full federal environmental review was required under the terms of the James Bay Agreement.[156]

The Quebec Liberal government subsequently announced that it would delay construction of the project for one year, to allow time for a single review to be conducted. In January 1992, the federal and provincial governments and Aboriginal peoples finally reached an agreement on complex terms of a joint review under the James Bay Agreement.[157] Before the five joint environmental review committees established under the agreement could complete their work, however, the newly elected Parti Québécois government announced in November 1994 that it was suspending the $13 billion project indefinitely.[158] The announcement by Premier Jacques Parizeau followed conclusions by the environmental review team that Hydro Quebec's environmental impact study was deficient.

The Impact of Federal Involvement
In the Rafferty-Alameda case, the federal environmental assessment proved to be little more than an irritant to the province and an embarrassment to

the federal government. The federal panel was left to consider the environmental impacts of a virtually completed project. However, in the James Bay and Al-Pac cases, federal involvement arguably did make a difference. The threat of full federal reviews pushed both Quebec and Alberta to agree to more aggressive reviews than they seemed inclined to pursue on their own. Although the first Al-Pac panel's recommendation that federal and provincial approvals be delayed pending further studies was not followed, the panel's negative assessment of the project nonetheless prompted the proponent to substantially improve its design for the mill.

In the James Bay case, federal pressure, however intermittent, was instrumental in leading the Quebec government to delay construction and agree to a single, comprehensive review. Although it would be a gross overstatement to attribute the cancellation of the project to the federal role in environmental assessment, the federal government's insistence on a single review did delay construction and thus may have made it easier for the Quebec government to respond to political and consumer pressures by cancelling the project before it had incurred massive construction costs.

In each of these cases, it is noteworthy that it was pressure from environmentalists, Aboriginal peoples, and ultimately the courts that forced the federal government to act. Time and again, the federal government revealed its reluctance to exercise its environmental authority in ways that could hinder economic development or provoke federal-provincial conflict. Even after the first unfavourable court decision in the *Rafferty-Alameda* case, the federal government still attempted to avoid a full environmental review, only to have its hands slapped by the court. Lucien Bouchard recalled that the government was 'forced into proselytizing' by the courts.[159] Later, there were allegations of Bouchard's successor making secret deals with the province to allow construction to proceed before completing the court-ordered review.

In the Al-Pac case, the federal government and the province apparently reached an accommodation in the second round of the review, which allowed the province to solicit a 'scientific' rationale to approve the project without threat of federal interference, even though the environmental studies recommended by the first panel had not been completed. And finally, in the James Bay case, the federal government clearly sought to avoid conflict with the province by consenting at one point to a two-stage review and by abstaining under the James Bay Agreement, despite apparent support from the provincial environment minister for a more aggressive federal role. The government continued to shirk its responsibilities under the James Bay Agreement by pleading constitutional limitations, until forced to acknowledge them by the courts. In the end, the strongest impression left by these three case studies is the profound reluctance of both the federal and provincial governments to jeopardize economic development in pursuit of environmental protection.

Just as CEPA prompted multilateral efforts to develop the Statement on Interjurisdictional Cooperation and prototype bilateral administrative and equivalency agreements, so too did the EARP litigation and Canadian Environmental Assessment Act (CEAA) prompt a multilateral response. Through CCME, the federal government and the provinces in 1991 reached agreement on a set of Cooperative Principles for Environmental Assessment, which express a commitment to reduce uncertainty and duplication of environmental assessments through cooperation, and to promote consistency across jurisdictions to limit 'forum shopping.'[160] A prototype bilateral agreement, the Draft Framework for Environmental Assessment Harmonization, was developed by a CCME task group and adopted by the council in 1992. The first such bilateral agreement was concluded by the federal government and Alberta in August 1993.[161]

Conclusion

In many respects, the period between 1985 and 1991 offered a replay of the early 1970s. As the salience of the environment re-emerged, the federal government again began to take a broader view of its own jurisdiction. With CEPA and CEAA, the federal government cast its jurisdictional net more widely than in the past, rejecting the supplementary federal role envisioned by earlier environmental statutes. The federal government also began to reclaim its regulatory and enforcement functions.

It is significant that these extensions of the federal role in environmental protection in the late 1980s occurred at the same time as the federal government was devolving powers to the provinces in other fields and cutting back many of its own spending programs. In fact, arguably the strongest assertions of federal authority to date were made, not only by a Conservative government intent on avoiding federal-provincial confrontation, but by an avowedly sovereignist federal Minister of the Environment. This suggests that growing public demand for environmental protection, rather than partisan ideology or developments in other policy areas, prompted renewed federal interest in the environment.

However, as anticipated and as in the early 1970s, there was ample evidence of residual hesitation. The dramatic increase in federal environmental assessment activity can be seen as the combined effect of a carelessly drafted federal regulation, increasingly professional environmental groups capable of capitalizing on that error, and a judiciary more comfortable in the post-

Charter era with its role as a guardian of public rights. Inasmuch as the federal government could not retreat completely from the position thrust upon it by the courts in the face of unprecedented public demand for environmental protection, the effect of the EARP decisions will be a lasting one in the field of environmental assessment. However, the EARP decisions are unlikely to presage an upheaval in other areas of federal environmental policy. The appearance of the word 'shall' in the EARP Guidelines Order is unusual among Canadian environmental statutes and regulations, which typically authorize, rather than require, the executive to take certain actions. Thus, Canadians will find few opportunities within the discretionary language of other federal statutes and regulations to force the federal government to take actions to protect the environment. Indeed, it is doubtful that an unexamined 'shall' ever will find its way into a federal statute again.

During this period, provincial governments also were increasingly active in the environmental field. Brown and Siddiq report an average increase in provincial expenditures on environmental protection of 6.6 per cent per year between 1985 and 1989, more than three times the overall rate of growth in provincial expenditures.[162] In light of the greater level of activity of both levels of government, there was potential for both competition and conflict. Public servants at both levels volunteered comments on competition between federal and provincial environment ministers to claim the environmental high ground. The Quebec minister asserted that 'the federal government, in wanting to take on responsibilities on these big industrial projects, will force the provinces, including Quebec, to occupy their field of jurisdiction.'[163] Indeed, soon after the passage of CEPA, Quebec, New Brunswick, British Columbia, and Ontario all revised their own environmental statutes to match the federal government's $1 million fines. And, in response to the EARP litigation and the proposed federal environmental assessment legislation, a number of provinces also revamped their own environmental assessment processes.

However, except in cases where both levels of government were pushed by court decisions, the competition between them was largely confined to symbolic announcements and enabling legislation, much as it was in 1970. When it came to standard setting and enforcement, there was a significant degree of intergovernmental coordination.[164] It was in the interests of budget-strapped federal and provincial governments alike to reconcile their administrative responsibilities. Moreover, politicians at both levels were mindful of the economic consequences of unrestrained competition in environmental regulation.

In addition, the provinces wished to defend their control over natural resources and economic development. Thus, CCME's efforts to draft statements of principles and model agreements can be seen not merely as an attempt by both orders of government to minimize administrative costs by coordinating their efforts, but as a conscious attempt by the provinces to restrain federal autonomy. The provinces' demands to be treated as full partners in federal environmental policy-making were notably one-way.

A crucial difference between the first and second waves of environmental concern was the greater role played by environmental groups. The opening up of environmental policy-making processes to include representatives of environmental organizations reflected a grass-roots rejection of the traditionally closed consultation processes. As one environmentalist argued, 'the public will no longer accept backroom deals between politicians and industry and they will not accept any more backroom deals between one order of government and another.'[165] This expansion of the scope of conflict had important implications for policy outcomes. In the 1970s and early 1980s, the absence of public demand for environmental programs, industry's resistance to regulation, and the provinces' protectiveness of their jurisdiction worked together to discourage federal environmental initiatives. However, by the late 1980s, the federal government increasingly was caught between hostile provinces and industry on the one hand, and demanding environmental groups providing an effective voice for growing public concern on the other. In that more pluralist environment, federal officials were forced to resist many provincial demands.

Addendum: Whither – or Wither – the Federal Role?

As the salience of environmental issues subsides in the mid-1990s, one is left with unanswered questions about the future roles of the federal and provincial governments in the environmental field. Does CEPA herald a more activist federal role in environmental protection, or will its fate be closer to that of the Canada Water Act? Will equivalency introduce an element of vertical or 'functional' federalism in Canadian environmental policy, or facilitate another federal withdrawal in the 1990s? Have Green Plan dollars provided the kind of federal leverage over provincial programs afforded by traditional shared-cost programs, or merely padded the federal government's list of accomplishments come election time? Will the Liberal government elected federally in November 1993 pursue the stronger federal role in environmental policy that the party demanded while in opposition, or respond to the combination of declining public attention to environmental issues and fiscal restraint by gradually with-drawing from the field, as previous Liberal governments did in the 1970s?

Early indications are that the 1990s will witness a federal retreat akin to that of the 1970s. With respect to CEPA, although the federal government fulfilled its promise to evaluate forty-four priority substances within five years, as of August 1994 it had issued regulations for only two of the twenty-five substances or classes of substances added to the List of Toxic Substances. Moreover, the federal government departed from its Green Plan commitment to regulate all substances found to be toxic, and is now promising only to develop 'action plans,' which may rely on voluntary, non-regulatory approaches.[166] Although the federal government is forg-ing ahead with evaluation of priority substances, with a commitment to evaluate 100 more by the year 2000 in addition to the original forty-four, its regulatory activities to actually control those substances found toxic are not proceeding apace. Equivalency is not having the intended effect of harmonizing provincial standards since only one equivalency agreement has been signed.[167]

The outcome of a legislatively mandated five-year review of CEPA will offer further indications of the federal government's intentions. It is telling that the parliamentary review was delayed by the environment minister, at the urging of the provinces, to grant a 'head start' to CCME efforts to rationalize federal and provincial roles.[168] In preparation for the review, Environment Canada, faced with the prospect of resource-inten-sive enforcement of its own regulations, advanced a proposal to relax the conditions on equivalency found in CEPA.[169]

However, the resulting report of the House of Commons Standing Committee on the Environment and Sustainable Development, issued in June 1995, suggests that the new government's own backbenchers are less concerned about the administrative costs and federal-provincial irritants associated with CEPA than their cabinet colleagues. Offering over 140 rec-ommendations to strengthen the act, the committee's report concluded that 'only federal action will ensure that the health of all Canadians is pro-tected' from the risks posed by toxic substances.[170] As observed by Kennett, the report is

at once an indictment of inaction in the administration of the federal government's 'flagship' environmental statute and a call for signifi-cantly increased federal environmental presence. The federal government's response to the CEPA report ... will be an important test of its willingness and ability to exercise environmental jurisdiction, its vision for federal-provincial relations in this area, and the extent to which it is prepared to match 'green' rhetoric with action.[171]

In the environmental assessment field, proclamation of the Canadian Environmental Assessment Act was delayed by two and a half years. The delay was caused by protracted efforts to develop regulations, which had to be ready when the act was proclaimed since they specify the conditions under which environmental assessments are required. Environment Canada's original regulatory proposal was 'gutted' by the Tory cabinet in response to industry and provincial objections prior to publication in the Canada Gazette.[172] The subsequent Liberal government, elected in November 1993, kept its promise to the environmental community by tightening the proposed regulations somewhat, as well as amending the act to ensure intervenor funding, but at the same time responded to provincial and industry objections by strengthening the commitment to harmonize federal and provincial assessment processes.

The $3 billion Green Plan offered a unique opportunity for the federal government to buy its way into the environmental protection field. When it was unveiled, federal officials predicted that Green Plan dollars would lubricate intergovernmental relations by providing federal dollars for joint federal-provincial initiatives, thus helping to establish the federal government in a visible but less confrontational role relative to the provinces. In practice, however, the Green Plan provided more grit than grease to the machinery of intergovernmental relations. The provinces continued to resent what they perceived as inadequate consultation both in the development of the original plan and subsequent spending announcements. If anything, the spending pattern of Green Plan funds – with heavy emphasis on research and education, and minimal attention to regulation – helped to re-establish the federal government in its traditional support role in the environmental field.

After their election, the new Liberal government initially embraced the Conservatives' Green Plan. By the mid-1990s, however, with increasing public and governmental emphasis on deficit reduction and the low salience of environmental issues, the Green Plan's days were numbered. The spending program was quietly terminated in early 1995, three years into its five-year mandate, and with only $847 million, or less than 30 per cent, of the original $3 billion commitment spent.[173] In striking contrast to the fanfare surrounding the Green Plan's development and release, there was no government press release announcing its demise and almost no media attention. At about the same time, the Liberal government announced its intentions to reduce Environment Canada's staff by almost one-quarter (from 5,700 to 4,300) and budget by almost one-third (from $737 million to $503 million) over a three-year period.[174]

With respect to intergovernmental relations, CCME's multilateral efforts began to bear fruit in the early 1990s. The federal government and Alberta signed two administrative agreements, concerning environmental assessment and the pollution control provisions of the Fisheries Act, as well as the only equivalency agreement under CEPA to date. The federal government has also signed administrative agreements concerning federal pulp and paper regulations with Quebec and British Columbia, CEPA administrative agreements with Saskatchewan and the Yukon, an environmental assessment agreement with Manitoba, and the so-called Atlantic Accord with the four Atlantic provinces. The agreements all express a commitment to a 'single window' approach, with the provinces staffing the window.

Even as this bewildering number of bilateral and multilateral accords was beginning to increase, CCME decided to move in a new direction. In November 1993, the ministers announced that harmonization would be the council's top priority in the coming two years.[175] While harmonization was already a stated goal of the Statement on Interjurisdictional Cooperation, the term is now being used more broadly. In addition to promoting consistency of standards between federal and provincial governments and across provinces – an effort that met with little success to date despite the good intentions of STOIC – a second goal of minimizing overlap and duplication has been given even greater emphasis. The harmonization initiative thus departs from recent multilateral and bilateral efforts which sought to achieve compatible coexistence. Overlap is now the enemy, and in a policy arena fraught with overlap, success could entail quite dramatic changes.

In contrast to STOIC and subsequent bilateral agreements, the harmonization initiative emerged as a result of what both federal and provincial officials described as a 'dramatic' change of heart by the federal government.[176] In the summer of 1993, federal officials, serving the new government of Prime Minister Kim Campbell, conveyed to their provincial counterparts in CCME a new commitment to eliminate overlap and rationalize federal and provincial roles in the field. The successor Liberal government maintained support for the initiative, which reinforced its own government-wide effort to 'renew the federation' by eliminating overlap and duplication. The olive branch was initially received with considerable skepticism by provincial representatives. Indeed, the emergence of several bilateral agreements in 1994 can be seen as a response to the provinces' demand for evidence that the federal government was acting in good faith.

CCME established a 'lead representatives committee' of federal and provincial officials, who first developed a Purpose, Objectives, and Principles document, which was approved by the council in June 1994.[177] The committee then prepared a draft Environmental Management Framework Agreement (EMFA) and accompanying schedules concerning matters ranging from environmental education to regulatory enforcement. The CCME approved this document for release for public consultations at their November 1994 meeting. Although the intention was for the council to approve the document as well as several additional schedules at their May 1995 meeting, the federal environment minister at the time, Sheila Copps, unexpectedly balked at the last minute at the environmental assessment schedule negotiated by her staff, sending the entire exercise into a tailspin. Indeed the meeting resulted in the Alberta and federal ministers exchanging insults via the media.[178] However, the initiative appeared to be back on track by the November 1995 CCME meeting, after which a revised draft framework agreement and ten of the eleven schedules (excluding the controversial environmental assessment schedule) were released for public comment.[179]

In many respects, the draft EMFA echoes the bilateral accords of the 1970s. Both federal and provincial governments express a shared commitment to maintaining consistently high environmental standards, while at the same time rationalizing federal and provincial roles to achieve 'one window' delivery of regulatory programs. For instance, while the draft compliance schedule notes that both orders of government are ultimately responsible for their own legislation, it is foreseen that the provinces will enforce both their own and federal standards, with the federal government only taking the lead on federal lands and in matters concerning international boundaries and agreements. Discussions thus appear to be moving 'back to the future,' where the federal government once again will conduct research ('out of the gumboots and back in the lab where they belong' in one provincial official's words), manage federal lands and oceans, and take the lead in negotiating international agreements (with extensive provincial consultation). The provinces, in contrast, will set their own standards, issue permits, monitor source performance, and enforce both their own and any federal regulations.

However, in other respects the draft EMFA envisions far more radical changes than either the accords or the more recent multilateral and bilateral agreements. The draft agreement enshrines the concept, long favoured by Quebec and Alberta, of 'national' standards developed by federal-provincial bodies as an alternative to 'federal' standards. The federal government's role is thus redefined from primary responsibility for setting national standards to mere participation as one of eleven governments involved in 'shared decision-making.' The EMFA Guidelines, Objectives and Standards schedule calls for the federal government to play a 'coordinating role to ensure that national discharge-based guidelines are developed,' but looks exclusively to the provinces to implement the guidelines. In fact, nowhere in the schedule is there any mention of federal regulations. While this would seem to be at odds with recent federal legislation, such as CEPA, elsewhere the Policy and Legislation schedule calls for amendment or even repeal of existing legislation as needed to eliminate overlap.

The implications of 'national,' as opposed to 'federal' standards may be profound. Federal and provincial governments typically are unwilling to restrict their autonomy by acceding to a decision rule of less than complete consensus in intergovernmental negotiations. However, unanimity makes it possible for any one government to veto a national standard stricter than it finds acceptable.[180] Moreover, while the EMFA frequently uses the term 'accountability,' there is no constitutional mechanism for federal and provincial governments acting within their own jurisdiction to hold each other to account. As with international agreements, there are no guarantees that individual governments within Canada will adhere to national agreements, even those to which they have consented. While this may sound cynical, the experience with the accords of the mid-1970s provides cause for such skepticism. It is also noteworthy that the draft EMFA does not require that the provinces adopt enforceable regulations in implementing national guidelines; voluntary 'codes of practice' could suffice. Thus, the concept of compliance with national standards offered by the Environmental Management Framework Agreement is weak in any case.

Many of the same conditions that both prompted and facilitated the federal retreat in the 1970s are again present in the 1990s. As public attention has waned, the federal government once again has been confronted by resource limitations and sustained opposition from both regulated industries and many of the provinces. The crucial difference this round could turn out to be the watchdog role played by environmental groups. Environmentalists now routinely have a place at the table in government-sponsored consultations, and they also retain considerable legal resources with respect to environmental assessment. Certainly environmentalists have expressed grave reservations concerning both the harmonization initiative and the CEPA review, but neither exercise has received meaningful press attention. Environmentalists' effectiveness in preventing a federal retreat in the 1990s ultimately will depend on their ability to mobilize credible support from a public increasingly preoccupied with other concerns.

7
Conclusions

The central premise of this book is that, in light of the diffuse benefits and concentrated costs of environmental protection, governments generally will be unwilling to pursue policies to protect the environment, although their reluctance may be briefly overcome during periods of exceptional public attentiveness to environmental issues. This premise has several implications for the relationship between federalism and environmental protection. First, it is argued here that both federal and provincial governments tend to value their environmental jurisdiction during periods of heightened salience of environmental issues. The rest of the time the federal government is ill-inclined to exercise its jurisdiction and takes advantage of jurisdictional uncertainty by 'passing the buck' to jurisdictionally defensive provinces. Second, it is anticipated that provincial governments' responsiveness to the concentrated interests of industry could lead them to compete for investment by lowering, or at least declining to strengthen, their environmental standards. Given the federal government's anticipated reluctance in the environmental field, the emergence of national standards to preclude this dynamic is by no means guaranteed. Third, it is argued that federal-provincial relations generally will be cooperative in light of the compatibility of provincial defensiveness concerning natural resources and the federal government's inclination to cede environmental responsibility to the provinces. However, intergovernmental competition and conflict could emerge during brief periods of heightened salience of environmental issues when both levels of government would be expected to adopt a broader view of their jurisdiction.

The material presented in Chapters 3 through 6 reviews the evolution of the federal government's role in environmental protection and of federal-provincial relations through two complete cycles of public opinion. This chapter considers the degree to which the evidence supports the theoreti-

cal arguments raised in Chapter 2 and summarized above, before return-
ing to broader questions of the desirability of collaboration versus
competition in the environmental field and the future direction of federal
environmental policy.

The Federal Role

Chapter 3 demonstrates that the federal government has not tested the
limits of its environmental jurisdiction to date. The extent of federal
authority remains uncertain largely because the federal government has
not provoked constitutional challenges by exercising its powers. The
courts have been quite generous in interpreting federal jurisdiction, but
they have had few opportunities to clarify the limits of that authority in
light of federal inaction.

As anticipated, however, the federal government's hesitance concerning
its constitutional jurisdiction has varied over time in response to cycles in
public attention to the environment. When public interest in the environment surged in the late 1960s, the same federal politicians who had
deflected calls for a stronger role in pollution control only a few years earlier began to envision much broader federal environmental authority. The
federal government passed a flurry of new environmental statutes predicated on previously unacknowledged sources of federal environmental
authority, and created an environment department to administer its new
statutes.

When public attention subsided in the early 1970s, however, politicians'
enthusiasm for environmental protection also diminished. Between 1972
and 1985, when environmental issues virtually disappeared from public
opinion polls, federal politicians gradually retreated from their earlier
assertions of authority. The pace of legislative activity slowed to a stand-
still. Moreover, the federal government declined to implement the more
controversial provisions of the environmental statutes it had just passed,
including sections of the Canada Water Act that had been hailed in 1970
as the centrepiece of the federal environmental program. Although better
progress was made in implementing the Fisheries Act Amendments, even
there regulatory activity ground to a halt by the late 1970s.

The late 1980s saw a replay of the late 1960s in many respects. As the
public rediscovered the environment, so too did politicians. Federal politicians again expressed confidence in the constitutional basis for a strong
federal role in environmental policy, and stressed the need for federal
involvement to establish uniform national standards. The federal government passed two new statutes, the Canadian Environmental Protection
Act and the Canadian Environmental Assessment Act, which embody the

strongest assertions of federal authority over the environment to date. Substantial new spending commitments were contained in the federal Green Plan, and Environment Canada once again began issuing new regulations and enforcing old ones. The resurgence of the federal role was hastened in 1989 by court decisions in the *Rafferty-Alameda* and *Oldman Dam* cases, which effectively forced the federal government to acknowledge the extent of its own constitutional authority and, what is even more important, forced the government to exercise this authority. Thus, in the late 1980s, the federal government advanced partly on its own steam and partly due to a strong push from behind from environmentalists and the courts.

Two general points can be made about the two periods of federal assertiveness. First, although federal government politicians were more willing to claim their jurisdiction during periods of heightened salience, they displayed considerable hesitance even then. This persistent reluctance was underscored by the federal government's response to the environmental impact assessment litigation of the late 1980s. The fact that the courts had to force the federal government to acknowledge and exercise its own jurisdiction clearly reveals the extent of federal reticence.

Second, although federal politicians were more inclined to pay the political price of imposing concentrated costs on industry during periods of high salience, they nonetheless sought to minimize those costs through the judicious use of subsidies and symbolic politics. The federal government responded to public concern with seemingly aggressive but often hollow commitments, then declined to follow through on them when public attention subsided. On the occasions when regulations were passed, subsidies often were used to cushion the blow, most notably in the case of the pulp and paper and smelting industries.

The temptation to resist imposition of concentrated costs is ever-present in all democratic political systems. One would expect similar trends in governmental activity in response to cycles in public opinion in both federal and unitary states. However, in the Canadian context, the institution of federalism provides a convenient means of escape from politically challenging environmental responsibilities for the federal government. Time and again, federal government spokespersons deflected calls for action by arguing that natural resources were a provincial responsibility. The federal government thus took advantage of overlapping jurisdiction to shirk responsibility for environmental protection.

The most important avenue through which the federal government retreated from implementation of its early environmental statutes was delegation to the provinces. In the mid-1970s, the federal government abdicated responsibility for implementation of its new statutes by formally delegating the task of enforcement to the provinces through bilateral federal-provincial environmental accords. A similar approach to enforcement was taken in the three provinces that did not sign formal agreements. When both the federal and provincial governments retreated from their earlier commitments as public attention faded, there was a shift in the balance of federal and provincial roles back toward the provinces. Preliminary evidence from bilateral agreements and the draft multilateral harmonization agreement suggests that a similar shift back to the provinces is occurring in the 1990s, as the second wave of public attention to the environment subsides.

The particular nature of the division of powers reinforces this trend. Rather than attempting to pass the buck back to the federal government, most provinces are highly motivated to defend their jurisdiction over natural resources. When public attention turned from the environment to economic issues in the 1970s, the provinces became increasingly protective of their authority to promote economic development of those resources, with the full support of resource-based industries. In the absence of public demand for environmental regulation, and faced with both provincial and industry opposition, the federal government obliged by leaving the field to the provinces.

The empirical evidence concerning the evolving federal role in environmental protection thus is compatible with that posited by public choice theory. A more water-tight case would demand insight into politicians' internal thought processes at the time key decisions were made – a virtually impossible task. The combination of cabinet secrecy and politicians' inclination to depict (and, no doubt, recall) their own motives in the most favourable light precludes definitive conclusions about why governments did not do more to protect the environment during periods of low salience.

Interprovincial Competition and National Standards

The focus of the empirical research presented in this book is the evolution of both the federal government's role in environmental protection, and federal-provincial relations concerning the environment. There has been no attempt to study provincial standard setting in depth. Detailed analysis of the dynamic of interprovincial economic competition discussed in Chapter 2 awaits further research. However, Chapters 3 to 6 do provide evidence of provincial reluctance to strengthen environmental standards for fear of placing local industry at a disadvantage relative to competitors in other provinces. During periods of heightened salience of environmental issues, this reluctance combined with public demands for action generated strong provincial support for national standards.

Thus, during the first 'green wave,' most provinces looked to the federal government to establish uniform national standards. However, the federal response during this period was mixed. On one hand, the first federal environment minister, Jack Davis, saw through the Fisheries Act Amendments, which strongly emphasized the need for national standards to overcome the threat of 'pollution havens.' On the other hand, the federal government at the same time passed the Canada Water Act, which expressly rejected the concept of uniform national standards. Moreover, in constitutional negotiations, the federal government did not seek constitutional clarification of its authority to establish national standards, despite encouragement from some provinces.

In any case, both the federal and provincial governments' commitment to national standards declined with the dwindling salience of environmental issues. This is particularly troubling since the risk of a race to the bottom is greatest during periods of public inattentiveness to the environment. The provinces' declining receptiveness to national standards is best illustrated by their resistance to the 1977 Fisheries Act Amendments. While they had embraced the national regulations promised by the 1970 amendments, in 1977 provincial spokespersons expressed concern that overly zealous federal regulators would ignore 'economic realities' within each province.

As the federal commitment to national standards simultaneously declined, the federal government issued only a handful of regulations. Interestingly, rather than imposing its own preferences, the federal government tended to act as a broker among the provinces, facilitating the development of intergovernmental consensus on national standards, and thus effectively pushing national standards toward the lowest common denominator.[1] The possibility remains, however, that the lowest common denominator that emerged in closed intergovernmental negotiations, in which stronger provinces placed pressure on weaker ones to strengthen their standards, was higher than would have prevailed had the weaker provinces been left entirely to their own devices. Consensual national standards are probably preferable to no national standards at all.

The impact of those consensual standards was greatly undermined, however, by weak enforcement. When the federal government declined to enforce its own standards, opting instead to delegate responsibility to the provinces, the situation reverted to one of voluntary provincial adherence to consensual norms, with all the attendant risks of defection. Many provincial permits did not meet national standards and, furthermore, were weakly enforced at best.

With the re-emergence of the environment on the national agenda in the late 1980s, both the federal and provincial governments expressed renewed commitment to national standards. A succession of federal environment ministers emphasized the crucial role of the federal government in establishing national standards. Although many provinces welcomed the promise of national standards offered by the new Canadian Environmental Protection Act, in general there was greater interest than in 1970 in harmonization of provincial standards through the Canadian Council of Ministers of the Environment (CCME). As the federal commitment wanes in the 1990s, it appears that the provinces' wishes will prevail. The draft harmonization agreement currently under consideration calls for 'national' standards developed through intergovernmental consensus, as opposed to 'federal' standards. Indeed, the draft agreement does not seem to anticipate the need for federal regulations ever again.

Provincial reluctance to regulate unilaterally suggests that devolution of regulatory powers within federal systems carries substantial risks. Those troubled by the prospects of interprovincial economic interdependence typically look to the federal government to establish national standards. However, with few exceptions, previous authors have casually assumed that the federal government will do just that. This study departs from previous work by critically examining federal politicians' willingness to intervene. In the field of environmental policy, the federal government's reluctance to issue and enforce national discharge standards over the last two decades suggests that previous authors have underestimated the obstacles to a federal response.

Federal-Provincial Relations and the Environment

For most of the last two and a half decades, federal-provincial relations concerning environmental protection have been remarkably cooperative. To a large extent, the harmonious tone of intergovernmental relations has been the result of federal deference to the provinces. The federal government has seldom threatened to invade the provinces' closely guarded natural resources jurisdiction, and thus, there has been little to fight about. However, there were exceptions during the early 1970s and late 1980s, when the federal government became more assertive with respect to its environmental jurisdiction.

The first 'green wave' saw considerable federal-provincial conflict, as the largest provinces sought to fend off federal intrusion. It is noteworthy, though, that many of the smaller provinces actually pressed for a stronger federal role, either because they were wary of interprovincial economic competition, or because they had limited administrative resources to do the job themselves. Although a sour climate of intergovernmental relations concerning the environment generally prevailed during this period, federal-provincial competition was confined to questions of jurisdiction and promises of future action; there was no evidence of federal-provincial competition with respect to regulatory standards.

Not surprisingly, as federal politicians again deferred to the provinces in the mid-1970s, intergovernmental harmony was restored. The detente of the 1970s and early 1980s was disrupted in 1988, however, when the federal government passed the Canadian Environmental Protection Act. An even greater source of tension was the subsequent court decisions that forced the federal government to perform environmental impact assessments of projects already approved by the provinces, and even to review the activities of the provincial governments themselves. In granting citizens enforceable claims to federal actions, the courts empowered environmentalists to drive a wedge between the federal and provincial governments, thus limiting opportunities for federal-provincial accommodation.

However, the same incentives that motivated federal and provincial governments to cooperate in the past are still present. The contentious climate of CCME meetings of the late 1980s subsided in the 1990s, as federal and provincial governments pursued rationalization of their roles.

Beyond Public Opinion

At a theoretical level, the hesitance of the federal government in the field of environmental policy forces reconsideration of the common assumption that governments invariably compete to extend their jurisdictional grasp. Intergovernmental competition for jurisdiction over environmental protection has been the exception to the rule, and federal and provincial governments have rarely, if ever, engaged in 'bidding wars' in developing their environmental standards.

The case of environmental protection suggests that the implications of federalism for public policy may be very different in policy fields where one or both levels of government are content to vacate the field, than where both are eager to assume responsibility, a proposition that warrants greater scholarly attention. This book represents a first step in that research agenda. Future work might begin by examining other policy fields characterized by diffuse benefits and concentrated costs, such as consumer protection, anti-trust law, and other forms of economic regulation. In addition, governments' occasional reluctance to assume responsibility for policy issues that do offer concentrated benefits, such as Aboriginal land claims and social assistance during the Depression, suggests a need for further research on how public attitudes toward target populations influenced policy.[2]

In the context of the growing literature on state-society interactions, this book places greater emphasis on societal than institutional forces. Canadian governments' failure to adequately address environmental problems cannot be attributed primarily to the institution of federalism, any more than environmental degradation itself is caused by federalism. The roots of both lie in the incentives to pollute and to tolerate pollution faced by different societal actors.

However, governments do devise their responses to electoral demands within an institutional context. Federalism can exacerbate the obstacles to collective action by giving expression to concentrated interests in two ways. First, when the provinces have jurisdiction over an issue, they face a temptation to compete to satisfy concentrated interests, which increases their reluctance to impose costs on such groups. Second, when the assignment of jurisdiction is unclear, either level of government can take advantage of overlapping jurisdiction to shirk responsibility for problems that involve the imposition of concentrated costs.

Although the primary focus of this research is the relationship between federalism and public policy, in the course of the research, it became clear that other institutions also play a role in shaping governments' strategies. The fusion of the executive and legislative functions in the parliamentary system of government tends to yield very general statutes, in which the executive is authorized to take a wide variety of actions, but is not required to take any action in particular.[3] Parliamentary government thus facilitates the coexistence of strong symbolic commitments with weak or non-existent implementation.

Politicians' Institutional Objectives

The argument thus far has depicted the distribution of costs and benefits as the independent variable which, when viewed through the lens of federal and parliamentary institutions, constrains policy choices and thus policy outcomes. However, as noted in Chapter 2, other causal factors may also be relevant. Neo-institutionalist scholars have argued that, rather than merely serving as a filter for politicians' responses to the electorate, institutions can take on life of their own, prompting state actors to represent the interests of the institution itself, rather than those of their constituents. This study reveals little concern on the part of federal government actors for defending, let alone extending, their jurisdiction.

However, there is considerable evidence of provincial sensitivity concerning jurisdiction.

Quebec usually led the provincial charge in opposition to federal initiatives, often with support from provinces that historically have been heavily reliant on development of natural resources. While Alberta and British Columbia, and in later years Saskatchewan, were preoccupied with defending provincial jurisdiction over natural resources, Quebec politicians and officials tended to view jurisdiction more broadly as an expression of nationalism. Interestingly, those provinces often were joined in their opposition by Ontario. To a larger degree than other provinces, Ontario's resistance was buoyed by personal resentment by provincial politicians and bureaucrats who perceived federal involvement as unnecessarily paternalistic in light of their own province's record on environmental issues.

'Province building' might have had a greater impact on environmental policy had the federal government not been in retreat already. As it was, provincial resistance generally reinforced the federal government's inclination to defer to the provinces. However, provincial opposition may have accounted for some of the residual hesitance displayed in federal environmental statutes passed during periods of heightened public concern.

Politicians' Personal Objectives

A second line of neo-institutionalist thought suggests that, to the extent that institutions are independent of electoral forces, they allow state actors to pursue their own personal objectives, rather than those of their constituents. Politicians may be motivated by altruistic concerns in addition to electoral forces. Federal and provincial politicians occasionally have displayed genuine dedication to environmental protection. Their claims to environmentalism are particularly convincing when they reveal willingness to sacrifice other personal or institutional goals in pursuit of environmental objectives. For instance, former federal environment minister Lucien Bouchard's commitment to his environment portfolio occasionally prevailed over his personal commitment to Quebec sovereignty, leading him to support federal 'interference' in Quebec's affairs. Similarly, the Quebec environment minister, Pierre Paradis, resorted to calling for a full federal review of the Quebec government's Great Whale project in an attempt to buttress his own fragile pro-environment position within the Quebec cabinet.

Notwithstanding these examples, it is noteworthy that to the extent that there were 'true believers' in government during the long hiatus in which there was almost no electoral pressure for environmental initiatives, they apparently had very little impact at either the federal or provincial level. Good intentions certainly did not prevent federal and provincial governments from backtracking on their environmental commitments when public attention waned.

Governmental Influence on Public Opinion

The argument that government actors respond primarily to public and interest group pressures is challenged by the possibility that governments are not merely passive recipients but determinants of public opinion. The research presented here offers remarkably little evidence of politicians attempting to shape public opinion. It is particularly relevant that when the salience of environmental issues declined in the early 1970s, neither the governing party nor the opposition parties within the federal Parliament sought to rekindle the issue, even though public opinion surveys continued to indicate a high degree of latent public concern for the environment. Their inaction during periods of low salience suggests that politicians of all parties took their cues from the electorate and interest groups, rather than vice versa.

Political Context

Politicians do not consider single issues in isolation from the broad array of political problems on their agenda, and it is thus important to consider the broader context in evaluating political actors' motives. In the language of game theory, Tsebelis argues that political actors are engaged in 'nested games,' in which the circumstances of larger or overlapping games influence players' payoffs and thus their choice of strategies in any one subgame.[4]

The constitutional context clearly influences both federal and provincial attitudes toward environmental jurisdiction. The fact that provincial jurisdiction over the environment is inextricably linked to provincial control of natural resources tends to make the provinces defensive of their environmental jurisdiction, even during periods of low public salience. In contrast, because federal environmental jurisdiction is more diffuse, the federal government has less to lose in other policy fields by yielding environmental protection to the provinces.

Developments in other policy fields also have had occasional impacts on federal policy. For instance, the federal government's retreat from environmental regulation likely was hastened by federal politicians' desire to make constitutional peace with the Western provinces after the energy wars of the late 1970s. Similarly, federal efforts in the mid-1990s to reduce federal-provincial overlap are undoubtedly influenced both by budgetary restraint in response to the deficit, and efforts to enhance the efficiency of the federation in response to an unexpectedly close referendum result in Quebec.

However, while the broader political context clearly influences actors' choices within the environmental field, it does not render the particular dynamics of the environmental policy game irrelevant. It is noteworthy that the federal government remained assertive with respect to its environmental jurisdiction in the late 1980s, despite the risk of exacerbating constitutional tensions. It is also significant that in the late 1970s, it was the environmental field that was offered as a sacrificial lamb to smooth over intergovernmental conflicts resulting from federal aggression in other policy fields.

Bureaucratic Resistance
The discussion thus far has tended to depict governments as unitary actors, implicitly assuming that cabinet speaks with a single voice on behalf of the government as a whole. Although strong traditions of party discipline in Canadian legislatures seldom call into question this characterization of executive-legislative relations, at least in majority governments, there are reasons to question the unity of the executive itself.

In Chapter 2 it is suggested that even if politicians are inclined to shirk their environmental responsibilities, they could be undermined by zealous bureaucrats in ministries or departments of the environment. The picture that emerges from Chapters 3 through 6, however, is one of conscientious bureaucrats severely constrained by limited administrative resources and political support. Since new regulations require cabinet approval, bureaucrats could only accomplish so much within the confines of hollow enabling statutes. Similarly, when regulations turned out to be flawed, as was the case with the regulations issued under the Fisheries Act, bureaucrats' hands were tied in the absence of cabinet support for regulatory reforms.

A similar picture emerges with respect to interdepartmental differences. Individual departments, such as the Department of Fisheries and Oceans, occasionally were more aggressive than Environment Canada. However, at the same time as they were pressing for more aggressive regulatory action, other departments representing industry clientele were lobbying to relax environmental standards. Critical decisions concerning budgets, new legislation, and regulations are still made at the cabinet level, where pro-environment forces historically have been outgunned by departments representing development interests, particularly during periods of low public attention to the environment. If cabinet is disinclined to pursue environmental protection measures, rogue bureaucrats or departments can only go so far. Thus, in the end, the mechanisms of cabinet and ministerial accountability worked surprisingly well most of the time.

Thus far, relatively little attention has been paid to the role of the courts. Although historically the courts have been a bit player in Canadian environmental policy-making, in the aftermath of *Oldman Dam* the role of the courts clearly demands greater attention. As an institution, the courts do not fit neatly within the categories of federal and provincial governments. Moreover, because there are no mechanisms to hold judges accountable to either politicians or the public – indeed lifetime tenure is designed to insulate the court from the whims of popular opinion – the institution of the courts may be especially responsive to institutional or 'good policy' motives of its members. 'Rogue judges' may ultimately exercise greater influence than 'rogue bureaucrats.'

As the relevance of other variables, such as political context and institutional interests, demonstrates, one cannot build a comprehensive theory around a single variable. Nor can any theory be confirmed by a study of only one policy field. However, this study of Canadian environmental policy does illustrate the need for reconsideration of common assumptions about governments' tendencies to seek jurisdiction, and about the implications for public policy of overlapping jurisdiction. The findings suggest that one cannot readily assume two heads of power are better than one. Overlap may well be inevitable in contemporary federal systems, but that merely demonstrates the need for greater attention to which particular federal-provincial arrangements best promote responsiveness and accountability in different policy fields.

Competition and Cooperation Revisited

In Chapter 1, the question was raised whether, in light of overlapping federal and provincial jurisdiction in the environmental field, intergovernmental competition or collaboration is preferable. The case of environmental protection offers no simple answer. Neither collaboration nor competition is an end in itself. A more important question is cooperation or competition between whom and for what purpose. In competing or cooperating, are governments responding to narrow interests or those of the broader public? While intergovernmental competition to respond to broad public demand is desirable, competition in response to industry threats is not. And while interjurisdictional cooperation to overcome such threats is desirable, cooperation that merely reflects neglect of environmental issues by all jurisdictions is hardly a sign of progress.

Among the provinces, the temptation to compete in defense of local industry is likely to prevail over the temptation to compete for green votes. Thus, in general, collaboration between provinces is to be preferred. Interprovincial efforts to establish national standards are clearly desirable in the absence of federal standards, particularly since such standards would not preclude individual provinces from going beyond national standards. However, national standards developed by interprovincial consensus are vulnerable to the risks that a 'joint decision trap' will yield standards at the lowest common denominator, and that independent implementation by individual provinces will cause voluntary agreements to unravel.

Collaboration is less desirable, however, when one considers the relationship between the federal government and the provinces. Varying degrees of collaboration between federal and provincial governments are conceivable in the environmental field. Federal and provincial governments can agree to rationalize implementation activities, as they did with the accords in the 1970s and recent bilateral agreements. The proposed harmonization agreement represents a further degree of collaboration, in which federal and provincial governments propose to share decision-making concerning environmental standards in addition to rationalizing implementation.

The purported advantages of collaboration include the potential to build on the strengths of each level of government, avoidance of duplication and intergovernmental conflict, and clarification of federal and provincial roles to limit buck passing. Thus, the federal and provincial governments claimed that the accords of the 1970s would both build on federal and provincial strengths and avoid duplication. However, in practice, the greatest savings to taxpayers lay in the fact that neither level of government aggressively pursued its mandates. Nor is it apparent that either level of government played to its strengths.

It is true that intergovernmental relations during the period of the accords were largely devoid of conflict. However, as Skogstad and Kopas note, the absence of federal-provincial conflict concerning the environment reflects the fact that the federal and provincial governments were equally inclined to turn a blind eye to polluters.[5] Harmonious intergovernmental relations can be viewed more as a reflection of the compatibility of the federal government's inclination to shirk responsibility and provincial governments' desire to defend their natural resources jurisdiction than as a consequence of particular intergovernmental arrangements. Indeed, rather than limiting buck passing, the accords were the primary mechanism through which the federal government abdicated its responsibilities.

While collaboration has been the norm for much of the past twenty-five years, its purported advantages have not been realized. However, while independence offers some important advantages in theory, in practice examples of independent action by federal and provincial governments in the environmental field have been few and far between. It is often argued that unilateralism can allow healthy federal-provincial competition to emerge. However, to date such competition has emerged only during brief periods of public attentiveness to the environment, and even then has been largely confined to the symbolic level.

Independence also creates opportunities for backup, such that if one level of government does not do the job the other will, and oversight, which entails federal and provincial governments keeping an eye on each other. Again, however, these advantages have seldom materialized because federal and provincial governments have rarely acted independently with respect to enforcement. An important exception lies in federal environmental reviews of several provincial projects in recent years, suggesting that such oversight is most likely to occur when individual citizens have leverage over the actions of one or both levels of government. A final advantage of independence is that it avoids the risks of a joint decision trap. However, despite formal independence, the federal government time and again has opted to collaborate with the provinces in setting national standards via consensus.

While independence has much to commend it, the dilemma is that federal and provincial governments' electoral incentives normally lead them to collaborate in the environmental field. Recent examples of environmental assessments suggest that external public or interest group pressure is essential if the federal government is to maintain its independence.

In any case, the success of either approach will rely to a large degree on the extent of direct accountability of both levels of government to their constituents. The potential savings associated with rationalization of enforcement and other administrative functions are increasingly attractive to federal and provincial governments in the current fiscal environment. However, past experience suggests that the risks of this approach outweigh the benefits unless there are meaningful mechanisms to hold both levels of government accountable for their commitments, not only to each other, but to their respective electorates. Beyond rationalized implementation, however, joint decision-making offers few benefits over federal standard setting and entails considerable risks.

Whither Canadian Environmental Policy?

More than twenty years after the first wave of environmentalism, Canadian federal and provincial governments are again at a turning point with respect to environmental policy. Both levels of government have emerged from the recent round of environmental fervor with new environmental commitments and new legislative tools to fulfil them. However, the record of unfulfilled promises of the early 1970s suggests that both levels of government could retreat from their recent commitments now that the salience of environmental issues has once again subsided. In placing particular emphasis on the pernicious influence of political institutions and the distribution of costs and benefits of environmental protection, neither of which are readily transformed, this book offers rather gloomy prospects for the future of Canadian environmental policy.

However, in closing, one can salvage some threads of optimism. First, the growing immediacy of environmental problems makes them increasingly difficult for even those diffusely affected to ignore. We may not have to wait twenty years for the next period of public attention to the environment. Second, the possibility remains that each cycle of public concern has a residual impact,[6] and that the combined effect of several such cycles will be a gradual improvement in public and governmental responsiveness to environmental problems. Governments tend to retreat at the margin, declining to fully implement statutes rather than revoking them, trimming budgets rather than eliminating entire departments. With each wave of public concern, some advances are institutionalized.

The second source of optimism lies in the fact that human beings are not robots responding to social and institutional forces in an unthinking way. My interviews revealed that many non-governmental actors do in fact have a strong intuitive understanding of the arguments about institutions and public policy presented in this book. It is no accident that industries facing process regulations historically have favoured provincial jurisdiction, since they benefit not only from a symbiotic relationship between resource owner and developer, but from the threat of jurisdictional mobility. Although, with the support of provincial governments, those interests generally have prevailed in environmental policy until recently, environmental groups have become increasingly capable of representing diffuse interests in recent years, as well as increasingly outspoken on jurisdictional questions. Just as industry groups have long perceived at which level of government their interests lie, environmentalists have become aware of how the political system affects their own interests. With increasing vigour, they are demanding a strong federal role to overcome interprovincial competition for investment and to provide an additional check on provincial enforcement.

Environmental groups are in a better position than ever before to pursue those objectives. They have found considerable sympathy within the courts in recent years, although the implications of recent court decisions beyond the field of environmental impact assessments may be limited. Perhaps more significant is the fact that the scope of environmental decision-making, traditionally limited to industry and government participants, has been extended in recent years to include environmental groups. Having won a place at the table, environmentalists will be in a better position to serve as watchdogs over future intergovernmental agreements. Finally, in recent years, environmentalists have increasingly bypassed governments and lobbied Canadian and international consumers directly, with considerable success. The details of federal-provincial arrangements will be less critical to the extent that environmentalists exercise such direct influence with consumers and the public.

Although environmental groups can effectively concentrate diffuse public interests, they nonetheless will be fighting an uphill battle in light of their scarce resources and industry's powerful threat of capital mobility. Ultimately, environmentalists' success or failure will lie in their ability to mobilize a public increasingly reassured by symbolic commitments and preoccupied with other pressing issues of the day. Yet, in the end, the very fact that the environment has risen to the top of the public agenda twice in recent memory offers some hope for our ability to overcome the many obstacles to collective action.

Notes

Chapter 1: Introduction

1 O.P. Dwivedi and R. Brian Woodrow, 'Environmental Policy-Making and Administration in Federal States: The Impact of Overlapping Jurisdiction in Canada,' in William M. Chandler and Christian W. Zollner, eds., *Challenges to Federalism: Policy-Making in Canada and the Federal Republic of Germany* (Kingston: Institute of Intergovernmental Relations, Queen's University, 1989).

2 Andrew R. Thompson, *Environmental Regulation in Canada: An Assessment of the Regulatory Process* (Vancouver: Westwater Research Centre 1980), 25.

3 Dominique Alhéritière, 'Les problèmes constitutionnels de la lutte contre la pollution de l'espace atmospherique au Canada,' *La Revue du Barreau Canadien* 50 (1972): 561-79, 571; O.P. Dwivedi, 'Environmental Administration in Canada,' *International Review of Administrative Sciences* 39 (1973): 149-57, 156; O.P. Dwivedi, 'The Canadian Government Response to Environmental Concerns,' in O.P. Dwivedi, ed., *Protecting the Environment: Issues and Choices – Canadian Perspectives* (Vancouver: Copp Clark 1974), 180; L.J. Lundqvist, 'Do Political Structures Matter in Environmental Politics? The Case of Air Pollution Control in Canada, Sweden, and the United States,' *Canadian Public Administration* 17 (1974): 119-42, 135; L.J. Lundqvist, *Environmental Policies in Canada, Sweden, and the United States: A Comparative Overview* (Beverly Hills: Sage Publications 1974); Kernaghan R. Webb, *Industrial Water Pollution Control and the EPS*, unpublished background study for the Law Reform Commission of Canada, May 1983, 1-4.

4 J. Owen Saunders, *Interjurisdictional Issues in Canadian Water Management* (Calgary: Canadian Institute of Resources Law 1988), 28-9; D.R. Percy, 'Federal/Provincial Jurisdictional Issues,' in H.I. Rueggeberg and A.R. Thompson, eds., *Water Law and Policy Issues in Canada* (Vancouver: Westwater Research Centre 1984), 86; Paul Muldoon and Marcia Valiante, *Toxic Water Pollution in Canada* (Calgary: Canadian Institute of Resources Law 1988), 26; Donna Tingley, 'Conflict and Cooperation on the Environment,' in Douglas Brown, ed., *Canada: The State of the Federation 1991* (Kingston: Institute of Intergovernmental Relations 1991), 132.

5 Robert T. Franson and Alastair R. Lucas, 'Legal Control of Hazardous Products in Canada,' in Science Council of Canada, *Canadian Law and the Control of Exposure to Hazards* (Ottawa: Science Council of Canada 1977), 25. See also H. Scott Fairley, 'The Constitutional Conundrum of Jurisdiction over the Environment,' in Canadian Bar Association, *Canada's Environmental Laws* (Toronto: Canadian Bar Association 1990), 1.

6 Alastair R. Lucas, 'Harmonization of Federal and Provincial Environmental Policies: The Changing Legal and Policy Framework,' in J. Owen Saunders, ed., *Managing Natural Resources in a Federal State* (Toronto: Carswell 1986), 39; Thompson, *Environmental Regulation*, 22; Saunders, *Interjurisdictional Issues*, 21; Muldoon and Valiante, *Toxic Water*, 27; Barry G. Rabe, 'Cross-Media Environmental Regulatory Integration: The Case of Canada,' *American Review of Canadian Studies* 19 (1989): 261-73, 262.

7 James Q. Wilson, 'The Politics of Regulation,' in James McKie, ed., *Social Responsibility and the Business Predicament* (Washington, DC: Brookings Institution 1975).

8 For instance, see Theda Skocpol, 'Bringing the State Back In: Strategies of Analysis in Current Research,' in Peter Evans, Dietrich Rueschemeyer, and Theda Skocpol, eds., *Bringing the State Back In* (Cambridge: Cambridge University Press 1985).

9 Frederick J. Fletcher and Donald C. Wallace, 'Federal-Provincial Relations and the Making of Public Policy in Canada: A Review of Case Studies,' in Richard Simeon, ed., *Division of Powers and Public Policy* (Toronto: University of Toronto Press 1985).

10 Alan C. Cairns, 'The Other Crisis of Canadian Federalism,' *Canadian Public Administration* 22 (1979): 175-95.

11 David R. Cameron, 'The Expansion of the Public Economy: A Comparative Analysis,' *American Political Science Review* 72 (1978): 1243-61; Fletcher and Wallace, 'Federal-Provincial Relations'; Keith Banting, *The Welfare State and Canadian Federalism* (Kingston: McGill-Queen's University Press 1987).

12 P.E. Trudeau, 'The Practice and Theory of Federalism,' in Michael Oliver, ed., *Social Purpose for Canada* (Toronto: University of Toronto Press 1961).

13 F.R. Scott, 'Centralization and Decentralization in Canadian Federalism,' in *Essays on the Constitution* (Toronto: University of Toronto Press 1977).

14 Alan C. Cairns, 'The Governments and Societies of Canadian Federalism,' in Douglas E. Williams, ed., *Constitution, Government, and Society in Canada: Selected Essays by Alan C. Cairns* (Toronto: McClelland and Stewart 1988), 167.

15 Albert Breton, 'Supplementary Statement,' *Report of the Royal Commission on the Economic Union and Development Prospects for Canada*, Volume 3 (Ottawa: Minister of Supply and Services Canada 1985), 493.

16 Trudeau, 'The Practice and Theory of Federalism.' The classic statement of this argument in the US is Louis Brandeis's depiction of the States as 'little laboratories of democracy.'

17 The classic statement of this argument can be found in James Madison's 'Federalist Paper No. 10,' reprinted in James Q. Wilson, *American Government*, 3rd ed. (Toronto: D.C. Heath 1986). It should be noted, however, that Madison

offered the argument in favour of national jurisdiction, since he was motivated to overcome the 'tyranny' of local majorities. Although the quite different argument, presented below, that diffuse interests can be better represented at the national level is often attributed to Madison (see, for instance, Jerry L. Mashaw and Susan Rose-Ackerman, 'Federalism and Regulation,' in George C. Eads and Michael Fix, eds., *The Reagan Regulatory Strategy* [Washington, DC: Urban Institute Press 1984], 121), in fact, Madison was concerned exclusively with shifting majorities, rather than Olsonian notions of obstacles to collective action.

18 A closely related argument is that multiple jurisdictions tend to better satisfy voter preferences, since citizens retain the option of 'voting with their feet' by moving to a jurisdiction that offers a more favourable package of environmental and economic services. C.M. Tiebout, 'A Pure Theory of Local Expenditures,' *Journal of Political Economy* 64 (1956): 416-24.

19 Mashaw and Rose-Ackerman, 'Federalism and Regulation,' 118.

20 Richard B. Stewart, 'Pyramids of Sacrifice? Problems of Federalism in Mandating State Implementation of National Environmental Policy,' *Yale Law Journal* 86 (1977): 1196-1272, 1213-14; Anthony Scott, 'Piecemeal Decentralization: The Environment,' in Robin Boadway, Thomas Courchene, and Douglas Purvis, eds., *Economic Dimensions of Constitutional Change* (Kingston: John Deutsch Institute for the Study of Economic Policy 1991).

21 Kenneth Norrie, Richard Simeon, and Mark Krasnick, *Federalism and Economic Union in Canada* (Toronto: University of Toronto Press 1986), 129. See also Martin Painter, 'Intergovernmental Relations in Canada: An Institutional Analysis,' *Canadian Journal of Political Science* 24 (1991): 269-88.

22 See, for instance, Mark Sproule-Jones, *Public Choice and Federalism in Australia and Canada* (Canberra: Australian National University 1975), 30.

23 Richard J. Schultz, 'Federalism and Telecommunications: Multiplication, Division and Sharing,' *Osgoode Hall Law Journal* 20 (1982): 745-61, 754; Steven Alexander Kennett, 'Interjurisdictional Water Resource Management in Canada: A Constitutional Analysis,' L.L.M. thesis, Queen's University, 1989, 99.

24 Cairns, 'The Other Crisis of Canadian Federalism.'

25 Breton, 'Supplementary Statement.'

26 See, for instance, Thompson, *Environmental Regulation in Canada*; Peter Nemetz, 'The Fisheries Act and Federal-Provincial Environmental Regulation: Duplication or Complementarity,' *Canadian Public Administration* 29 (1986): 401-24; Webb, *Industrial Water Pollution Control and the EPS*; Dale Gibson, 'Environmental Protection and Enhancement Under a New Canadian Constitution,' in Stanley M. Beck and Ivan Bernier, eds., *Canada and the New Constitution*, vol. 2 (Montreal: Institute for Research on Public Policy 1983); Franson and Lucas, 'Legal Control of Hazardous Products,' 48.

27 Fritz Scharpf, 'The Joint-Decision Trap: Lessons from West German Federalism and European Integration,' *Public Administration* 66 (1988): 239-78. A similar argument is offered in Banting, *The Welfare State and Canadian Federalism*.

28 An important exception is R.A. Young, Philippe Faucher, and André Blais, 'The Concept of Province-Building: A Critique,' *Canadian Journal of Political Science* 17 (1984): 783-818. The authors argue that not all provinces have attempted to extend their jurisdiction, nor resisted federal incursions.

29 Norrie, Simeon, and Krasnick, *Federalism and Economic Union in Canada*, 123.

30 Garth Stevenson, 'The Division of Powers,' in R.D. Olling and M.W. Westmacott, eds., *Perspectives on Canadian Federalism* (Scarborough: Prentice-Hall 1988), 41.

31 Cairns, 'The Governments and Societies of Canadian Federalism,' 150-1.

32 Richard Simeon, *Federal-Provincial Diplomacy: The Making of Recent Policy in Canada* (Toronto: University of Toronto Press 1972), 185.

33 Grace Skogstad, 'Federalism and Agricultural Policy,' in Herman Bakvis and William M. Chandler, eds., *Federalism and the Role of the State* (Toronto: University of Toronto Press 1987); D.V. Smiley, *The Federal Condition in Canada* (Toronto: McGraw-Hill Ryerson 1987), 21; Garth Stevenson, 'The Division of Powers,' 113; Garth Stevenson, *Unfulfilled Union: Canadian Federalism and National Unity*, 3rd ed. (St. Catharines: Gage 1989), 159, 174. An exception which places greater emphasis on 'buck passing' strategies is James Struthers, *No Fault of Their Own: Unemployment and the Canadian Welfare State 1914-1941* (Toronto: University of Toronto Press 1983).

34 See Tingley, 'Conflict and Cooperation,' 132; Canadian Environmental Law Association, cited in Colin P. Stevenson, 'A New Perspective on Environmental Rights After the Charter,' *Osgoode Hall Law Journal* 21 (1983): 390-421, 412; David Estrin and J. Swaigen, *Environment on Trial: A Handbook of Ontario Environmental Law* (Toronto: Canadian Environmental Law Research Foundation 1978), 13; Barbara Rutherford and Paul Muldoon, 'Designing an Environmentally Responsible Constitution,' *Alternatives* 18 (1992): 26-33, 30; Ian Jackson, in the House of Commons, Standing Committee on the Environment, *Minutes of Proceedings and Evidence*, 23 October 1991, 12:26. Although these authors have expressed concern about 'buck passing,' they have not offered a theory for when and why governments seek to avoid responsibility for environmental protection.

Chapter 2: Federalism, Policy-Making, and Intergovernmental Politics

1 Mancur Olson, *The Logic of Collective Action* (Cambridge: Harvard University Press 1965).

2 James Q. Wilson, 'The Politics of Regulation,' in James McKie, ed., *Social Responsibility and the Business Predicament* (Washington, DC: Brookings Institution 1975). A similar point is made in an earlier article by Theodore Lowi, 'American Business, Public Policy, Case-Studies, and Political Theory,' *World Politics* 16 (1964): 677.

3 Garth Stevenson, 'The Division of Powers,' in Richard Simeon, ed., *Division of Powers and Public Policy* (Toronto: University of Toronto Press 1985).

4 G. Bruce Doern, 'Introduction: The Regulatory Process in Canada,' in G. Bruce Doern, ed., *The Regulatory Process in Canada* (Toronto: Macmillan 1978), 14.

5 George J. Stigler, 'The Theory of Economic Regulation,' *Bell Journal of Economics and Management* 2 (1971): 3-21.
6 Douglas G. Hartle, *Public Policy Decision Making and Regulation* (Toronto: Institute for Research on Public Policy 1979), 91.
7 Michael J. Trebilcock, Douglas Hartle, J. Robert S. Prichard, and Donald Dewees, *The Choice of Governing Instrument* (Ottawa: Economic Council of Canada 1982).
8 Hartle, *Public Policy Decision Making*, 87; Anne Schneider and Helen Ingram, 'Social Construction of Target Populations: Implications for Politics and Policy,' *American Political Science Review* 87 (1993): 334-47.
9 Although discharge fees could be considered a form of taxation, I consider them to be a form of regulation since the intent is to promote behavioural change, rather than to raise government revenues.
10 William J. Baumol and Wallace E. Oates, *The Theory of Environmental Policy*, 2nd ed. (New York: Cambridge University Press 1988), Chapter 14.
11 Daniel A. Farber, 'Politics and Procedure in Environmental Law,' *Journal of Law, Economics, and Organization* 8 (1992): 59-81, 60.
12 Jack L. Walker, 'The Origins and Maintenance of Interest Groups in America,' *American Political Science Review* 77 (1983): 390-406; Leslie A. Pal, *Interests of State: The Politics of Language, Multiculturalism, and Feminism in Canada* (Montreal: McGill-Queen's University Press 1993).
13 Farber, 'Politics and Procedure,' 61.
14 R. Brian Woodrow, 'The Development and Implementation of Federal Pollution Control Policy,' Ph.D. thesis, University of Toronto, 1977, 124.
15 E. Donald Elliott, Bruce A. Ackerman, and John C. Millian, 'Toward a Theory of Statutory Evolution: The Federalization of Environmental Law,' *Journal of Law, Economics, and Organization* 1 (1985): 313-40.
16 See, for instance, D.P. Emond, 'Environmental Law and Policy: A Retrospective Examination of the Canadian Experience,' in Ivan Bernier and Andrée Lajoie, eds., *Consumer Protection, Environmental Law, and Corporate Power* (Toronto: University of Toronto Press 1985), 134.
17 Hartle, *Public Policy Decision Making*, 17; also, Donald N. Dewees, *Evaluation of Policies for Regulating Environmental Pollution* (Ottawa: Economic Council of Canada 1980), 24.
18 Anthony Downs, 'Up and Down with Ecology – The "Issue-Attention Cycle,"' *The Public Interest* 27 (1972): 38-50.
19 A simple model offered by Peltzman is illustrative. (Sam Peltzman, 'Towards a More General Theory of Regulation,' *Journal of Law and Economics* 19 (1976): 211-41.) He posits that politicians would seek to maximize political support, M, such that

$$M = abs\ [(n \times f) - (N - n) \times h],$$

where

n = number of voters in the regulated group;
f = probability that regulated interests will oppose;
N = total number of voters;
h = probability that diffuse beneficiaries will support.

Because *n* is small, *f* normally will be much larger than *h*, reflecting the logic of collective action. However, since (*N* - *n*) is much larger than *n*, *M* would be very sensitive to changes in *h*.

20 Farber, 'Politics and Procedure,' 66.

21 Frank R. Baumgartner and Bryan D. Jones, *Agendas and Instability in American Politics* (Chicago: University of Chicago Press 1993). Unlike Downs, Baumgartner and Jones envision that each brief period of instability results in a substantial and lasting change in issue construction and policy actors. However, while they provide empirical support for their model of long periods of relative stability punctuated by brief periods of issue salience and legislative attention, they do not offer evidence that the public and governmental attitudes that prevail at the peak in salience are institutionalized. Their implicit assumption that all issue definitions are potentially stable ignores the fact that mobilization of some interests is more difficult to sustain than others.

22 B. Guy Peters and Brian W. Hogwood, 'In Search of the Issue-Attention Cycle,' *Journal of Public Policy* 47 (1985): 238-53.

23 Peltzman, 'Towards a More General Theory of Regulation,' 227.

24 Albert Breton, *Centralization, Decentralization and Intergovernmental Competition* (Kingston: Institute of Intergovernmental Relations 1990), 7. A similar point is made by George Tsebelis, in *Nested Games: Rational Choice in Comparative Politics* (Berkeley: University of California Press 1990), 98.

25 Peter Leslie, *Federal State, National Economy* (Toronto: University of Toronto Press 1987), 59. In addition, Leslie identifies two other types of jurisdiction: authority to pursue particular objectives (e.g., 'Peace, Order, and good Government'), and authority over matters concerning a particular clientele (e.g., 'Indians').

26 Keith Banting, *The Welfare State and Canadian Federalism* (Kingston: McGill-Queen's University Press 1987), Chapter 4.

27 Richard Simeon and Ian Robinson, *State, Society, and the Development of Canadian Federalism* (Toronto: University of Toronto Press 1990), 339.

28 My thinking on this point has been greatly influenced by Kent Weaver's work on blame avoidance. See R. Kent Weaver, *Automatic Government: The Politics of Indexation* (Washington, DC: Brookings Institution 1988); and 'The Politics of Blame Avoidance,' *Journal of Public Policy* 6 (1986): 371-98.

29 For an analysis of strategic behaviour by citizens and governments in the face of spillovers, see Susan Rose-Ackerman, 'Does Federalism Matter? Political Choice in a Federal Republic,' *Journal of Political Economy* 89 (1981): 152-65.

30 Wallace E. Oates, *Fiscal Federalism* (New York: Harcourt Brace Javanovich 1972).

31 Paul E. Peterson and Mark C. Rom, *Welfare Magnets: A New Case for a National Standard* (Washington, DC: Brookings 1990).

32 Nancy Burns and Glenn Beamer, 'The Politics of Budget Constraints,' paper presented to the 1993 Annual Meeting of the American Political Science Association, September 1993.

33 James A. Brander, 'Economic Policy Formation in a Federal State: A Game Theoretic Approach,' in R. Simeon, ed., *Intergovernmental Relations* (Toronto: University of Toronto Press 1985); Eli M. Noam, 'Government Regulation of

Business in a Federal State: Allocation of Power Under Deregulation,' *Osgoode Hall Law Journal* 20 (1982): 762-79.

34 James R. Markusen, Edward R. Morey, and Nancy Olewiler, 'Competition in Regional Environmental Policies when Plant Locations are Endogenous,' *Journal of Public Economics* 56 (1995): 55-770.

35 Baumol and Oates, *The Theory of Environmental Policy*, Chapter 17; Richard O. Zerbe, 'Optimal Environmental Jurisdictions,' *Ecology Law Quarterly* 4 (1974): 193-245; Wallace E. Oates and Robert M. Schwab, 'Economic Competition Among Jurisdictions: Efficiency Enhancing or Distortion Inducing?' *Journal of Public Economics* 35 (1988): 333-54.

36 Zerbe, 'Optimal Environmental Jurisdictions,' 202.

37 Baumol and Oates, *Theory of Environmental Policy*, 289.

38 Kathryn Harrison, 'The Regulator's Dilemma: Regulation of Pulp Mill Effluents in a Federal State,' *Canadian Journal of Political Science*, forthcoming.

39 This could also occur if environmental risks are perceived to be geographically concentrated, as in the case of hazardous waste disposal facilities. The 'not in my backyard' syndrome is formally modelled in Markusen, Morey, and Olewiler, 'Competition.'

40 Although the argument here is presented in terms of obstacles to collective action, it differs little from that of structural neo-Marxists. See, for instance, Fred Block, 'The Ruling Class Does Not Rule,' *Socialist Revolution* 7 (1977): 6-28.

41 See, for instance, Oates, *Fiscal Federalism*; and Peterson and Rom, *Welfare Magnets*.

42 Brander, 'Economic Policy Formation in a Federal State,' 62.

43 Gerard Bélanger, 'The Division of Powers in a Federal System: A Review of the Economic Literature,' in Richard Simeon, ed., *Division of Powers and Public Policy* (Toronto: University of Toronto Press 1985), 13.

44 Albert Breton and Anthony Scott, *The Economic Constitution of Federal States* (Toronto: University of Toronto Press 1978).

45 Jerry L. Mashaw and Susan Rose-Ackerman, 'Federalism and Regulation,' in George C. Eads and Michael Fix, eds., *The Reagan Regulatory Strategy* (Washington, DC: Urban Institute Press 1984).

46 Rose-Ackerman, 'Does Federalism Matter?'

47 Noam, 'Government Regulation of Business,' 767; Rose-Ackerman, 'Does Federalism Matter?'

48 The analogy is from Weaver, 'The Politics of Blame Avoidance.'

49 Richard J. Schultz, *Federalism, Bureaucracy, and Public Policy* (Montreal: McGill-Queen's University Press 1980).

50 B. Dan Wood, 'Principals, Bureaucrats, and Responsiveness in Clean Air Enforcements,' *American Political Science Review* 82 (1988): 213-34.

51 Downs, 'Up and Down with Ecology.'

52 See A. Paul Pross, *Group Politics and Public Policy* (Toronto: Oxford University Press 1986); Leslie A. Pal, *Interests of State*.

53 G. Bruce Doern and Thomas Conway, *The Greening of Canada: Federal Institutions and Decisions* (Toronto: University of Toronto Press 1994).

54 Tsebelis, *Nested Games*.

Chapter 3: The Constitutional Framework

1 One exception is the provision for reference of constitutional questions to the Supreme Court. Another exception can be found in the *Oldman Dam* decision, discussed later in this chapter, in which the courts interpreted a federal regulation as establishing a non-discretionary duty of the federal government to perform environmental assessments. While the *Oldman Dam* decision provided citizens with an opportunity to sue the federal government for inaction, rather than for its actions, it is argued in Chapter 6 that this aggressive judicial approach is unlikely to find application in other areas of environmental law. The Charter of Rights and Freedoms also might be interpreted as establishing positive duties for governments, for instance in the area of official language minority education. Although there has been some speculation that Section 7 of the Charter, concerning 'life, liberty and security of the person' may create a right to a healthful environment, Hatherly argues that for the legal system to accept such a right 'would involve a radical departure from the conventional appreciation of the nature of legal rights.' (Mary E. Hatherly, 'Constitutional Jurisdiction in Relation to Environmental Law,' unpublished background paper for the Law Reform Commission of Canada 1984, 272.) See also Colin P. Stevenson, 'A New Perspective on Environmental Rights After the Charter,' *Osgoode Hall Law Journal* 21 (1983): 390-421.

2 Urquhart has argued that the Supreme Court's word is not always the end of the matter, since federal and provincial governments can reach informal agreements to circumvent awkward Court rulings. (Ian Urquhart, 'Federalism, Ideology, and Charter Review: Alberta's Response to Morgentaler,' *Canadian Journal of Law and Society* 4 [1989]: 157-73.) The fact remains that such accommodations are feasible only if a constitutional decision is unfavourable to both levels of government, thus creating an incentive for them to negotiate. Even then, the best they can achieve is some form of workable arrangement consistent with the terms of the Court's interpretation of the constitution. Short of constitutional amendment, they cannot undo the Court's decision.

3 In rare circumstances losing in court may be perceived to have political benefits. Despite 'devastating constitutional losses' in a Supreme Court ruling in 1938, which held four bills passed by the Alberta Social Credit government to be ultra vires, the government pressed on, passing ten more statutes that were declared ultra vires and eleven others that were disallowed by the federal government. See Richard Simeon and Ian Robinson, *State, Society, and the Development of Canadian Federalism* (Toronto: University of Toronto Press 1990), 82. It is noteworthy that after the initial defeats the provincial government had little left to lose constitutionally. Nonetheless, the case indicates that a government may invite defeat in the courts in order to claim credit for trying, or to generate demands for constitutional reform.

4 Robert T. Franson and Alastair R. Lucas, *Canadian Environmental Law* (Vancouver: Butterworths 1976), 251.

5 Although S.109 originally applied only to the four provinces that entered Confederation in 1867, subsequent judicial interpretation and constitutional amendments have ensured that the section now applies to all provinces.

Gerard V. LaForest, *Natural Resources and Public Property* (Toronto: University of Toronto Press 1969), 30.

6 Under common law, provinces other than Quebec own the beds of all navigable rivers. Bora Laskin, 'Jurisdictional Framework for Water Management,' in *Resources for Tomorrow*, Conference Background Papers, vol. 1 (Ottawa: Queen's Printer 1961-2), 211-26. The situation under Quebec's civil law is more complex, but the result is similar. See Dominique Alhéritière, *La gestion des eaux en droit constitutionnel canadien* (Quebec: Editeur Officiel du Quebec 1976), 28. The provinces also own the beds of most lakes of substantial size by virtue of their ownership of public lands.

7 A.R. Thompson and H.R. Eddy, 'Jurisdictional Problems in Natural Resource Management,' in W.D. Bennett, A.D. Chambers, A.R. Thompson, H.R. Eddy, and A.J. Cordell, eds., *Essays on Aspects of Resource Policy* (Ottawa: Science Council of Canada 1973), 76.

8 Dale Gibson, 'Constitutional Jurisdiction over Environmental Management in Canada,' *University of Toronto Law Journal* 23 (1973): 54-87.

9 LaForest, *Natural Resources and Public Property*, Chapter 9.

10 For a discussion of two important cases – *Canadian Industrial Gas and Oil Ltd. (CIGOL)* v. *Saskatchewan*, and *Central Canada Potash* v. *Saskatchewan* – see John Richards and Larry Pratt, *Prairie Capitalism: Power and Influence in the New West* (Toronto: McClelland and Stewart 1979), Chapter 11.

11 Peter Leslie, *Federal State, National Economy* (Toronto: University of Toronto Press 1987), 59.

12 J. Owen Saunders, *Interjurisdictional Issues in Canadian Water Management* (Calgary: Canadian Institute of Resources Law 1988).

13 J. Peter Meekison and Roy J. Romanow, 'Western Advocacy and Section 92A of the Constitution,' in J.P. Meekison, R.J. Romanow, and W.D. Moull, *Origins and Meaning of Section 92A: The 1982 Constitutional Amendment on Resources* (Montreal: Institute for Research on Public Policy 1985).

14 *Interprovincial Co-operatives Ltd.* v. *The Queen in Right of Manitoba* (1975), 53 *Dominion Law Reports*, 321-59.

15 Dale Gibson, 'Interjurisdictional Immunity in Canadian Federalism,' *Canadian Bar Review* 47 (1969): 40-61.

16 *Interprovincial Co-operatives Ltd.* v. *The Queen.*

17 Dale Gibson, 'The Constitutional Context of Canadian Water Planning,' *Alberta Law Review* 7 (1969): 71-92.

18 Hatherly, 'Constitutional Jurisdiction in Relation to Environmental Law,' 272.

19 *Reference re: Offshore Mineral Rights* (BC), [1967] *Supreme Court Reports*, 792.

20 Although the Section only applies to the four original provinces, the federal government also obtained various public assets when other provinces entered Confederation.

21 Regulations concerning pollution of parks are authorized by the National Parks Act (R.S.C. 1970, C. N-13). The National Harbours Board Act (R.S.C. 1970, C. N-8) provides authority to limit discharges into federal harbours. Similar provisions are found in the Harbour Commissions Act and the Government Harbours and Piers Act.

22 These categories are based on the 'functional/global' distinction offered by Paul Emond, 'The Case for a Greater Federal Role in the Environmental Protection Field: An Examination of the Pollution Problem and the Constitution,' *Osgoode Hall Law Journal* 10 (1972): 647-80.

23 The Supreme Court upheld a broad pollution control provision of the federal Fisheries Act, which prohibits acts potentially harmful to fish. See *Northwest Falling Contractors Ltd.* v. *The Queen,* [1980] 53 *Canadian Criminal Cases* (2d), 353. However, the court found another section of the same statute to be ultra vires, on the grounds that it was a blanket prohibition of water pollution without sufficient connection to fisheries jurisdiction (*Fowler* v. *The Queen,* [1980] 2 *Recueils des arrêts de la Cour suprême du Canada,* 213). See Alastair R. Lucas, 'Constitutional Law – Federal Fisheries Power – Provincial Resource Management and Property and Civil Rights Powers – *Fowler* v. *The Queen* and *Northwest Falling Contractors Ltd.* v. *The Queen,*' *University of British Columbia Law Review* 16 (1982): 145-54.

24 Andrew R. Thompson, *Environmental Regulation in Canada: An Assessment of the Regulatory Process* (Vancouver: Westwater Research Centre 1980), 24.

25 See Peter C. Thompson, 'Institutional Constraints in Fisheries Management,' *Journal of the Fisheries Research Board* 31 (1974): 1965-81; Richard W. Parisien, 'The Fisheries Act: Origins of Federal Delegation of Administrative Jurisdiction to the Provinces,' unpublished report (Environment Canada 1972); H. Scott Fairley, 'Canadian Federalism, Fisheries and the Constitution: External Constraints on Internal Ordering,' *Ottawa Law Review* 12 (1980): 257-318.

26 Laskin, 'Jurisdictional Framework.'

27 Parisien, 'The Fisheries Act.'

28 As a result of peculiarities of Quebec civil law prior to Confederation, the federal government has complete authority over both coastal and inland fisheries in Quebec. However, since fishing from abutting lands is particularly common in Quebec, the provincial government retains a substantial voice in fisheries management as the owner of most riparian lands. See Parisien, 'The Fisheries Act.'

29 Franson and Lucas, *Canadian Environmental Law,* 491.

30 *A.G. Canada* v. *A.G. Ontario,* [1937] *A.C.,* 326 (Canada P.C.).

31 Henry Landis, 'Legal Controls of Pollution in the Great Lakes Basin,' *Canadian Bar Review* 48 (1970): 66-157, 134.

32 Robert T. Franson and Alastair R. Lucas, 'Legal Control of Hazardous Products in Canada,' in Science Council of Canada, *Canadian Law and the Control of Exposure to Hazards* (Ottawa: Science Council of Canada 1977), Chapter 2.

33 Alastair R. Lucas, 'Natural Resources and Environmental Management: A Jurisdictional Primer,' in Donna Tingley, ed., *Environmental Protection and the Canadian Constitution* (Edmonton: Environmental Law Centre [Alberta] Society 1987).

34 Michael A. Jaeger, 'Back to the Future: Environmental Federalism in an Era of Sustainable Development,' *Journal of Environmental Law and Practice* 3 (1993): 3-39.

35 *Grand Council of the Crees (of Quebec) and Cree Regional Authority*, appellants, v. *A.G. Canada, A.G. Quebec, Hydro-Quebec and National Energy Board*, respondents, 24 February 1994.
36 Margaret Mellon, Leslie Ritts, Steven Garrod, and Marcia Valiante, *The Regulation of Toxic and Oxidant Pollution in North America* (Toronto: CCH Canada 1986), 97.
37 *Boggs* v. *The Queen*, [1981] 1 *Supreme Court Reports*, 49, 60.
38 *R.* v. *Cosman's Furniture* (1972), 73 *Dominion Law Reports*, 312.
39 Gibson, 'Constitutional Jurisdiction over Environmental Management.'
40 Peter W. Hogg, *Constitutional Law of Canada*, 2nd ed. (Toronto: Carswell 1985), 416.
41 Franson and Lucas, *Canadian Environmental Law*, 256.
42 Franson and Lucas, 'The Legal Control of Hazardous Products in Canada,' 15.
43 Franson and Lucas, *Canadian Environmental Law*, Chapter 2.
44 Andrew Thompson, 'Regulation as a Bargaining Process,' paper presented to *Boardrooms, Backrooms and Backyards*, a conference sponsored by the Canadian Environmental Law Research Foundation, March 1982.
45 D.R. Percy, 'Federal/Provincial Jurisdictional Issues,' in H.I. Rueggeberg and A.R. Thompson, eds., *Water Law and Policy Issues in Canada* (Vancouver: Westwater Research Centre 1984), 86.
46 *A.G. Ontario* v. *Canada Temperance Federation*, [1946] 193 *A.C.*, 207.
47 Gibson, 'Constitutional Jurisdiction over Environmental Management,' 84.
48 See, for instance, Gibson, 'Constitutional Context of Water Management,' and Emond, 'The Case for a Greater Federal Role in the Environmental Protection Field.'
49 Landis, 'Legal Controls in the Great Lakes Basin'; Alhéritière, *La gestion des eaux*; André Tremblay, 'La priorité des compétences provinciales dans la lutte contre la pollution des eaux,' in Philippe Crabbé and Irene M. Spry, eds., *Natural Resource Development in Canada* (Ottawa: University of Ottawa Press 1973); Gerald A. Beaudoin, 'La protection de l'environnement et ses implications en droit constitutionnel,' *McGill Law Journal* 23 (1977): 207-24; Michel Yergeau and Jacques St-Denis, 'La protection de l'environnement: un survoi du cadre legislatif,' *Assurances* 56 (1988): 10-30; W.R. Lederman, 'Unity and Diversity in Canadian Federalism: Ideals and Methods of Modernization,' *Canadian Bar Review* 53 (1975): 597-620; Hogg, *Constitutional Law of Canada*, 598; Gerald LeDain, 'Sir Lyman Duff and the Constitution,' *Osgoode Hall Law Journal* 12 (1974): 261-338, 293.
50 Lederman, 'Unity and Diversity in Canadian Federalism,' 610-11.
51 Beaudoin, 'La protection de l'environnement,' 210.
52 *R.* v. *Crown Zellerbach Canada Ltd.*, [1988] 84 *National Reporter*, 1.
53 Gibson, 'Constitutional Context for Canadian Water Planning'; Gerard V. LaForest, 'Interprovincial Rivers,' *Canadian Bar Review* 50 (1972): 39-49.
54 Laskin, 'Jurisdictional Framework'; David R. Percy, 'New Approaches to Inter-Jurisdictional Problems,' in Barry Sadler, ed., *Water Policy for Western Canada: The Issues of the Eighties* (Calgary: University of Calgary Press 1983).

55 Dale Gibson, 'The Environment and the Constitution: New Wine in Old Bottles,' in O.P. Dwivedi, ed., *Protecting the Environment: Issues and Choices – The Canadian Perspective* (Vancouver: Copp Clark 1974), 119.

56 *Canada Metal Co. Ltd. v. The Queen* (1983), 144 *Dominion Law Reports,* 124-32.

57 Rueggeberg and Thompson, *Water Law and Policy,* 21.

58 *Interprovincial Co-operatives Ltd. v. The Queen* (1975), 53 *Dominion Law Reports,* 321-59. There have been a number of commentaries on the case: Joost Blom, 'The Conflict of Laws and the Constitution – *Interprovincial Co-operatives Ltd. v. The Queen,' University of British Columbia Law Review* 11 (1977): 144-57; Michael Terry Hertz, '"Interprovincial," the Constitution, and the Conflict of Laws,' *University of Toronto Law Journal* 26 (1976): 84-107; William H. Hurlburt, 'Conflict of Laws – Choice of Law – Place of Tort,' *Canadian Bar Review* 54 (1976): 173-8; Saunders, *Interjurisdictional Issues,* 18.

59 Ritchie, in *Interprovincial Co-operatives v. The Queen,* 350.

60 It is understandable that the federal government would not use the *Interprovincial Co-operatives* case as an opportunity to assert its jurisdiction over interprovincial pollution, even if it valued the jurisdiction. At the time of the offense, the federal government had not taken any action to control the particular problem at issue, and thus was not in a credible position to fend off provincial 'incursions.' However, it is noteworthy that the federal government did not simply stay out of the dispute – it argued in favour of the constitutionality of the Manitoba statute. Ontario's support of Manitoba also illustrates the extent of provincial jurisdictional defensiveness, since the Manitoba government's actions indirectly challenged the adequacy of Ontario's own environmental standards.

61 Ritchie, in *Interprovincial Co-operatives v. The Queen,* 346.

62 Laskin, in *Interprovincial Co-operatives v. The Queen,* 338.

63 *R. v. Crown Zellerbach Canada Ltd.,* [1988] 84 *National Reporter,* 1-68.

64 *R. v. Crown Zellerbach Canada Ltd.,* 36.

65 The conclusion is somewhat surprising in light of Justice LeDain's stated reluctance, in earlier work, to allocate jurisdiction over environmental protection to the federal government as a matter of national concern. LeDain, 'Sir Lyman Duff.'

66 L. Alan Willis, 'The Crown Zellerbach Case on Marine Pollution: National and International Dimensions,' *The Canadian Yearbook of International Law* 26 (1988): 235-52.

67 LaForest, in *R. v. Crown Zellerbach Canada Ltd.,* 62-3.

68 LaForest, in *R. v. Crown Zellerbach Canada Ltd.,* 51.

69 LaForest, in *R. v. Crown Zellerbach Canada Ltd.,* 53.

70 LaForest, in *R. v. Crown Zellerbach Canada Ltd.,* 54.

71 Alastair Lucas, 'The New Environmental Law,' in R. Watts and D. Brown, eds., *Canada: The State of the Federation, 1989* (Kingston: Institute of Intergovernmental Relations 1989), 183.

72 Alastair R. Lucas, 'R. v. *Crown Zellerbach Canada Ltd.,' University of British Columbia Law Review* 23 (1989): 369.

73 *Canadian Wildlife Federation Inc.* v. *Minister of the Environment,* [1989] 3 *Canadian Environmental Law Reports* (NS), 287; *Canadian Wildlife Federation Inc.* v. *Minister of the Environment,* [1990] 4 *Canadian Environmental Law Reports* (NS), 1; *Canadian Wildlife Federation Inc.* v. *Canada,* 4 [1990] *Canadian Environmental Law Reports,* 201-26.

74 The Court reversed an earlier trial court decision. See *Friends of the Old Man River Society* v. *Canada* (Minister of Transport), 2 *Canadian Environmental Law Reports* (NS), 234; *Friends of the Old Man River Society* v. *Canada* (Minister of Transport), [1991] 5 *Canadian Environmental Law Reports* (NS), 1.

75 Other questions of administrative law included whether provincial governments were bound by the federal regulation, whether the regulation was authorized by the Department of Environment Act, and whether the Appeals Court judge was acting within his discretion in reversing the lower court decision and ordering the two federal ministers to comply with the terms of the EARP Guidelines Order. The Supreme Court answered each of these questions in the affirmative.

76 *Re: Friends of the Oldman River Society and The Queen in right of Alberta et al.; Attorney-General of Quebec et al., Interveners* (1992), 88 *Dominion Law Reports,* 1-60.

77 *Re: Friends of the Oldman River Society,* 46.

78 Ibid., 44-5.

79 For an example of those who see room for greater federal involvement, see Marie-Ann Bowden, '*Friends of the Oldman River Society* v. *Canada et al:* Two Steps Forward, One Step Back,' *Saskatchewan Law Review* 56 (1992): 209-21. For commentaries perceiving more restrictive federal jurisdiction, see Joseph de Pencier, 'Oldman River Dam and Federal Environmental Assessment Now and in the Future,' *Journal of Environmental Law and Practice* 2 (1992): 293-312; and Mark Warkentin, '*Friends of the Oldman River Society* v. *Canada* (Minister of Transport),' *University of British Columbia Law Review* 26 (1992): 313-29.

80 Steven A. Kennett, 'Federal Environmental Jurisdiction After Oldman,' *McGill Law Review* 38 (1993): 180-203.

81 *Re: Friends of the Oldman River Society,* 45.

82 *Northwest Falling* v. *The Queen; Fowler* v. *The Queen.*

83 Kennett, 'Federal Environmental Jurisdiction After Oldman.' The sectoral/global and restrictive/comprehensive typology focus on different aspects of environmental jurisdiction. The sectoral/global distinction refers to the scope of activities or subjects covered by a particular head of power. The restrictive/comprehensive distinction describes the nature of the environmental authority associated with a particular head of power, however narrow or far-reaching the scope of the head of power itself.

84 Factum of the Friends of the Oldman River Society, 18.

85 *Re: Friends of the Oldman River Society,* 49.

86 David Vanderzwaag and Linda Duncan, 'Canada and Environmental Protection: Confident Political Faces, Uncertain Legal Hands,' in Robert Boardman, ed., *Canadian Environmental Policy: Ecosystems, Politics, and Process* (Toronto: Oxford University Press 1992), 11.

87 Ross Howard, 'Oldman Dam Ruling Stuns Federal Officials – Bouchard Noncommittal, Calls Decisions "Interesting,"' *Globe and Mail*, 15 March 1990, A5.
88 *Sa Majesté La Reine*, plaignante, c. *Hydro Québec*, accusée, et Le Procureur General du Québec, intervenant, 1991 R.J.Q. 2736-47.
89 *R. c. Hydro-Québec*, (1995) A.Q. No. 143, No. 200-10-000150-925.
90 Gibson, 'Interjurisdictional Immunity.'
91 Saunders, *Interjurisdictional Issues*, 19.
92 Thompson, *Environmental Regulation*, 19. See also Percy, 'Federal/Provincial Jurisdictional Issues,' 86; and Paul Muldoon and Marcia Valiante, *Toxic Water Pollution in Canada* (Calgary: Canadian Institute of Resources Law 1988), 26. Even an author with a more provincialist perspective concluded, 'bien que les textes constitutionnels ne soient pas toujours concluants, ils sont toutefois assez indicatifs pour que ni les legislatures provinciales ni le legislateur central ne hissent la Constitution comme paravent pour masquer leur inaction' (Beaudoin, 'La protection de l'environnement,' 223-4).
93 One exception would appear to be the recent *Grand Council of Crees* case, which involved a bold attempt by the National Energy Board to achieve environmental objectives through reliance on the trade and commerce power. However, it is noteworthy that the assertion of jurisdiction in that case was made by a relatively independent regulatory agency, rather than by politicians overseeing a traditional department.

Chapter 4: The Emergence of Federal Involvement, 1969-72

1 O.P. Dwivedi, 'The Canadian Government Response to Environmental Concern,' in O.P. Dwivedi, ed., *Protecting the Environment: Issues and Choices – Canadian Perspectives* (Vancouver: Copp Clark 1974).
2 Ronald Ingelhart, *The Silent Revolution* (Princeton: Princeton University Press 1977).
3 Responses to this question over the years were summarized in *The Gallup Report*, 28 May 1990, 2.
4 The wording of the question has changed slightly over the years. Prior to 1969, respondents were asked to identify the 'most urgent problem.' Between 1969 and April 1972, the question sought the 'nation's greatest problem.' Since November 1972, Gallup has sought the 'most important problem.'
5 Gallup poll #331, August 1968.
6 *The Gallup Report*, 12 April 1971.
7 See also *The Gallup Report*, 'Concern with Pollution Drops Among Canadians,' 26 February 1975.
8 Gallup polls #355 (September 1972), #361 (September 1973), #364 (March 1974), and #369 (October 1974).
9 R.B. Woodrow, 'The Development and Implementation of Federal Pollution Control Policy Programs in Canada, 1966-1974,' Ph.D. thesis, University of Toronto, 1977, 85.
10 *The Gallup Report*, 2 December 1970; *The Gallup Report*, 15 September 1976. The survey was conducted in August 1982.

11 Woodrow, 'Development and Implementation of Federal Pollution Control Policy,' 73.

12 Hazel Erskine, 'The Polls: Pollution and Its Costs,' *Public Opinion Quarterly* 36 (1972): 120.

13 Riley E. Dunlap, 'Trends in Public Opinion Toward Environmental Issues: 1965-1990,' in Riley E. Dunlap and Angela G. Mertig, eds., *American Environmentalism: The U.S. Environmental Movement, 1970-1990* (Philadelphia: Taylor and Francis 1992), 92. See also Riley E. Dunlap, 'Public Opinion and Environmental Policy,' in James P. Lester, ed., *Environmental Politics and Policy* (Durham: Duke University Press 1989); and Robert Cameron Mitchell, 'Public Opinion and Environmental Politics in the 1970s and 1980s,' in Norman J. Vig and Michael E. Kraft, eds., *Environmental Policy in the 1980s: Reagan's New Agenda* (Washington, DC: Congressional Quarterly Press 1984).

14 Dunlap, 'Trends in Public Opinion,' 97.

15 Dunlap, 'Trends in Public Opinion,' 95-101.

16 J.W. Parlour and S. Schatzow, 'The Mass Media and Public Concern for Environmental Problems in Canada, 1960-1972,' *International Journal of Environmental Studies* 13 (1978): 9-17.

17 Henry Green, *Newspapers in Canada*, Urban Pollution Task Report, Media #1, 96, as cited in Woodrow, 'Development and Implementation of Federal Pollution Control Policy,' 76.

18 Woodrow, 'Development and Implementation of Federal Pollution Control Policy,' 77.

19 J. Holmes and P. Keilhofer, *Development of Environmental Concern within the Canadian House of Commons*, Urban Pollution Task Report, Arbiters #7, 11, as cited in Woodrow, 'Development and Implementation of Federal Pollution Control Policy,' 92.

20 Woodrow, 'Development and Implementation of Federal Pollution Control Policy,' 124.

21 Minister of Resources and Development Winters in House of Commons, *Debates*, 30 January 1953, 1491. Hansard reports many similar statements over the years. See 14 July 1955, 6109; 19 December 1962, 2815; 5 May 1964, 2928-9.

22 Gary H. Muntz, 'Federal Government Policy and the Issue of Inland Water Pollution,' M.A. thesis, University of Guelph, 1972, 22.

23 Woodrow, 'Development and Implementation of Federal Pollution Control Policy,' 99.

24 See, for instance, Dale Gibson, 'The Constitutional Context of Canadian Water Planning,' *Alberta Law Review* 7 (1969): 71-92.

25 House of Commons, *Debates*, 14 April 1969, 7458. See also *Debates*, 23 June 1969, 10557; 23 January 1969, 4763.

26 Pierre Trudeau, in House of Commons, *Debates*, 14 February 1969, 5524.

27 House of Commons, *Debates*, 23 June 1969, 10570.

28 See testimony by R.M. Fowler, President, Canadian Pulp and Paper Association, and Robert Bonner, Executive Vice-President, MacMillan-Bloedel, in House of

Commons, Standing Committee on National Resources and Public Works, *Canada Water Act*, 5 March 1970.

29 Woodrow, 'Development and Implementation of Federal Pollution Control Policy,' 117. See also testimony from Canadian Wildlife Federation and Pollution Probe in Standing Committee on National Resources and Public Works, *Canada Water Act*, 12 and 24 March 1970.

30 House of Commons, *Debates*, 23 June 1969, 10548. See also, *Debates*, 26 January 1971, 2789.

31 Woodrow, 'Development and Implementation of Federal Pollution Control Policy,' 104.

32 David Crane, 'Ottawa Plans Joint Effort to Eliminate Water Pollution,' *Globe and Mail*, 26 August 1969, 1.

33 *Globe and Mail*, 'Water Act Changes Suggested by Lang,' 19 July 1969, 2.

34 James W. Parlour, 'The Politics of Water Pollution Control: A Case Study of the Formation of the Canada Water Act, Part I: Comprehensive Water Resource Management,' *Journal of Environmental Management* 12 (1981): 43.

35 Muntz, 'Federal Government Policy,' 82.

36 Parlour, 'Formation of the Canada Water Act.'

37 Woodrow, 'Development and Implementation of Federal Pollution Control Policy,' 146.

38 Donald Newman, 'Greene Gets Agreement From All Provinces; Phosphate Pollution to be Criminal Offense,' *Globe and Mail*, 19 February 1970, 1.

39 Stanley B. Stein, 'An Opinion on the Constitutional Validity of the Proposed Canada Water Act,' *University of Toronto Faculty Law Review* 28 (1970): 74-82; Henry Landis, 'Legal Controls of Pollution in the Great Lakes Basin,' *Canadian Bar Review* 48 (1970): 66-157; André Tremblay, 'La priorité des compétences provinciales dans la lutte contre la pollution des eaux,' in Philippe Crabbé and Irene M. Spry, eds., *Natural Resource Development in Canada* (Ottawa: University of Ottawa Press 1973). Although Ontario, Alberta, British Columbia, and Quebec all opposed the Canada Water Act for various reasons, only the latter two challenged its constitutionality. See Woodrow, 'Development and Implementation of Federal Pollution Control Policy,' 327.

40 This argument is made by Gerard LaForest, 'Jurisdiction over Natural Resources: Provincial or Federal,' in Philippe Crabbé and Irene M. Spry, eds, *Natural Resource Development in Canada* (Ottawa: University of Ottawa Press 1973), 229.

41 J. Owen Saunders, *Interjurisdictional Issues in Canadian Water Management* (Calgary: Canadian Institute of Resources Law 1988), 28-9.

42 Mr. Mather, in House of Commons, *Debates*, 19 January 1970, 2568.

43 J.J. Greene, in House of Commons, Standing Committee on National Resources and Public Works, *Minutes of Proceedings and Evidence*, 2 February 1970, 30. See also House of Commons, *Debates*, 20 November 1969, 1046.

44 James W. Parlour, 'The Politics of Water Pollution Control: A Case Study of the Canadian Fisheries Act Amendments and the Pulp and Paper Effluent Regulations, 1970,' *Journal of Environmental Management* 13 (1981): 146.

45 Jack Davis, 'The Fish and the Law that Guards Against Pollution,' *Globe and Mail*, 7 August 1969, 7.
46 House of Commons, Committee on Fisheries and Forestry, *Minutes of Proceedings and Evidence*, 30 April 1970, 19:7.
47 Davis, 'The Fish and the Law,' 7.
48 *Globe and Mail*, 'Maritime Pulp Mills Singled out for Attack in New Fisheries Act,' 2 February 1970, 3.
49 Parlour, 'Canadian Fisheries Act Amendments,' 131.
50 House of Commons, *Debates*, 20 April 1970, 6052.
51 Davis, 'The Fish and the Law'; and Davis in House of Commons, *Debates*, 27 January 1971, 2830; and 6 February 1971, 3433.
52 Jack Davis in House of Commons, *Debates*, 20 April 1970, 6052.
53 Parlour, 'Formation of the Canada Water Act,' 32.
54 Woodrow, 'Development and Implementation of Federal Pollution Control Policy,' 379.
55 As cited in Muntz, 'Federal Government Policy,' 58-9.
56 House of Commons, *Debates*, 19 February 1971, 3574.
57 Section 9 of the Clean Air Act did authorize federal action if an individual source led to a violation of one or more of the objectives. However, the act made no provision for the more pressing need to control numerous smaller sources that collectively could contribute to violations of objectives, as did the comparable US legislation adopted the previous year.
58 Lennart J. Lundqvist, *Environmental Policies in Canada, Sweden, and the United States: A Comparative Overview* (Beverly Hills: Sage Publications 1974), 30.
59 House of Commons, Committee on Fisheries and Forestry, *Minutes of Proceedings and Evidence*, 27 April 1971, 7:12.
60 House of Commons, Committee on Fisheries and Forestry, *Minutes of Proceedings and Evidence*, 29 April 1971, 8:8.
61 Dominique Alhéritière, 'Les problèmes constitutionnels de la lutte contre la pollution de l'espace atmospherique au Canada,' *La Revue du Barreau Canadien* 50 (1972): 561-79.
62 See also K.C. Lucas, 'The Federal Role in Air Pollution Control in Canada,' Environment Canada, APCP 71-19, 1971.
63 House of Commons, Committee on Fisheries and Forestry, *Minutes of Proceedings and Evidence*, 10 March 1971, 1:13.
64 Peter Nemetz, 'Federal Environmental Regulation in Canada,' *Natural Resources Journal* 26 (1986): 558.
65 For a review of provincial legislation, see Robert T. Franson and Alastair R. Lucas, *Canadian Environmental Law* (Toronto: Butterworths – Continuing Service 1976).
66 Canada, Federal-Provincial Conference, 'Briefing Book,' Ottawa, 16-17 February 1970. See also Malcolm Reid, 'Provinces Unite Against Pollution,' *Globe and Mail*, 5 August 1969, 1.
67 Donald Newman, 'Premiers Decide to Co-operate in Expanding Pollution Agency,' *Globe and Mail*, 5 August 1970, 1.

68 Woodrow, 'Federal Pollution Control,' 203-6; Parlour, 'Formation of the Canada Water Act'; Andrew R. Thompson, *Environmental Regulation in Canada: An Assessment of the Regulatory Process* (Vancouver: Westwater Research Centre 1980), 22; Saunders, *Interjurisdictional Issues*, 37; O.P. Dwivedi and R. Brian Woodrow, 'Environmental Policy-Making and Administration in Federal States: The Impact of Overlapping Jurisdictions in Canada,' in William M. Chandler and Christian W. Zollner, eds., *Challenges to Federalism: Policy-Making in Canada and the Federal Republic of Germany* (Kingston: Institute of Intergovernmental Relations, Queen's University 1989).

69 See, for instance, Geoffrey Stevens, 'Robarts calls for federal aid to provinces and industry to fight pollution,' *Globe and Mail*, 18 February 1970, 8; and *Globe and Mail*, 'Blame Ottawa for Placentia pollution, fishermen told,' 29 May 1969, 4.

70 Woodrow, 'Development and Implementation of Federal Pollution Control,' 210; *Vancouver Sun*, 'Sneers at Davis' Anti-pollution Measures: Campbell Blast Ends Throne Debate,' 5 February 1971, 8; *Reclamation*, 'No Intrusion,' January 1970, 3.

71 *Edmonton Journal*, 'Anti-pollution Act Won't Do Job: Province,' 26 August 1969, 2.

72 Woodrow, 'Federal Pollution Control Policy,' 214.

73 Woodrow, 'Development and Implementation of Federal Pollution Control Policy,' 272.

74 Woodrow, 'Development and Implementation of Federal Pollution Control Policy,' 327.

75 Woodrow, 'Development and Implementation of Federal Pollution Control Policy,' 325; *Reclamation*, 'Comments on New Canada Water Act,' October 1969, 5; Roger Davies, 'What do the Provinces Think?,' *Water and Pollution Control*, November 1969, 64; *Globe and Mail*, 'Quebec Leads Criticism of Ottawa Anti-pollution Plan,' 27 August 1969, 8.

76 Frances Russell, 'No Water Laws Fight, Robarts Says,' *Globe and Mail*, 20 May 1970, 8.

77 Davies, 'What do the Provinces Think?'

78 Statement by the Honourable Jean-Jacques Bertrand to the Federal-Provincial Conference, 16-17 February 1970, 6-7, cited in Woodrow, 'Development and Implementation of Federal Pollution Control Policy,' 326. See also *Globe and Mail*, 'Quebec to Oppose Anti-pollution Bill,' 14 February 1970, 2; and *Globe and Mail*, 'Quebec Leads Criticism of Ottawa Anti-pollution Plan,' 27 August 1969, 8.

79 J.J. Greene, in House of Commons, *Debates*, 20 November 1969, 1048.

80 Otto Lang, quoted in the *Globe and Mail*, 'Water Act Won't Work in Ontario: Kerr,' 30 January 1970, 4.

81 British Columbia did raise objections after the fact, ironically arguing that the approach under the Fisheries Act would undermine federal-provincial cooperation under the Canada Water Act, a statute for which the provincial government previously had expressed no great admiration. See Iain Hunter, 'Pollution control "in utter chaos,"' *Vancouver Sun*, 14 August 1970, 1.

82 House of Commons, Standing Committee on Fisheries and Forestry, *Minutes of Proceedings and Evidence*, 27 April 1971, 7:11.
83 Canadian Intergovernmental Conference Secretariat, *The Constitutional Review: 1968-1971*, Secretary's Report, 196.
84 Donald V. Smiley, *Canada in Question: Federalism in the Eighties*, 3rd ed. (Toronto: McGraw-Hill 1980), 71.
85 J.W. MacNeill, *Environmental Management* (Ottawa: Information Canada 1971).
86 Canadian Intergovernmental Conference Secretariat, *The Constitutional Review*, 192-3.
87 See 'Notes for the Use of the Honourable John P. Robarts on the Constitutional Aspects of Environmental Management,' Second Working Session of the Constitutional Conference, 14-15 September 1970, Ottawa; 'Proposals of the Province of British Columbia to the Working Sessions of the Constitutional Conference and Federal-Provincial Conference,' Ottawa, 14-16 September 1970.
88 Nova Scotia and Manitoba's comments are summarized in Canadian Intergovernmental Conference Secretariat, *The Constitutional Review*, 193.
89 'Constitutional Conference, Second Working Session, September 14 and 15, 1970: Statement of Conclusions,' 15 September 1970, 3.
90 Canadian Intergovernmental Conference Secretariat, *The Constitutional Review*, 194. BC proposed that the provinces should have exclusive jurisdiction concerning environmental matters contained within their own borders, subject only to federal authority to establish national standards. Quebec recommended exclusive provincial powers to legislate with respect to air and water pollution within provincial borders, joint federal and provincial authority with respect to international matters, and a constitutional court, rather than federal authority, to resolve interprovincial disputes.
91 Woodrow, 'Development and Implementation of Federal Pollution Control Policy,' 462.
92 Statement by D.V. Heald, attorney general for Saskatchewan, Special Joint Committee on the Constitution of Canada, *Minutes of Proceedings and Evidence*, 17 November 1970, 12:32.
93 The McGuigan Report and other constitutional proposals over a fifteen-year period are reviewed in Dale Gibson, 'Environmental Protection and Enhancement under a New Canadian Constitution,' in Stanley M. Beck and Ivan Bernier, eds., *Canada and the New Constitution*, vol. 2 (Montreal: Institute for Research on Public Policy 1983).
94 *Vancouver Sun*, 'BC Claims Water Management Rights,' 19 March 1971, 9.

Chapter 5: The Federal Retreat, 1972-85

1 O.P. Dwivedi and R. Brian Woodrow, 'Environmental Policy-Making and Administration in a Federal State: The Impact of Overlapping Jurisdiction in Canada,' in William M. Chandler and Christian W. Zollner, eds., *Challenges to Federalism: Policy-Making in Canada and the Federal Republic of Germany* (Kingston: Institute of Intergovernmental Relations, Queen's University, 1989).

2 Gallup Canada polls #355 (September 1972), #361 (September 1973), #364 (March 1974), and #369 (October 1974).
3 Ian McAllister and Donely T. Studlar, 'Trends in Public Opinion on the Environment in Australia,' *International Journal of Public Opinion Research* 5 (1993): 353-61; Riley E. Dunlap, 'Trends in Public Opinion Toward Environmental Issues: 1965-1990,' in Riley E. Dunlap and Angela G. Mertig, eds., *American Environmentalism: The U.S. Environmental Movement, 1970-1990* (Philadelphia: Taylor and Francis 1992).
4 *The Gallup Report*, 28 May 1990.
5 *The Gallup Report*, 2 December 1970; and 15 September 1976.
6 James Parlour and Steven Schatzow, 'The Mass Media and Public Concern for Environmental Problems in Canada, 1960-1972,' *International Journal of Environmental Studies* 13 (1978): 9-17.
7 Anthony Downs, 'Up and Down with Ecology – The "Issue-Attention Cycle,"' *The Public Interest* 27 (1972): 38-50.
8 Riley E. Dunlap, 'Public Opinion and Environmental Policy,' in James P. Lester, ed., *Environmental Politics and Policy* (Durham: Duke University Press 1989).
9 Robert H. Durr, 'What Moves Policy Sentiment?' *American Political Science Review* 87 (1993): 158-70. Nevitte and Kanji rule out this explanation because they found no correlation between individual wealth and level of environmental concern. See Neil Nevitte and Mebs Kanji, 'Explaining Environmental Concern and Action in Canada,' *Applied Behavioral Science Review* 3 (1995): 85-102. However, the authors analyzed data for only one year, and thus cannot assess whether trends in the national economy influence environmental concern. While there may be insignificant differences between levels of concern among the wealthy and the poor in a given year, both may be less attentive to the environment when the economy takes a turn for the worse.
10 The debate between Everett Carl Ladd, who emphasized the significance of low salience, and Louis Harris, who emphasized the high degree of public concern, is described in Robert Cameron Mitchell, 'Public Opinion and Environmental Politics in the 1970s and 1980s,' in Norman J. Vig and Michael E. Kraft, eds., *Environmental Policy in the 1980s: Reagan's New Agenda* (Washington, DC: Congressional Quarterly Press 1984).
11 John R. Zaller, *The Nature and Origins of Mass Opinion* (New York: Cambridge University Press 1992).
12 James A. Stimson, *Public Opinion in America: Moods, Cycles, and Swings* (Boulder: Westview 1991), 3.
13 Dunlap, 'Public Opinion and Environmental Policy,' 134.
14 Dunlap, 'Public Opinion and Environmental Policy,' 131.
15 G. Bruce Doern and Thomas Conway, *The Greening of Canada: Federal Institutions and Decisions* (Toronto: University of Toronto Press 1994), 117-18.
16 Several developments in the late 1970s increased the visibility of problems related to toxic substances and hazardous wastes. In 1979, derailment of a train containing tankers of pressurized chlorine gas forced evacuation of 250,000 residents of Mississauga, Ontario, for several days. Also in the late 1970s, Canadian and US scientists reported that they had detected dioxins in fish and

the eggs of fish-eating birds in the Great Lakes region. The discovery was cause for concern because the extreme toxicity of dioxins was already well documented. Finally, an environmental disaster at Love Canal, New York, prompted international attention to the problem of unsafe disposal of hazardous wastes. Love Canal, located just outside Niagara Falls, was used as a disposal site for chemical wastes in the 1940s and 1950s after plans to complete the canal were abandoned. In the late 1970s, residents of homes built on or near the site, which had subsequently been covered by clay, began to complain of chemical odours and health problems. Hundreds of families were subsequently relocated, over 200 homes were demolished, and over $200 million was spent on cleanup and relocation.

17 Under categories of air pollution, conservation, environment, pollution, water pollution, and wilderness, one finds over 1,000 citations in 1970. The number declined to 150 in 1975, and 65 by 1985 (British Columbia Legislative Library, *Newspaper Index* [Vancouver: Precision Micrographic Services, continuing service]). Thanks are owed to George Hoberg, who provided these data.

18 John Quarles, *Cleaning Up America: An Insider's View of the Environmental Protection Agency* (Boston: Houghton Mifflin 1976), 214.

19 R.B. Woodrow, 'The Development and Implementation of Federal Pollution Control Policy Programs in Canada, 1966-1974,' Ph.D. thesis, University of Toronto, 1977, 455.

20 Woodrow, 'The Development and Implementation of Federal Pollution Control Policy,' 457.

21 Doern and Conway, *The Greening of Canada*, 20.

22 Jack Davis, in House of Commons, *Debates*, 21 March 1972, 1008.

23 A.T. Davidson, in House of Commons, Standing Committee on Fisheries and Forestry, *Minutes of Proceedings and Evidence*, 15 May 1973, 12:10.

24 *Canadian Environmental Control Newsletter*, 5 May 1973, 136.

25 Woodrow, 'The Development and Implementation of Federal Pollution Control Policy,' 453.

26 Doern and Conway, *The Greening of Canada*, 61-2.

27 Jack Davis, in House of Commons, *Debates*, 26 January 1973, 686. The decision subsequently was overturned on appeal, affirming provincial authority, but leaving the extent of concurrent federal authority ill-defined.

28 Factum of Government of Canada, *Interprovincial Co-operatives Ltd. and Dryden Chemicals Ltd.* v. *The Queen* in Right of Ontario, 26 March 1975, 23.

29 George Baker, parliamentary secretary to the Minister of the Environment, in House of Commons, *Debates*, 29 June 1976, 14972.

30 The federal response is quoted in Warner Troyer, *No Safe Place* (Vancouver: Clark, Irwin 1992), 123. The provincial response is noted in Ross Howard, *Poisons in Public* (Toronto: James Lorimer 1980), 25.

31 Doern and Conway, *The Greening of Canada*, 13.

32 Environment Canada, 'Environment Canada: Its Role, Goals and Organization,' 1975, 6.

33 Environment Canada, 'A Ten-Year Planning Guideline for Environment Canada, 1976-1986,' December 1974, 86.

34 Letter from Prime Minister Trudeau to Roméo LeBlanc, Minister of Fisheries and Environment, 9 November 1978 (emphasis added).

35 Doern and Conway, *The Greening of Canada*, 54.

36 Len Marchand, in House of Commons, *Debates*, 23 January 1979, 2492-3.

37 Allan J. MacEachen, in House of Commons, *Debates*, 23 January 1979, 2465.

38 Cited by Lorne Giroux, 'A Statement by the Canadian Environmental Advisory Council on Enforcement Practices of Environment Canada,' in Canadian Environmental Advisory Council, *Review of the Proposed Environmental Protection Act* (Ottawa: Canadian Environmental Advisory Council 1987), 97. See also Doreen C. Henley, 'The Advocacy Approach,' in Linda F. Duncan, ed., *Environmental Enforcement: Proceedings of the National Conference on the Enforcement of Environmental Law* (Edmonton: Environmental Law Centre [Alberta] Society 1985).

39 Environment Canada, *Annual Report* (Ottawa, 1983-4), 1.

40 M. Paul Brown and Raymond P. Coté, 'Environmental Advocacy Revisited: An Approach for the 1990s,' mimeo, 3.

41 See for instance, Environment Canada, Corporate Planning Group, 'Environment Canada: Its Evolving Mission,' September 1982, 10, 12.

42 Tom Conway, 'Taking Stock of the Traditional Regulatory Approach,' in G. Bruce Doern, ed., *Getting it Green* (Ottawa: CD Howe 1990), 36.

43 House of Commons, *Debates*, 22 April 1985, 3496.

44 Task Force on Program Review, *Environmental Quality Strategic Review* (Ottawa: Supply and Services Canada 1986), 39.

45 Woodrow, 'The Development and Implementation of Federal Pollution Control Policy,' 103, 495.

46 Charles Caccia, in House of Commons, *Debates*, 22 October 1979, 454.

47 A single page of Hansard offers an example of two future environment ministers, Tom McMillan in opposition and Charles Caccia as a government backbencher, demanding a stronger federal role. (House of Commons, *Debates*, 9 July 1981, 11387.) Yet as ministers, both sought to work through the provinces whenever possible.

48 Bruce H. Wildsmith, 'Fisheries, Harmonization and the Economic Union,' in Mark Krasnick, ed., *Case Studies in the Division of Powers* (Toronto: University of Toronto Press 1985), 238.

49 B. Guy Peters and Brian W. Hogwood, 'In Search of the Issue-Attention Cycle,' *Journal of Public Policy* 47 (1985): 238-53.

50 Two minor amendments to environmental statutes are not reviewed here. Consistent with the tenor of the times, the Motor Vehicle Safety Act was amended in 1977 to allow the minister to grant manufacturers exemptions from federal regulations, including emission control regulations. A minor amendment also was made to the Pest Control Products Act in 1982.

51 Honourable Jeanne Sauvé, in Standing Committee on Fisheries and Forestry, *Minutes of Proceedings and Evidence*, 6 May 1975, Issue 23.

52 The issue finally was clarified by *Reference re: Ownership of the Bed of the Strait of Georgia and Related Areas* (1976), 1 *British Columbia Law Reports,* affirmed [1984] 1 *Supreme Court Reports*, 388.

53 'Task Force Report on Environmental Contaminants Legislation,' September 1972, Appendix B.
54 Legislation was not introduced until 1974. The bill then died once on the order paper before it was passed in 1975 and finally proclaimed in 1976.
55 See testimony by Pollution Probe in Standing Committee on Fisheries and Forestry, *Minutes of Proceedings and Evidence*, 17 June 1975. See also remarks by Joe Clark, on 11 April 1975, 16:14.
56 J.F. Castrilli, 'Control of Toxic Chemicals in Canada: An Analysis of Law and Policy,' *Osgoode Hall Law Journal* 20 (1982): 322-401.
57 Testimony by the Honourable Roméo LeBlanc, House of Commons, *Debates*, 16 May 1977, 5670.
58 House of Commons, *Debates*, 16 May 1977, 5669; also, Standing Committee on Fisheries and Forestry, *Minutes of Proceedings and Evidence*, 16 June 1977, 33A:64-66.
59 House of Commons, Standing Committee on Fisheries and Forestry, *Minutes of Proceedings and Evidence*, 16 June 1977, 62.
60 House of Commons, Standing Committee on Fisheries and Forestry, *Minutes of Proceedings and Evidence*, 16 June 1977, Issue 33.
61 Quebec's silence is especially puzzling in light of that province's sensitivity to federal intrusions in provincial jurisdiction. With respect to PEI, see Standing Committee on Fisheries and Forestry, *Minutes of Proceedings and Evidence*, 16 June 1977, 33A:3.
62 Letter from Neil Byers, Saskatchewan Minister of the Environment to Roméo LeBlanc, federal Minister of the Environment, 14 June 1977, reprinted in Standing Committee on Fisheries and Forestry, *Minutes of Proceedings and Evidence*, 16 June 1977, 33A:5.
63 J.F. MacTavish, Deputy Minister of the Environment, Nova Scotia, in Standing Committee on Fisheries and Forestry, *Minutes of Proceedings and Evidence*, 16 June 1977, 33:6. Similar arguments by Newfoundland, British Columbia, Alberta, and New Brunswick can be found at 33A:1, 33:17-18, 33A:40, and 33A:4, respectively.
64 Submission of Walter Solodzuk, Deputy Minister of the Environment, Alberta, in Standing Committee on Fisheries and Forestry, *Minutes of Proceedings and Evidence*, 16 June 1977, 33A:32. See also 33A:41.
65 Standing Committee on Fisheries and Forestry, *Minutes of Proceedings and Evidence*, 16 June 1977, 33A:8.
66 Standing Committee on Fisheries and Forestry, *Minutes of Proceedings and Evidence*, 14 June 1977, 31A:31.
67 The proposed amendments were supported by the Canadian Wildlife Federation and, not surprisingly, by groups representing fishers. Standing Committee on Fisheries and Forestry, *Minutes of Proceedings and Evidence*, 9 June 1977.
68 Mr. Wenman, in Standing Committee on Fisheries and Forestry, *Minutes of Proceedings and Evidence*, 14 June 1977, 31:35; Bill Jarvis, in House of Commons, *Debates*, 28 June 1977, 7166.

69 Lloyd Crouse, in House of Commons, *Debates*, 16 May 1977, 5673. See also Lloyd Crouse, in *Debates*, 28 June 1977, 7164, and Bill Jarvis, in *Debates*, 28 June 1977, 7165.
70 Les Edgeworth, in Standing Committee on Fisheries and Forestry, *Minutes of Proceedings and Evidence*, 8 June 1977, 29:25 and 29:34.
71 Doern and Conway, *The Greening of Canada*, 220.
72 The arrangement was documented in the so-called Lucas-Weir memorandum, which was signed by the Assistant Deputy Ministers of Fisheries and the Environmental Protection Service in 1971.
73 Letter from Prime Minister Trudeau to Roméo LeBlanc, Minister of Fisheries and Environment, 9 November 1978.
74 Confidential interview, June 1991.
75 House of Commons, *Debates*, 16 December 1980, 5801.
76 House of Commons, *Debates*, 16 December 1980, 5801.
77 Michael Whittington, 'Department of Environment,' in G. Bruce Doern, ed., *Spending Tax Dollars: Federal Expenditures 1980-1* (Ottawa: Carleton University 1980), 101.
78 Statistics Canada, *Human Activity and the Environment 1991* (Ottawa, Statistics Canada 1991), 101.
79 Doern and Conway, *The Greening of Canada*, 39.
80 Memorandum from A.W. May, Deputy Minister of Fisheries and Oceans, to Jacques Gerin, Deputy Minister of Environment Canada, 2 June 1983.
81 A. Paul Pross, 'Water and Environmental Law: Bureaucratic Constraints,' in Susan Guppy, Yvonne Fern, and Bruce Wildsmith, eds., *Water and Environmental Law* (Halifax: Institute for Resource and Environmental Studies, Dalhousie University 1981).
82 Regulations were issued for secondary lead smelters, chlor-alkali plants, asbestos mining and milling, and polyvinyl chloride manufacturing. Guidelines were issued for cement manufacture, asphalt paving, coke ovens, arctic mining, incinerators, wood pulping, and thermal power generation.
83 Paul M. Brown, 'Organizational Design as Policy Instrument: Environment Canada in the Canadian Bureaucracy,' in Robert Boardman, ed., *Canadian Environmental Policy: Ecosystems, Politics, and Process* (Toronto: Oxford University Press 1992), 29.
84 Environment Canada, 'The Clean Air Act Report 1984-5,' 3.
85 Les Edgeworth, 'Canada's Approach to Environmental Pollution Control for the Pulp and Paper Industry,' presented by F.G. Hurtubise to the 15th EUCEPA Conference, Rome, 7-12 May 1973, 5. Regulations were issued under the Fisheries Act for pulp and paper mills, chlor-alkali plants, petroleum refineries, metal mining, potato processing plants, and meat and poultry plants.
86 Confidential interview, June 1991.
87 A revision of the pulp and paper regulations was ready for review by the Privy Council Office, and a proposed regulation for the textile industry was even further advanced.
88 Woodrow, 'The Development and Implementation of Federal Pollution Control Policy,' 434.

89 J. Owen Saunders, *Interjurisdictional Issues in Canadian Water Management* (Calgary: Canadian Institute of Resources Law 1990), 37; Dwivedi and Woodrow, 'Environmental Policy-Making and Administration in Federal States,' 281.
90 By the 1976-7 fiscal year, only three of the bilateral committees had even met. Environment Canada, *Canada Water Act Annual Report, 1976-7.*
91 Andrew R. Thompson, *Environmental Regulation in Canada: An Assessment of the Regulatory Process* (Vancouver: Westwater Research Centre 1980), 22.
92 Saunders, *Interjurisdictional Issues,* 27.
93 Murray Rankin and Peter Finkle, 'The Enforcement of Environmental Law: Taking the Environment Seriously,' *University of British Columbia Law Review* 17 (1982): 35-57.
94 Thompson, *Environmental Regulation in Canada,* 33.
95 David Estrin 'Tokenism and Environmental Protection,' in O.P. Dwivedi, ed., *Protecting the Environment* (Vancouver: Copp Clark 1974); Peter Nemetz, 'Federal Environmental Regulation in Canada,' *Natural Resources Journal* 26 (1986): 552-608, 552; Conway, 'Taking Stock of the Traditional Regulatory Approach'; Rankin and Finkle, 'The Enforcement of Environmental Law,' 35-57; Peter A. Victor and Terrence N. Burrell, *Environmental Protection Regulation: Water Pollution, and the Pulp and Paper Industry* (Ottawa: Economic Council of Canada 1981); Ted Schrecker, *The Political Economy of Environmental Hazards* (Ottawa: Law Reform Commission of Canada 1984). For a review of recent changes in the process, see George Hoberg, 'Environmental Policy: Alternative Styles,' in Michael Atkinson, ed., *Governing Canada: State Institutions and Public Policy* (Toronto: HBJ Holt 1993).
96 Lynne B. Huestis, 'Policing Pollution: The Prosecution of Environmental Offenses,' Working Paper, Law Reform Commission of Canada, September 1984, 41.
97 Conway, 'Taking Stock of the Traditional Regulatory Approach,' 36.
98 Huestis, 'Policing Pollution,' 55-6.
99 Kathryn Harrison, 'Is Cooperation the Answer? Canadian Environmental Enforcement in Comparative Context,' *Journal of Policy Analysis and Management* 14 (Spring 1995): 221-45.
100 Kernaghan Webb, 'Between Rocks and Hard Places: Bureaucrats, Law and Pollution Control,' in Robert Paehlke and Douglas Torgeson, eds., *Managing Leviathan* (Peterborough: Broadview Press 1990).
101 Webb, 'Between Rocks and Hard Places.'
102 K.E.A. de Silva, *The Pulp and Paper Modernization Grants Program – An Assessment* (Ottawa: Economic Council of Canada 1988).
103 Harrison, 'Is Cooperation the Answer?'
104 Thompson, *Environmental Regulation in Canada*; Huestis, 'Policing Pollution'; Lorne Giroux, 'Delegation of Administration,' in Donna Tingley, ed., *Environmental Protection and the Canadian Constitution* (Edmonton: Environmental Law Centre [Alberta] Society 1987).
105 Only in Quebec were arrangements formally documented through Orders in Council. John MacLatchy, 'Delegation of the Fisheries Act and Current Administration of the Pollution Provisions,' Environment Canada, mimeo,

April 1989; Richard W. Parisien, 'The Fisheries Act: Origins of Federal Delegation of Administrative Jurisdiction to the Provinces,' unpublished report (Ottawa: Environment Canada 1972.)

106 MacLatchy, 'Delegation of the Fisheries Act,' 3. Interestingly, Environment Canada did historically administer the Fisheries Act pulp and paper effluent regulations in Manitoba and Saskatchewan, even though administration of the act in inland waters had been delegated to both of those provinces.

107 Confidential interview with Environment Canada official, July 1991.

108 Standing Committee on Fisheries and Forestry, *Minutes of Proceedings and Evidence*, 5 May 1970, #20.

109 Confidential interviews, June 1991.

110 Jack Davis, 'Objectives of the Department of the Environment,' in Conference Board of Canada, *Pollution Control in Canada: Government and Industry Viewpoints*, September 1971.

111 Parisien, 'The Fisheries Act.'

112 House of Commons, *Debates*, 21 March 1972, 1008.

113 The Canada-New Brunswick Accord for the Protection and Enhancement of Environmental Quality is reprinted in Standing Committee on Fisheries and Forestry, *Minutes and Proceedings of Evidence*, 8 June 1977, 29A:51.

114 It is noteworthy that the federal role was described as one of developing national 'guidelines' and 'requirements,' rather than enforceable 'regulations.' It also is noteworthy that the provinces avoided a commitment to establish 'regulations' to satisfy national standards, in favour of the more innocuous 'requirements.'

115 Federal-Provincial Relations Office, *Federal-Provincial Programs and Activities: A Descriptive Inventory 1989-1990* (Ottawa: Federal-Provincial Relations Office 1990), 11-27.

116 Office of the Secretariat, Committee of Regional Executives, Environment Canada, 'A Summary of Federal-Provincial Agreements, Western and Northern Region,' March 1989.

117 Lynne Huestis, 'Pilot Study Report, S. 33 Fisheries Act,' Department of Justice, Federal Statutes Compliance Project, December 1985, 53-67.

118 P. Nemetz, D. Uyeno, P. Vertinsky, J. Vertinsky, and A. Vining, 'Regulation of Toxic Chemicals in the Environment,' Economic Council of Canada, Working Paper #20, February 1981, 159.

119 Confidential interviews, May to October 1991.

120 Huestis, 'Policing Pollution,' 89-90.

121 Raymond Robinson, in House of Commons, Special Committee on Regulatory Reform, *Minutes of Proceedings and Evidence*, 14 September 1980, 6:46.

122 Kathryn Harrison, 'Passing the Buck: Federalism and Canadian Environmental Policy,' Ph.D. thesis, University of British Columbia, 1993, 376-81.

123 Huestis, 'Pilot Study Report,' 53; Kernaghan R. Webb, 'Industrial Water Pollution Control and the EPS,' unpublished background study for the Law Reform Commission of Canada, May 1983, 5-187.

124 Between 1970 and 1987, EPS laid only two charges under the Fisheries Act in Quebec, neither of which concerned the pulp and paper industry, even though

Quebec mills had the lowest rates of compliance in the country (Lorne Giroux, 'Statement by the Canadian Environmental Advisory Council'). Huestis also reported that in 1985, although there were no Quebec environmental standards for the entire mining industry, EPS did not take any action to enforce federal regulations under the Fisheries Act for that sector (Huestis, 'Pilot Study Report,' 65).

125 Huestis, 'Policing Pollution,' 93-7.
126 David Estrin, 'Mirror Legislation,' in Donna Tingley, ed., *Environmental Protection and the Canadian Constitution* (Edmonton: Environmental Law Centre [Alberta] Society 1989), 60.
127 Woodrow, 'The Development and Implementation of Federal Pollution Control Policy,' 480.
128 Christina Anne Wilson, 'The Canadian Council of Resource and Environment Ministers as a Site for Elite Accommodation in Canada, 1963 to 1974,' M.A. thesis, University of Western Ontario, 1984, 116; Wayne Cheveldayoff, 'Ignored by Ottawa, Provinces, Council of Ministers on Resources, Environment to Fold,' *Globe and Mail*, 5 October 1973, 9.
129 Doern and Conway, *The Greening of Canada*, 125.
130 Don Munton, 'The Provinces and Canada-United States Environmental Relations,' in Tom Keating and Don Munton, eds., *The Provinces and Canadian Foreign Policy* (Toronto: Canadian Institute of International Affairs 1985), 93.
131 Michael Keating, 'Canada Decides to go it Alone in Acid Rain Fight,' *Globe and Mail*, 7 March 1984, 1-2.
132 Michael Keating, 'Acid Rain Agreement Hailed as Victory,' *Globe and Mail*, 6 February 1985, 1.
133 Robert Egel, 'Canada's Acid Rain Policy: Federal and Provincial Roles,' in Jurgen Schmandt, Hilliard Roderick, and Judith Clarkson, eds., *Acid Rain and Friendly Neighbors: The Policy Dispute between Canada and the United States* (Durham: Duke University Press 1988).
134 Rick Boychuk, 'Federal Action Needed on Acid Rain: Lévesque,' *Montreal Gazette*, 11 April 1985, A5. See also *Halifax Chronicle-Herald*, 'Quebec Anticipated N.S. Backing in Talks on Acid Rain Problem,' 9 November 1979, 12; and *Montreal Gazette*, 'Ottawa, Quebec Vow to Team up in War Against Acid Rain Pollution,' 4 December 1984, A6.
135 In 1979, a Conservative minister of the environment, John Fraser, stated, 'unless I have evidence that the provinces are not prepared to co-operate, I do not intend to use the constitutional power of the federal government at this time' (House of Commons, *Debates*, 22 October 1979, 457). His Liberal successor, John Roberts, echoed that sentiment in stating, 'I believe it is the provinces that must take a lead role, since property, civil rights and the administration of justice, including civil procedures, are clearly within their domain and constitutional responsibility' (House of Commons, *Debates*, 9 July 1981, 11391).
136 Confidential interview, October 1991.
137 Personal interview with Charles Caccia, June 1991.
138 See Keating, 'Canada Decides to Go It Alone'; *Globe and Mail*, 'Ottawa Tells Quebec to Help Cut Acid Rain,' 2 June 1984, 5; *Vancouver Sun*, 'Acid Rain

Cleanup Hinges on Federal Aid,' 6 February 1985, A8; *Montreal Gazette*, 'Ontario, Ottawa Clash Over Acid Funds,' 3 October 1985, B4.

139 Personal interview, Charles Caccia, June 1991.

140 Confidential interview.

141 Michael Whittington, 'Environmental Policy,' in G. Bruce Doern and V. Seymour Wilson, *Issues in Canadian Public Policy* (Toronto: Macmillan 1974); Michael Jenkin, *The Challenge of Diversity: Industrial Policy in the Canadian Federation* (Ottawa: Science Council of Canada 1983), 120-4; Grace Skogstad and Paul Kopas, 'Environmental Policy in a Federal System: Ottawa and the Provinces,' in Robert Boardman, ed., *Canadian Environmental Policy*.

142 Confidential interview, October 1991.

143 Whittington, 'Environmental Policy'; Dwivedi and Woodrow, 'Environmental Policy-Making,' 272.

144 A former secretary general of CCREM stated, 'a principal strength of the Council is that it has no formal [policy-making] power.' Cited in Whittington, 'Environmental Policy.'

145 Confidential interviews, 1990-1.

146 Confidential interview, July 1991.

147 Task Force on Program Review, *Environmental Quality Strategic Review*, 34-5.

148 Confidential interview, June 1991.

149 Task Force on Program Review, *Environmental Quality Strategic Review*, 70.

150 Barry G. Rabe, 'Cross-Media Environmental Regulatory Integration: The Case of Canada,' *American Review of Canadian Studies* 19 (1989): 261-73; Woodrow, 'The Development and Implementation of Federal Pollution Control Policy,' 203-6, 541; Thompson, *Environmental Regulation in Canada*, 22; Saunders, *Interjurisdictional Issues*, 21; Alastair R. Lucas, 'Harmonization of Federal and Provincial Environmental Policies: The Changing Legal and Policy Framework,' in J. Owen Saunders, *Managing Natural Resources in a Federal State* (Toronto: Carswell 1986).

151 Confidential interview, April 1991.

152 See Peter Nemetz, 'The Fisheries Act and Federal-Provincial Environmental Regulation: Duplication or Complementarity?' *Canadian Public Administration* 29 (1986): 401-24.

153 Confidential interview, May 1991.

Chapter 6: The Second Wave

1 E.E. Schattschneider, *The Semi-Sovereign People* (San Francisco: Holt, Rinehart and Winston 1960).

2 M. Paul Brown, 'Organizational Design as Policy Instrument: Environment Canada in the Canadian Bureaucracy,' in Robert Boardman, ed., *Canadian Environmental Policy: Ecosystems, Politics, and Process* (Toronto: Oxford University Press 1992), 31.

3 G. Bruce Doern and Thomas Conway, *The Greening of Canada: Federal Institutions and Decisions* (Toronto: University of Toronto Press 1994), 64.

4 Task Force on Program Review, *Environmental Quality Strategic Review* (Ottawa: Supply and Services Canada 1986), 39.

5 Confidential interview, June 1991.
6 *The Gallup Report*, 28 May 1990; Gallup Canada polls #109-1 (September 1991) and #204-1 (April 1992).
7 The data are from Gallup Canada poll #907-1, conducted in July 1989.
8 Doern and Conway, *The Greening of Canada*, 118.
9 See testimony by Doug Miller, in House of Commons, *Minutes of Proceedings and Evidence of the Standing Committee on the Environment*, September 1991, 6A:18.
10 Riley E. Dunlap, 'Trends in Public Opinion Toward Environmental Issues: 1965-1990,' in Riley E. Dunlap and Angela G. Mertig, eds., *American Environmentalism: The U.S. Environmental Movement, 1970-1990* (Philadelphia: Taylor and Francis 1992).
11 Ian McAllister and Donely T. Studlar, 'Trends in Public Opinion on the Environment in Australia,' *International Journal of Public Opinion Research* 5 (1993): 353-61.
12 Data are from Gallup Canada polls #907-1 (July 1989), and #012-1 (December 1990); and *The Gallup Poll*, 31 January 1994.
13 The 'hiccup' in mid-1988 in the salience of economic concerns reflects a sudden rise in attention to the issue of free trade prior to the federal election in the fall of 1988.
14 As cited in Statistics Canada, *Human Activity and the Environment 1994* (Ottawa: Statistics Canada 1994).
15 See, for instance, Decima Research, 'Report to Environment Canada on Nation-Wide Survey on Attitudes Toward Environmental Issues and Priorities,' September 1987.
16 *British Columbia Report*, 'First Let's Save the Economy,' 26 April 1993.
17 Roughly a quarter of respondents looked to both levels of government equally. Miller, in House of Commons, *Minutes of Proceedings and Evidence of the Standing Committee on the Environment*, 6A:2.
18 *Times Colonist* (Victoria), 'Ottawa Guide on Environment,' 6 February 1990, D9.
19 Statistics Canada, *Human Activity and the Environment 1991* (Ottawa: Statistics Canada 1991), 101.
20 Task Force on Program Review, *Environmental Quality Strategic Review*, 39.
21 Doern and Conway, *The Greening of Canada*, 222.
22 House of Commons, *Minutes of Proceedings and Evidence of the Legislative Committee on Bill C-75*, 3 February 1988, 14:18.
23 Lucien Bouchard, 'Notes for an Address at the Symposium "Le Saint-Laurent, un fleuve a reconquerir,"' 3 November 1989.
24 Lucien Bouchard, *On the Record* (Toronto: Stoddart Publishing 1994), Chapter 14.
25 Confidential interview, June 1993.
26 Ross Howard, 'Federal Environment Plan Bogs Down,' *Globe and Mail*, 2 February 1990, A1; Rosemary Speirs, 'Mulroney on Thin Ice,' *Toronto Star*, 20 January 1990, D1.

27 *Province* (Vancouver), 'Bouchard Sees Red Over Green Plan,' 8 April 1991, 19; Bouchard, *On the Record*, 208.
28 Environment Canada, *A Framework for Discussion on the Environment* (Ottawa: Supply and Services Canada 1990); G. Bruce Doern, *The Federal Green Plan: Assessing the 'Prequel'* (Ottawa: CD Howe Institute 1990).
29 Government of Canada, 'Green Plan Consultation National Wrap-Up Session Workshop Reports,' August 1990. The cost figure is from Ross Howard, 'Ottawa to Pay $1-million to Promote Green Plan,' *Globe and Mail*, 12 October 1990, A5.
30 Frank Dabbs, 'Industries Fear that Federal "Green" Plan is "Son of NEP,"' *Financial Post*, 11 January 1990, 17.
31 Tamsin Carlisle, 'Mixed Reactions in Alberta over Green Plan,' *Financial Post*, 28 December 1990, 12.
32 Confidential interviews, July 1991.
33 Government of Canada, *Canada's Green Plan* (Ottawa: Ministry of Supply and Services 1990).
34 George Hoberg and Kathryn Harrison, 'It's Not Easy Being Green: The Politics of Canada's Green Plan,' *Canadian Public Policy* 20 (1994): 119-37.
35 Government of Canada, *Canada's Green Plan*, 46.
36 Jean Charest, in House of Commons, *Minutes of Proceedings and Evidence of the Standing Committee on the Environment*, 31 October 1991, 15:6.
37 Personal interview, September 1991.
38 Rianne Mahon, 'Canadian Public Policy: The Unequal Structure of Representation,' in Leo Panitch, ed., *The Canadian State: Political Economy and Political Power* (Toronto: University of Toronto Press 1977).
39 Task Force on Program Review, *Environmental Quality Strategic Review* (Ottawa: Task Force Program Review 1986), 83.
40 Lynn McDonald, in House of Commons, *Debates*, 17 September 1987, 9059.
41 See, for instance, Anne McIlroy, 'Environmentalists Fear Power Shift to Provinces,' *Vancouver Sun*, 25 March 1990, A6.
42 Confidential interview, July 1991.
43 Barbara Rutherford, in House of Commons, *Minutes of Proceedings and Evidence of the Standing Committee on the Environment*, 6 November 1991, 17:11.
44 Jeff Buttle, 'Cutback in Environmental Role Feared,' *Vancouver Sun*, 10 May 1990, B4.
45 Confidential interview, July 1991.
46 Confidential interview, July 1991.
47 Confidential interview, May 1991.
48 Jerry L. Mashaw and Susan Rose-Ackerman, 'Federalism and Regulation,' in George C. Eads and Michael Fix, eds., *The Reagan Regulatory Strategy* (Washington, DC: Urban Institute Press 1984). On behalf of the pipeline industry, see Gerald Maier, in House of Commons, *Minutes of Proceedings and Evidence of the Standing Committee on the Environment*, 7 November 1991, 18:36. On behalf of the oil industry, see Jack McLeod, in House of Commons, *Minutes of Proceedings and Evidence of the Standing Committee on the Environment*, 10 October 1991, 10:6.

49 Melvin Smith, in House of Commons, *Minutes of Proceedings and Evidence of the Standing Committee on the Environment*, 7 November 1991, 18:8. See also Keith Hendrick, 18:6.
50 Constitutional Committee of the Québec Liberal Party, 'A Québec Free to Choose,' January 1991, 38.
51 Government of Canada, *Shaping Canada's Future Together* (Ottawa: Supply and Services Canada 1991), 10.
52 Brief by the Rawson Academy of Aquatic Science and the Canadian Arctic Resources Committee, House of Commons, *Minutes of Proceedings and Evidence of the Standing Committee on the Environment*, 23 October 1991, 12A:3-4. See also testimony by Franklin Gertler, 16:28, and Paul Muldoon, 17:8.
53 Franklin Gertler, in House of Commons, *Minutes of Proceedings and Evidence of the Standing Committee on the Environment*, 5 November 1991, 16:30.
54 Barbara Rutherford, in House of Commons, *Minutes of Proceedings and Evidence of the Standing Committee on the Environment*, 6 November 1991, 17:12.
55 As cited in House of Commons, *Minutes of Proceedings and Evidence of the Standing Committee on the Environment*, 31 October 1991, 15:9.
56 Elizabeth May, in House of Commons, *Minutes of Proceedings and Evidence of the Standing Committee on the Environment*, 6 November 1991, 17:16.
57 Confidential interview, June 1991.
58 Doern and Conway, *The Greening of Canada*, 13.
59 On CEPA, see Alastair Lucas, 'The New Environmental Law,' in R. Watts and D. Brown, eds., *Canada: The State of the Federation, 1989* (Kingston: Institute of Intergovernmental Relations 1989); Lorne Giroux, 'Les nouvelles technologies et le regime de la protection de l'environnement au Canada: la nouvelle Loi canadienne sur la protection de l'environnement,' *Les Cahiers de Droit* 30 (1989): 747-76; and Donna Tingley, 'Conflict and Cooperation on the Environment,' in Douglas Brown, ed., *Canada: The State of the Federation, 1991* (Kingston: Institute of Intergovernmental Relations 1991).
60 The Ocean Dumping Control Act, the Environmental Contaminants Act, and the Clean Air Act were then repealed, though regulations issued to date under these statutes were retained under CEPA. Provisions of the Canada Water Act, other than Part III, which was incorporated in CEPA, remain on the books.
61 Glen Toner, 'Whence and Whither: ENGOs, Business and the Environment,' mimeo, undated; George Hoberg, 'Environmental Policy: Alternative Styles,' in Michael Atkinson, ed., *Governing Canada: State Institutions and Public Policy* (Toronto: HBJ Holt 1993).
62 Toner, 'Whence and Whither.'
63 Environment Canada, 'From Cradle to Grave: A Management Approach to Toxic Chemicals,' September 1986.
64 Tingley, 'Conflict and Cooperation,' 141-2.
65 Confidential interview, July 1991.
66 See for instance, Ron McLeod, 'The Provincial Perspective,' in Donna Tingley, ed., *Environmental Protection and the Canadian Constitution* (Edmonton: Environmental Law Centre [Alberta] Society 1987), 15.
67 McLeod, 'The Provincial Perspective,' 13.

68 M.K. Evans, 'Peace, Order and Good Government: Constructing a Constitutional Mandate for Environment Canada,' in Department of Justice, *Seminar on Enforcement of Environmental Law: January 26-27, 1988*, mimeo, 4.
69 J.F. Castrilli, 'Control of Toxic Chemicals in Canada: An Analysis of Law and Policy,' *Osgoode Hall Law Journal* 20 (1982): 322-401, 359.
70 Evans, 'Peace, Order and Good Government,' 13.
71 S.C. 1989, c. 9, as noted in Rodney Northey, 'Federalism and Comprehensive Environmental Reform: Seeing Beyond the Murky Medium,' *Osgoode Hall Law Journal* 29 (1989): 127-81, 146.
72 Linda F. Duncan, 'Trends in Enforcement: Is Environment Canada Serious about Enforcing Its Laws?' in Donna Tingley, ed., *Into the Future: Environmental Law and Policy for the 1990s* (Edmonton: Environmental Law Centre [Alberta] Society 1990), 55.
73 See, for instance, Charles Caccia, in House of Commons, *Debates*, 26 April 1988, 14820; Sergio Marchi, in *Debates*, 4 May 1988, 15132; and Pauline Jewett, in *Debates*, 5 May 1988, 15156-7.
74 Charles Caccia, in House of Commons, *Debates*, 16 September 1987, 9019.
75 Charles Caccia, in House of Commons, *Minutes of Proceedings and Evidence of the Legislative Committee on Bill C-75*, 8 February 1988. Also House of Commons, *Debates*, 26 April 1988, 14821.
76 In fact, the opposition to equivalency was joined by two former environment ministers who had helped to preside over the progressive weakening of the federal role in environmental protection. See Charles Caccia, in House of Commons, *Debates*, 26 April 1988, 14846, and 4 May 1988, 15132; and John Roberts, 'Meeting the Environmental Challenge,' in Thomas Axworthy and Pierre Elliott Trudeau, eds., *Towards a Just Society: The Trudeau Years* (Markham: Viking 1990) 175-6.
77 William A. Neff, 'Mirror Legislation,' in Tingley, ed., *Environmental Protection and the Canadian Constitution* (Edmonton: Environmental Law Centre [Alberta] Society 1987), 64.
78 Linda Duncan and Elizabeth Swanson, 'Submission to the Parliamentary Committee on Bill C-74: Canadian Environmental Protection Act,' 10 December 1987.
79 See, for instance, Richard D. Lindgren, 'Toxic Substances in Canada: The Regulatory Role of the Federal Government,' in Tingley, ed., *Into the Future: Environmental Law and Policy for the 1990s* (Edmonton: Environmental Law Centre [Alberta] Society 1990), 41.
80 Confidential interview, June 1991. The legal issue is discussed in Alastair R. Lucas, '*R. v. Crown Zellerbach Canada Ltd.*,' *University of British Columbia Law Review* 23 (1989): 355-71.
81 Tingley, 'Conflict and Cooperation,' 145.
82 House of Commons, *Minutes of Proceedings and Evidence of the Standing Committee on the Environment*, 26 September 1991, 6:32.
83 Tom McMillan, 'Luncheon Address,' in Tingley, ed. *Environmental Protection and the Canadian Constitution* (Edmonton: Environmental Law Centre [Alberta] Society 1987), 53.

84   Lucas, 'The New Environmental Law,' 184.
85   The court distinguished an affirmative decision-making responsibility, such as a requirement to issue a permit, from mere authority to take action, and thus held that although the Department of Transport was required by the Guidelines Order to conduct an environmental review of the *Oldman Dam*, since it was required to issue a permit for construction, the Department of Fisheries and Oceans was not. *Re: Friends of the Oldman River Society and The Queen in right of Alberta et al.; Attorney-General of Quebec et al., Intervenors* (1992), 88 *Dominion Law Reports*, 1-60.
86   Monique Ross, 'An Evaluation of Joint Environmental Impact Assessments,' in Monique Ross and J. Owen Saunders, eds., *Growing Demands on a Shrinking Heritage: Managing Resource-Use Conflicts* (Calgary: Canadian Institute of Resources Law 1992).
87   Schattschneider, *The Semi-Sovereign People*, Chapter 1.
88   Confidential interview, July 1991.
89   Graeme Hamilton and Philip Authier, 'Green Law Makes Brassard see red,' *Gazette* (Montreal), 7 October 1994, A1, A8.
90   For a detailed comparison of the two, see Joseph de Pencier, 'The Federal Environmental Assessment Process: A Practical Comparison of the EARP Guidelines Order and the Canadian Environmental Assessment Act,' *Journal of Environmental Law and Practice* 3 (1993): 329-43.
91   See Ted Schrecker, 'The Canadian Environmental Assessment Act: Tremulous Step Forward, or Retreat into Smoke and Mirrors,' *Canadian Environmental Law Reports* 5 (1991): 192-246. However, after that article was published, the bill was amended in response to environmentalists' criticisms to reduce the number of times the bill evoked the opinion of the minister or other responsible authority. For a later critique of the act, see Robert. B. Gibson, 'The New Canadian Environmental Assessment Act: Possible Responses to its Main Deficiencies,' *Journal of Environmental Law and Practice* 2 (1992): 223-55.
92   *Western Report*, 'Fjordbotten: No Means No,' 25 December 1989, 30.
93   Confidential interview, 1991.
94   Confidential interviews, July 1991.
95   Confidential interview, July 1991.
96   Confidential interview, May 1991.
97   Confidential interview, July 1991.
98   House of Commons, Legislative Committee on Bill C-13, *Minutes of Proceedings and Evidence*, 19 November 1991, 10:10.
99   'Amendments to Bill C-78: An Act to Establish a Federal Environmental Assessment Process. A Submission to the House of Commons Legislative Committee on Bill C-78 by the Ministers of Environment of British Columbia, Alberta, Saskatchewan, Manitoba, Ontario, New Brunswick, Prince Edward Island, Nova Scotia, Newfoundland, Yukon, Northwest Territories,' 4 December 1990.
100 Geoffrey York, 'Quebec's Anger Surprised Ottawa,' *Globe and Mail*, 24 March 1992, A7.

101 Peter O'Neil, 'Senate Bucks Pressure From Quebec and Passes Environment Bill,' *Vancouver Sun*, 24 June 1992, A4; also Geoffrey York, 'Senate Panel Passes Key Environmental Bill,' *Globe and Mail*, 23 June 1992, A5.

102 *Calgary Herald*, 'Bouchard Won't Yield Jurisdiction,' 11 May 1990, A3.

103 Confidential interview, June 1991. See also Canadian Council of Ministers of the Environment, 'Summary of Discussions and Decisions,' 6 May 1991, 3. It is not clear how federal officials planned to avoid involvement in light of the strict requirements of the act, but the regulations specifying conditions for federal reviews did remain to be written.

104 Glenn Bohn, 'Study Reveals Majority of Pulp Mills Break Law,' *Vancouver Sun*, 15 March 1989, A1; William F. Sinclair, *Controlling Pollution from Canadian Pulp and Paper Manufacturers: A Federal Perspective* (Ottawa: Minister of Supply and Services Canada 1990).

105 John Reynolds, in House of Commons, *Minutes of Proceedings and Evidence of the Special Committee to Pre-Study Bill C-78*, 4 December 1990, 13:19.

106 Environment Canada, 'Canadian Environmental Protection Act: Enforcement and Compliance Policy,' 1987.

107 Duncan, 'Trends in Enforcement,' 52.

108 Canadian Council of Ministers of the Environment, 'Report of the Task Force on Federal-Provincial Partnerships for Environmental Protection,' January 1990.

109 Confidential interview, July 1991.

110 Donald V. Smiley, 'An Outsider's Observations of Federal-Provincial Relations Among Consenting Adults,' in Richard Simeon, ed., *Confrontation and Collaboration – Intergovernmental Relations in Canada Today* (Toronto: Institute of Public Administration of Canada 1979).

111 Confidential interview, July 1991.

112 Confidential interviews, June 1991.

113 Confidential interview, July 1991.

114 Canadian Council of Ministers of the Environment, 'Statement of Interjurisdictional Cooperation on Environmental Matters,' 1990.

115 Confidential interview, May 1991.

116 Confidential interview, May 1991.

117 *Gazette* (Montreal), 'New Dam Political Trade-off: Ex-aide,' 12 September 1988, A8.

118 *Canadian Wildlife Federation Inc.* v. *Canada*, [1990] 4 *Canadian Environmental Law Reports*, 201-26.

119 The court did rule that if the federal environment minister did not appoint a full EARP panel by 30 January 1990, the license would be quashed. However, the minister complied and the license remained in effect.

120 The province's initial position was that it had agreed to halt construction of the dams themselves, but not associated work on the overall project. However, on 11 October 1990 Saskatchewan announced that it was resuming construction of the dams as well, indirectly referring to an agreement (discussed below) granting federal approval of the move. George N. Hood, *Against the Flow:*

Rafferty-Alameda and the Politics of the Environment (Saskatoon: Fifth House Publishers 1994), 150-1.

121   Hood, *Against the Flow*, 124-8.

122   Ross Howard and David Roberts, 'Rafferty Dam Goes Ahead,' *Globe and Mail*, 13 October 1990, A1.

123   Ross Howard and David Roberts, 'De Cotret Denies Making Deal with Saskatchewan on Dams,' *Globe and Mail*, 26 October 1990, A1.

124   David Roberts, 'Minister "Didn't Care" if Dam Panel Quit,' *Globe and Mail*, 2 November 1990, A1; Hood, *Against the Flow*, 140.

125   *Canada (A.G.)* v. *Saskatchewan Water Corporation*, [1990] 5 *Canadian Environmental Law Reports*, 252 (Sask. QB).

126   Anne McIlroy, 'Panel Lists 18 Reasons Dam Needs More Study,' *Vancouver Sun*, 11 September 1991, A8.

127   Larry Pratt and Ian Urquhart, *The Last Great Forest: Japanese Multinationals and Alberta's Northern Forests* (Edmonton: NeWest Press 1994), 139, 141, 151.

128   Andrew Nikiforuk and Ed Struzik, 'The Great Forest Sell-Off,' *Report on Business Magazine*, November 1989; George Oake, 'Alberta's Pulp Mill Plans Raise a Stink,' *Toronto Star*, 2 December 1989, D5.

129   'Agreement Concerning Environmental Impact Assessments of Projects in Alberta with Implications for Canada and Alberta,' 15 May 1986.

130   Scott McKeen and Roy Cook, 'Forestry Staff Stay Away From Pulp Mill Hearings,' *Edmonton Journal*, 22 November 1989, A7.

131   Christopher Donville, 'Ottawa Condemns Alberta Pulp Mill Proposal,' *Globe and Mail*, 1 November 1989, A1. Federal officials stress that it was the proponent's environmental impact assessment, rather than the project itself that was being rejected. However, not surprisingly, that fine distinction was lost on the media and on Alberta politicians.

132   Brian Lahoi, 'Fjordbotten Suspicious of "Unreasonable Standards,"' *Edmonton Journal*, 1 February 1990, A3.

133   Graham Fraser, 'Bouchard Backs Comments on Pulp Mill,' *Globe and Mail*, 2 November 1989, B1.

134   Confidential interview, July 1991.

135   Alberta-Pacific Environmental Impact Assessment Review Board, 'The Proposed Alberta-Pacific Pulp Mill: Report of the EIA Review Board,' March 1990.

136   Christopher Donville, 'Alberta Accepts Pulp Mill Report,' *Globe and Mail*, 3 March 1990, A3.

137   Scott McKeen, 'Al-Pac Review Taught a Lesson,' *Calgary Herald*, 16 October 1889, A5.

138   Scott McKeen, 'Ottawa Ducks Al-Pac Debate,' *Edmonton Journal*, 8 September 1990, G1; Scott McKeen, 'Critical Report on Pulp Mill Won't be Heard by Al-Pac Panel,' *Edmonton Journal*, 29 August 1990, A1.

139   Johanna Powell, 'Alberta Says Yes to $1.6B Al-Pac Mill,' *Financial Post*, 21 December 1991, 1.

140   Robert Bourassa, *Power from the North* (Scarborough: Prentice-Hall 1985).

141   'Power to Burn,' *Maclean's*, 21 May 1990, 50.

142 François Froest, 'Grande-Baleine: Lucien Bouchard Menace Québec de Tenir des Audiences Publiques,' *La Presse*, 2 December 1990, A17.
143 Although consensus was reached on the wording of the agreement in June, it was not signed by Quebec until November, and the federal government until February, 1991.
144 *Gazette* (Montreal), 'Paradis Reverses Stand on James Bay,' 20 September 1990, A1.
145 *Ottawa Citizen*, 'Quebec Says "hands off" Energy Policy,' 26 October 1990, F5. The pretext for her remarks was a National Energy Board decision that it would only grant Hydro Quebec the necessary licenses for export of electricity from the project on the condition that it undergo a full federal environmental review. Quebec subsequently appealed the NEB decision successfully, but the Supreme Court restored the original decision. The *Grand Council of Crees* decision is reviewed in Chapter 3.
146 Graeme Hamilton, 'Quebec Lax on Environment: Bouchard,' *Gazette* (Montreal), 30 October 1990, A1.
147 *Globe and Mail*, 'Dam Move Called Dangerous Precedent,' 18 October 1990, A1.
148 Geoffrey York and Barrie McKenna, 'Quebec Permitted to Start Hydro Project,' *Globe and Mail*, 21 November 1990, A1.
149 Graeme Hamilton, 'Cree Threaten More Hydro Project Delays,' *Gazette* (Montreal), 27 March 1991, A1.
150 Philip Authier, 'Ottawa Flip-Flops on Hydro Project, Paradis Charges,' *Gazette* (Montreal), 23 November 1990, A7.
151 Graeme Hamilton, 'Ottawa Gives Quebec the Go-ahead on Great Whale,' *Gazette* (Montreal), 20 November 1990, A1.
152 Peggy Curran, 'De Cotret Puts Foot Down on Great Whale Project,' *Gazette* (Montreal), 22 November 1990, A4. Public opinion polls taken at the time indicated that 80 per cent of Canadians, including 72 per cent of Quebecers, agreed that there should be a full review of the Great Whale project before construction proceeded. See Anne McIlroy, 'Most Quebecers Want Environmental Review of James Bay: Poll,' *Gazette* (Montreal), 17 November 1990, A1.
153 Kevin Dougherty, 'New James Bay Snag?' *Financial Post*, 23 May 1991, 4.
154 André Picard and Geoffrey York, 'Ottawa to Assess Hydro Project,' *Globe and Mail*, 10 July 1991, A5.
155 André Picard, 'Ottawa Chided by Judge Over Great Whale Project,' *Globe and Mail*, 18 July 1991, A3.
156 *Cree Regional Authority* v. *Quebec (Procureur Général)*, Federal Court Trial Division, 10 September 1991, [1991] 47 Federal Trial Reports, 251-71.
157 'Protocole D'Accord: Evaluation Environnementale Du Project Grande Baleine,' 23 January 1992; André Picard, 'Great Whale Project to Get Review,' *Globe and Mail*, 25 January 1992, A5.
158 Rhéal Séguin, Ann Gibbon, and Graham Fraser, 'Quebec Shelves Great Whale Project,' *Globe and Mail*, 19 November 1994, A1, A13.
159 Bouchard, *On the Record*, 213.

160 Steven A. Kennett, 'Hard Law, Soft Law and Diplomacy: The Emerging Paradigm for Intergovernmental Cooperation in Environmental Assessment,' *Alberta Law Review* 31 (1993): 644-61.
161 Canada-Alberta Agreement for Environmental Assessment Cooperation, August 1993.
162 M. Paul Brown and Fazley Siddiq, 'The Dimensions of Provincial Environmental Protection Spending,' paper presented at the Annual Meeting of the Canadian Political Science Association, Kingston, June 1991.
163 Philip Authier, 'Federal Environmental Impact Plans May Force Quebec to Move: Paradis,' *Gazette* (Montreal), 20 June 1990, A7.
164 Kathryn Harrison, 'The Regulator's Dilemma: Regulation of Pulp Mill Effluents in a Federal State,' *Canadian Journal of Political Science*, forthcoming.
165 William J. Andrews, in House of Commons, *Minutes of Proceedings and Evidence of the Standing Committee on the Environment*, 24 October 1991, 13:43.
166 In a recent federal report, regulation is not even mentioned initially among the strategies available to the federal government to control listed substances. (See Environment Canada and Health and Welfare Canada, 'Preparing the Second Priority Substances List under the Canadian Environmental Protection Act,' April 1993, 1.)
167 'An Agreement on the Equivalency of Federal and Alberta Regulations for the Control of Toxic Substances in Alberta,' June 1994. The agreement suspends the effect of federal regulations for pulp mills, lead smelters, and vinyl chloride plants in Alberta.
168 Confidential interviews, May to June 1994.
169 Environment Canada, 'Environment Canada Regulatory Review – Environmental Protection Program: A Discussion Document,' November 1993, vii.
170 House of Commons, Standing Committee on Environment and Sustainable Development, *It's About Our Health! Towards Pollution Prevention*, June 1995. It is noteworthy that, although the Liberal-dominated parliamentary committee that reviewed CEPA was extremely critical of implementation efforts to date, they declined to assign blame to the previous Conservative government, presumably at least in part because no change of approach had been evident since the election of the Liberal government.
171 Steven A. Kennett, 'The Environmental Management Framework Agreement: Reforming Federalism in Post-Referendum Canada,' *Resources* 52 (1995): 1-5, 3.
172 Confidential interview, June 1994. See also Geoffrey York, 'New Regulations Gut Environmental Assessment Law,' *Globe and Mail*, 26 September 1993, A4.
173 'Canada's Green Plan Strikes Out,' *Vancouver Sun*, 20 April 1995, A4.
174 Environment Canada, 'Program Review and Environment Canada,' 27 February 1995.
175 This development is discussed in greater detail in Kathryn Harrison, 'Prospects for Intergovernmental Harmonization in Environmental Policy,' in Douglas M. Brown and Janet Hiebert, eds., *Canada: The State of the Federation, 1994* (Kingston: Institute of Intergovernmental Relations 1994); and Kennett, 'The Environmental Management Framework Agreement.'

176 Confidential interviews, May to June 1994.
177 Canadian Council of Ministers of the Environment, 'Rationalizing the Management Regime for the Environment: Purpose, Objectives and Principles,' June 1994.
178 'Copps Attacks "Racist" Barb,' *Vancouver Sun*, 27 September 1995, A4.
179 Canadian Council of Ministers of the Environment, 'Environmental Management Framework Agreement, Discussion Draft,' October 1995.
180 Although in theory it is also possible for a 'green' government to veto a national standard it considers too weak, the effect of that veto is to revert to the undesirable default condition of no national standard. Thus, a government seeking high national standards cannot serve its interests by exercising a veto in the same way a government seeking to relax national standards can.

Chapter 7: Conclusions

1 Kathryn Harrison, 'The Regulator's Dilemma: Regulation of Pulp Mill Effluents in a Federal State,' *Canadian Journal of Political Science*, forthcoming.
2 Anne Schneider and Helen Ingram, 'Social Construction of Target Populations: Implications for Politics and Policy,' *American Political Science Review* 87 (1993): 334-47.
3 Ronald Brickman, Sheila Jasanoff, and Thomas Ilgen, *Controlling Chemicals: The Politics of Regulation in Europe and the United States* (Ithaca: Cornell University Press 1985); George Hoberg, 'Governing the Environment: Comparing Policy in Canada and the United States,' in Keith Banting, George Hoberg, and Richard Simeon, eds., *Degree of Freedom: Canada and the United States in a Changing World* (Montreal: McGill-Queen's University Press, forthcoming).
4 George Tsebelis, *Nested Games: Rational Choice in Comparative Perspective* (Berkeley: University of California Press 1990).
5 Grace Skogstad and Paul Kopas, 'Environmental Policy in a Federal System: Ottawa and the Provinces,' in Robert Boardman, ed., *Canadian Environmental Policy: Ecosystems, Politics, and Process* (Toronto: Oxford University Press 1992), 47.
6 Anthony Downs, 'Up and Down with Ecology – The "Issue-Attention Cycle,"' *The Public Interest* 27 (1972): 38-50; Frank R. Baumgartner and Bryan D. Jones, *Agendas and Instability in American Politics* (Chicago: University of Chicago Press 1993).

Bibliography

Alhéritière, Dominique. 'Les problèmes constitutionnels de la lutte contre la pollution de l'espace atmospherique au Canada.' *La Revue du Barreau Canadien* 50 (1972): 561-79

–. *La gestion des eaux en droit constitutionnel canadien.* Quebec: Editeur Officiel du Quebec 1976

Banting, Keith. *The Welfare State and Canadian Federalism.* Kingston: McGill-Queen's University Press 1987

Baumgartner, Frank R., and Bryan D. Jones. *Agendas and Instability in American Politics.* Chicago: University of Chicago Press 1993

Baumol, William J., and Wallace E. Oates. *The Theory of Environmental Policy.* 2nd ed. New York: Cambridge University Press 1988

Beaudoin, Gerald A. 'La protection de l'environnement et ses implications en droit constitutionnel.' *McGill Law Journal* 23 (1977): 207-24

Bélanger, Gerard. 'The Division of Powers in a Federal System: A Review of the Economic Literature.' In Richard Simeon, ed., *Division of Powers and Public Policy.* Toronto: University of Toronto Press 1985

Block, Fred. 'The Ruling Class Does Not Rule.' *Socialist Revolution* 7 (1977): 6-28

Blom, Joost. 'The Conflict of Laws and the Constitution – *Interprovincial Co-operatives Ltd.* v. *The Queen.*' *University of British Columbia Law Review* 11 (1977): 144-57

Bourassa, Robert. *Power from the North.* Scarborough: Prentice-Hall 1985

Bowden, Marie-Ann. '*Friends of the Oldman River Society* v. *Canada et al*: Two Steps Forward, One Step Back.' *Saskatchewan Law Review* 56 (1992): 209-21

Brander, James A. 'Economic Policy Formation in a Federal State: A Game Theoretic Approach.' In R. Simeon, ed., *Intergovernmental Relations.* Toronto: University of Toronto Press 1985

Breton, Albert. 'Supplementary Statement.' *Report of the Royal Commission on the Economic Union and Development Prospects for Canada.* Vol. 3. Ottawa: Minister of Supply and Services Canada 1985

–. *Centralization, Decentralization and Intergovernmental Competition.* Kingston: Institute of Intergovernmental Relations 1990

Breton, Albert, and Anthony Scott. *The Economic Constitution of Federal States*. Toronto: University of Toronto Press 1978

Brickman, Ronald, Sheila Jasanoff, and Thomas Ilgen. *Controlling Chemicals: The Politics of Regulation in Europe and the United States*. Ithaca: Cornell University Press 1985

Brown, M. Paul. 'Organizational Design as Policy Instrument: Environment Canada in the Canadian Bureaucracy.' In Robert Boardman, ed., *Canadian Environmental Policy: Ecosystems, Politics, and Process*. Toronto: Oxford University Press 1992

Brown, M. Paul, and Fazley Siddiq. 'The Dimensions of Provincial Environmental Protection Spending.' Paper presented at the Annual Meeting of the Canadian Political Science Association, Kingston, June 1991

Burns, Nancy, and Glenn Beamer. 'The Politics of Budget Constraints.' Paper presented at the Annual Meeting of the American Political Science Association, September 1993

Cairns, Alan C. 'The Other Crisis of Canadian Federalism.' *Canadian Public Administration* 22 (1979): 175-95

–. 'The Governments and Societies of Canadian Federalism.' In Douglas E. Williams, ed., *Constitution, Government, and Society in Canada: Selected Essays by Alan C. Cairns*. Toronto: McClelland and Stewart 1988

Cameron, David R. 'The Expansion of the Public Economy: A Comparative Analysis.' *American Political Science Review* 72 (1978): 1243-61

Castrilli, J.F. 'Control of Toxic Chemicals in Canada: An Analysis of Law and Policy.' *Osgoode Hall Law Journal* 20 (1982): 322-401

Castrilli, J.F., and Toby Vigod. *Pesticides in Canada: An Examination of Federal Law and Policy*. Ottawa: Law Reform Commission of Canada 1989

Conway, Tom. 'Taking Stock of the Traditional Regulatory Approach.' In G. Bruce Doern, ed., *Getting it Green*. Ottawa: CD Howe 1990

Crabbé, Philippe, and Irene M. Spry. *Natural Resource Development in Canada*. Ottawa: University of Ottawa Press 1973

de Pencier, Joseph. '*Oldman River Dam* and Federal Environmental Assessment Now and in the Future.' *Journal of Environmental Law and Practice* 2 (1992): 293-312

de Silva, K.E.A. *Pulp and Paper Modernization Grants Program – An Assessment*. Ottawa: Economic Council of Canada 1988

Dewees, Donald N. *Evaluation of Policies for Regulating Environmental Pollution*. Ottawa: Economic Council of Canada 1980

Doern, G. Bruce. 'Introduction: The Regulatory Process in Canada.' In G. Bruce Doern, ed., *The Regulatory Process in Canada*. Toronto: Macmillan 1978

–. *The Federal Green Plan: Assessing the 'Prequel.'* Ottawa: CD Howe Institute 1990

Doern, G. Bruce, and Thomas Conway. *The Greening of Canada: Federal Institutions and Decisions*. Toronto: University of Toronto Press 1994

Downs, Anthony. 'Up and Down with Ecology – The "Issue-Attention Cycle."' *The Public Interest* 27 (1972): 38-50

Duncan, Linda F. 'Trends in Enforcement: Is Environment Canada Serious about Enforcing Its Laws?' In Donna Tingley, ed., *Into the Future: Environmental Law and Policy for the 1990s*. Edmonton: Environmental Law Centre (Alberta) Society 1990

Dunlap, Riley E. 'Public Opinion and Environmental Policy.' In James P. Lester, ed., *Environmental Politics and Policy*. Durham: Duke University Press 1989

–. 'Trends in Public Opinion Toward Environmental Issues: 1965-1990.' In Riley E. Dunlap and Angela G. Mertig, eds., *American Environmentalism: The U.S. Environmental Movement, 1970-1990*. Philadelphia: Taylor and Francis 1992

Durr, Robert H. 'What Moves Policy Sentiment?' *American Political Science Review* 87 (1993): 158-70

Dwivedi, O.P. 'Environmental Administration in Canada.' *International Review of Administrative Sciences* 39 (1973): 149-57

–. 'The Canadian Government Response to Environmental Concerns.' In O.P. Dwivedi, ed., *Protecting the Environment: Issues and Choices – Canadian Perspectives*. Vancouver: Copp Clark 1974

Dwivedi, O.P., and R. Brian Woodrow. 'Environmental Policy-Making and Administration in Federal States: The Impact of Overlapping Jurisdiction in Canada.' In William M. Chandler and Christian W. Zollner, eds., *Challenges to Federalism: Policy-Making in Canada and the Federal Republic of Germany*. Kingston: Institute of Intergovernmental Relations, Queen's University 1989

Egel, Robert. 'Canada's Acid Rain Policy: Federal and Provincial Roles.' In Jurgen Schmandt, Hilliard Roderick, and Judith Clarkson, eds., *Acid Rain and Friendly Neighbors: The Policy Dispute between Canada and the United States*. Durham: Duke University Press 1988

Elliott, E. Donald, Bruce A. Ackerman, and John C. Millian. 'Toward a Theory of Statutory Evolution: The Federalization of Environmental Law.' *Journal of Law, Economics, and Organization* 1 (1985): 313-40

Emond, D.P. 'Environmental Law and Policy: A Retrospective Examination of the Canadian Experience.' In Ivan Bernier and Andrée Lajoie, eds., *Consumer Protection, Environmental Law, and Corporate Power*. Toronto: University of Toronto Press 1985

Emond, Paul. 'The Case for a Greater Federal Role in the Environmental Protection Field: An Examination of the Pollution Problem and the Constitution.' *Osgoode Hall Law Journal* 10 (1972): 647-80

Erskine, Hazel. 'The Polls: Pollution and Its Costs.' *Public Opinion Quarterly* 36 (1972): 120-35

Estrin, David. 'Tokenism and Environmental Protection.' In O.P. Dwivedi, ed., *Protecting the Environment*. Vancouver: Copp Clark 1974

–. 'Mirror Legislation.' In Donna Tingley, ed., *Environmental Protection and the Canadian Constitution*. Edmonton: Environmental Law Centre (Alberta) Society 1987

Estrin, David, and J. Swaigen. *Environment on Trial: A Handbook of Ontario Environmental Law*. Toronto: Canadian Environmental Law Research Foundation 1978

Fairley, H. Scott. 'Canadian Federalism, Fisheries and the Constitution: External Constraints on Internal Ordering.' *Ottawa Law Review* 12 (1980): 257-318

–. 'The Constitutional Conundrum of Jurisdiction over the Environment.' In Canadian Bar Association, *Canada's Environmental Laws*. Toronto: Canadian Bar Association 1990

Farber, Daniel A. 'Politics and Procedure in Environmental Law.' *Journal of Law, Economics, and Organization* 8 (1992): 59-81

Fletcher, Frederick J., and Donald C. Wallace. 'Federal-Provincial Relations and the Making of Public Policy in Canada: A Review of Case Studies.' In Richard Simeon, ed., *Division of Powers and Public Policy*. Toronto: University of Toronto Press 1985

Franson, M.A.H., R.T. Franson, and A.R. Lucas. *Environmental Standards: A Comparative Study of Canadian Standards, Standard Setting Processes and Enforcement*. Edmonton: Environmental Council of Alberta 1982

Franson, Robert T., and Alastair R. Lucas. *Canadian Environmental Law*. Vancouver: Butterworths – Continuing Service 1976

–. 'Legal Control of Hazardous Products in Canada.' In Science Council of Canada, *Canadian Law and the Control of Exposure to Hazards*. Ottawa: Science Council of Canada 1977

Gibson, Dale. 'Interjurisdictional Immunity in Canadian Federalism.' *Canadian Bar Review* 47 (1969): 40-61

–. 'The Constitutional Context of Canadian Water Planning.' *Alberta Law Review* 7 (1969): 71-92

–. 'Constitutional Jurisdiction over Environmental Management in Canada.' *University of Toronto Law Journal* 23 (1973): 54-87

–. 'The Environment and the Constitution: New Wine in Old Bottles.' In O.P. Dwivedi, ed., *Protecting the Environment: Issues and Choices – Canadian Perspectives*. Vancouver: Copp Clark 1974

–. 'Environmental Protection and Enhancement under a New Canadian Constitution.' In Stanley M. Beck and Ivan Bernier, eds., *Canada and the New Constitution*. Vol. 2. Montreal: Institute for Research on Public Policy 1983

Gibson, Robert. B. 'The New Canadian Environmental Assessment Act: Possible Responses to Its Main Deficiencies.' *Journal of Environmental Law and Practice* 2 (1992): 223-55

Giroux, Lorne. 'A Statement by the Canadian Environmental Advisory Council on Enforcement Practices of Environment Canada.' In Canadian Environmental Advisory Council, *Review of the Proposed Environmental Protection Act*. Ottawa: Canadian Environmental Advisory Council 1987

–. 'Delegation of Administration.' In Donna Tingley, ed., *Environmental Protection and the Canadian Constitution*. Edmonton: Environmental Law Centre (Alberta) Society 1987

–. 'Les nouvelles technologies et le regime de la protection de l'environ-
nement au Canada: la nouvelle Loi canadienne sur la protection de
l'environnement.' *Les Cahiers de Droit* 30 (1989): 747-76
Harrison, Kathryn. 'Passing the Buck: Federalism and Canadian
Environmental Policy.' Ph.D. thesis, University of British Columbia, 1993
–. 'Prospects for Intergovernmental Harmonization in Environmental Policy.'
In Douglas M. Brown and Janet Hiebert,eds., *Canada: The State of the
Federation, 1994*. Kingston: Institute of Intergovernmental Relations 1994
–. 'Is Cooperation the Answer? Canadian Environmental Enforcement in
Comparative Context.' *Journal of Policy Analysis and Management* 14 (Spring
1995): 221-45
–. 'The Regulator's Dilemma: Regulation of Pulp Mill Effluents in a Federal
State.' *Canadian Journal of Political Science*, forthcoming
Hartle, Douglas G. *Public Policy Decision Making and Regulation*. Toronto:
Institute for Research on Public Policy 1979
Hatherly, Mary E. 'Constitutional Jurisdiction in Relation to Environmental
Law.' Unpublished background paper for the Law Reform Commission of
Canada 1984
Henley, Doreen C. 'The Advocacy Approach.' In Linda F. Duncan,
*Environmental Enforcement: Proceedings of the National Conference on the
Enforcement of Environmental Law*. Edmonton: Environmental Law Centre
(Alberta) Society 1985
Hertz, Michael Terry. '"Interprovincial," the Constitution, and the Conflict of
Laws.' *University of Toronto Law Journal* 26 (1976): 84-107
Hoberg, George. 'Environmental Policy: Alternate Styles.' In Michael
Atkinson, ed., *Governing Canada: State Institutions and Public Policy*. Toronto:
HBJ Holt 1993
–. 'Governing the Environment: Comparing Policy in Canada and the United
States.' In Keith Banting, George Hoberg, and Richard Simeon, eds., *Degrees
of Freedom: Canada and the United States in a Changing World*. Montreal:
McGill-Queen's University Press, forthcoming
Hoberg, George, and Kathryn Harrison. 'It's Not Easy Being Green: The
Politics of Canada's Green Plan.' *Canadian Public Policy* 20 (1994): 119-37
Hogg, Peter W. *Constitutional Law of Canada*. 2nd ed. Toronto: Carswell 1985
Howard, Ross. *Poisons in Public*. Toronto: James Lorimer 1980
Huestis, Lynne B. 'Policing Pollution: The Prosecution of Environmental
Offenses.' Working Paper, Law Reform Commission of Canada, September
1984
–. 'Pilot Study Report, S. 33 Fisheries Act.' Department of Justice, Federal
Statutes Compliance Project, December 1985
Hurlburt, William H. 'Conflict of Laws – Choice of Law – Place of Tort.'
Canadian Bar Review 54 (1976): 173-8
Ilgen, Thomas. 'Between Europe and America, Ottawa and the Provinces:
Regulating Toxic Substances in Canada.' *Canadian Public Policy* 11 (1985):
578-90

Ingelhart, Ronald. *The Silent Revolution*. Princeton: Princeton University Press 1977

Jaeger, Michael A. 'Back to the Future: Environmental Federalism in an Era of Sustainable Development.' *Journal of Environmental Law and Practice* 3 (1993): 3-39

Jenkin, Michael. *The Challenge of Diversity: Industrial Policy in the Canadian Federation*. Ottawa: Science Council of Canada 1983

Kennett, Steven Alexander. 'Interjurisdictional Water Resource Management in Canada: A Constitutional Analysis.' L.L.M. thesis, Queen's University, 1989

–. 'Hard Law, Soft Law and Diplomacy: The Emerging Paradigm for Intergovernmental Cooperation in Environmental Assessment.' *Alberta Law Review* 31 (1993): 644-61

–. 'Federal Environmental Jurisdiction After *Oldman*.' *McGill Law Review* 38 (1993): 180-203

LaForest, Gerard V. *Natural Resources and Public Property*. Toronto: University of Toronto Press 1969

–. 'Interprovincial Rivers.' *Canadian Bar Review* 50 (1972): 39-49

–. 'Jurisdiction over Natural Resources: Provincial or Federal.' In Philippe Crabbé and Irene M. Spry, eds, *Natural Resource Development in Canada*. Ottawa: University of Ottawa Press 1973

Landis, Henry. 'Legal Controls of Pollution in the Great Lakes Basin.' *Canadian Bar Review* 48 (1970): 66-157

Laskin, Bora. 'Jurisdictional Framework for Water Management.' In *Resources for Tomorrow*. Conference Background Papers. Vol. 1. Ottawa: Queen's Printer 1961-2

LeDain, Gerald. 'Sir Lyman Duff and the Constitution.' *Osgoode Hall Law Journal* 12 (1974): 261-338

Lederman, W.R. 'Unity and Diversity in Canadian Federalism: Ideals and Methods of Modernization.' *Canadian Bar Review* 53 (1975): 597-620

Leslie, Peter. *Federal State, National Economy*. Toronto: University of Toronto Press 1987

Lindgren, Richard D. 'Toxic Substances in Canada: The Regulatory Role of the Federal Government.' In Donna Tingley, ed., *Into the Future: Environmental Law and Policy for the 1990s*. Edmonton: Environmental Law Centre (Alberta) Society 1990

Lowi, Theodore. 'American Business, Public Policy, Case-Studies, and Political Theory.' *World Politics* 16 (1964): 677

Lucas, Alastair R. 'Constitutional Law – Federal Fisheries Power – Provincial Resource Management and Property and Civil Rights Powers – *Fowler* v. *The Queen* and *Northwest Falling Contractors Ltd.* v. *The Queen*.' *University of British Columbia Law Review* 16 (1982): 145-54

–. 'Harmonization of Federal and Provincial Environmental Policies: The Changing Legal and Policy Framework.' In J. Owen Saunders, ed., *Managing Natural Resources in a Federal State*. Toronto: Carswell 1986

–. 'Natural Resources and Environmental Management: A Jurisdictional
Primer.' In Donna Tingley, ed., *Environmental Protection and the Canadian
Constitution*. Edmonton: Environmental Law Centre (Alberta) Society 1987

–. 'R. v. Crown Zellerbach Canada Ltd.' *University of British Columbia Law Review*
23 (1989): 355-71

–. 'The New Environmental Law.' In R. Watts and D. Brown, eds., *Canada:
State of the Federation, 1989*. Kingston: Institute of Intergovernmental
Relations 1989

Lundqvist, Lennart J. *Environmental Policies in Canada, Sweden, and the United
States: A Comparative Overview*. Beverly Hills: Sage Publications 1974

–. 'Do Political Structures Matter in Environmental Politics? The Case of Air
Pollution Control in Canada, Sweden, and the United States.' *Canadian
Public Administration* 17 (1974): 119-42

MacNeill, J.W. *Environmental Management*. Ottawa: Information Canada 1971

Mahon, Rianne. 'Canadian Public Policy: The Unequal Structure of
Representation.' In Leo Panitch, ed., *The Canadian State: Political Economy
and Political Power*. Toronto: University of Toronto Press 1977

Markusen, James R., Edward R. Morey, and Nancy Olewiler. 'Competition in
Regional Environmental Policies when Plant Locations are Endogenous.'
Journal of Public Economics 56 (1995): 55-77.

Mashaw, Jerry L., and Susan Rose-Ackerman. 'Federalism and Regulation.' In
George C. Eads and Michael Fix, eds., *The Reagan Regulatory Strategy*.
Washington, DC: Urban Institute Press 1984

McAllister, Ian, and Donely T. Studlar. 'Trends in Public Opinion on the
Environment in Australia.' *International Journal of Public Opinion Research* 5
(1993): 353-61

McLeod, Ron. 'The Provincial Perspective.' In Donna Tingley, ed.,
Environmental Protection and the Canadian Constitution. Edmonton:
Environmental Law Centre (Alberta) Society 1987

McMillan, Tom. 'Luncheon Address.' In Tingley, ed., *Environmental Protection
and the Canadian Constitution*. Edmonton: Environmental Law Centre
(Alberta) Society 1987

Meekison, J. Peter, and Roy J. Romanow. 'Western Advocacy and Section 92A
of the Constitution.' In J.P. Meekison, R.J. Romanow, and W.D. Moull, eds.,
*Origins and Meaning of Section 92A: The 1982 Constitutional Amendment on
Resources*. Montreal: Institute for Research on Public Policy 1985

Mellon, Margaret, Leslie Ritts, Steven Garrod, and Marcia Valiante. *The
Regulation of Toxic and Oxidant Pollution in North America*. Toronto: CCH
Canada 1986

Mitchell, Robert Cameron. 'Public Opinion and Environmental Politics in the
1970s and 1980s.' In Norman J. Vig and Michael E. Kraft, eds.,
Environmental Policy in the 1980s: Reagan's New Agenda. Washington, DC:
Congressional Quarterly Press 1984

Muldoon, Paul, and Marcia Valiante. *Toxic Water Pollution in Canada*. Calgary:
Canadian Institute of Resources Law 1988

Munton, Don. 'The Provinces and Canada-United States Environmental
Relations.' In Tom Keating and Don Munton, eds., *The Provinces and
Canadian Foreign Policy.* Toronto: Canadian Institute of International Affairs
1985

Muntz, Gary H. 'Federal Government Policy and the Issue of Inland Water
Pollution.' M.A. thesis, University of Guelph, 1972

National Task Force on Environment and Economy. *Report of the National
Task Force on Environment and Economy.* Toronto: Canadian Council of
Ministers of the Environment 1987

Neff, William A. 'Mirror Legislation.' In Donna Tingley, ed., *Environmental
Protection and the Canadian Constitution.* Edmonton: Environmental Law
Centre (Alberta) Society 1987

Nemetz, Peter. 'The Fisheries Act and Federal-Provincial Environmental
Regulation: Duplication or Complementarity?' *Canadian Public
Administration* 29 (1986): 401-24

–. 'Federal Environmental Regulation in Canada.' *Natural Resources Journal* 26
(1986): 552-608

Nemetz, P., D. Uyeno, P. Vertinsky, J. Vertinsky, and A. Vining. 'Regulation of
Toxic Chemicals in the Environment.' Ottawa: Economic Council of
Canada 1981

Nevitte, Neil, and Mebs Kanji. 'Explaining Environmental Concern and
Action in Canada.' *Applied Behavioral Science Review* 3 (1995): 85-102

Noam, Eli M. 'Government Regulation of Business in a Federal State:
Allocation of Power under Deregulation.' *Osgoode Hall Law Journal* 20
(1982): 762-79

Norrie, Kenneth, Richard Simeon, and Mark Krasnick. *Federalism and
Economic Union in Canada.* Toronto: University of Toronto Press 1986

Northey, Rodney. 'Federalism and Comprehensive Environmental Reform:
Seeing Beyond the Murky Medium.' *Osgoode Hall Law Journal* 29 (1989):
127-81

Oates, Wallace E. *Fiscal Federalism.* New York: Harcourt Brace Jovanovich
1972

Oates, Wallace E., and Robert M. Schwab. 'Economic Competition Among
Jurisdictions: Efficiency Enhancing or Distortion Inducing?' *Journal of Public
Economics* 35 (1988): 333-54

Olson, Mancur. *The Logic of Collective Action.* Cambridge: Harvard University
Press 1965

Painter, Martin. 'Intergovernmental Relations in Canada: An Institutional
Analysis.' *Canadian Journal of Political Science* 24 (1991): 269-88

Pal, Leslie A. *Interests of State: The Politics of Language, Multiculturalism, and
Feminism in Canada.* Montreal: McGill-Queen's University Press 1993

Parisien, Richard W. 'The Fisheries Act: Origins of Federal Delegation of
Administrative Jurisdiction to the Provinces.' Unpublished report,
Environment Canada 1972

Parlour, James W. 'The Politics of Water Pollution Control: A Case Study of
the Formation of the Canada Water Act, Part I: Comprehensive Water

Resource Management.' *Journal of Environmental Management* 12 (1981): 31-64
–. 'The Politics of Water Pollution Control: A Case Study of the Canadian Fisheries Act Amendments and the Pulp and Paper Effluent Regulations, 1970.' *Journal of Environmental Management* 13 (1981): 127-49
Parlour, James W., and Steven Schatzow. 'The Mass Media and Public Concern for Environmental Problems in Canada, 1960-1972.' *International Journal of Environmental Studies* 13 (1978): 9-17
Peltzman, Sam. 'Towards a More General Theory of Regulation.' *Journal of Law and Economics* 19 (1976): 211-41
Percy, David R. 'New Approaches to Inter-Jurisdictional Problems.' In Barry Sadler, ed., *Water Policy for Western Canada: The Issues of the Eighties*. Calgary: University of Calgary Press 1983
–. 'Federal/Provincial Jurisdictional Issues.' In H.I. Rueggeberg and A.R. Thompson, eds., *Water Law and Policy Issues in Canada*. Vancouver: Westwater Research Centre 1984
Peters, B. Guy, and Brian W. Hogwood. 'In Search of the Issue-Attention Cycle.' *Journal of Public Policy* 47 (1985): 238-53
Peterson, Paul E., and Mark C. Rom. *Welfare Magnets: A New Case for a National Standard*. Washington, DC: Brookings Institution 1990
Pross, A. Paul. 'Water and Environmental Law: Bureaucratic Constraints.' In Susan Guppy, Yvonne Fern, and Bruce Wildsmith, eds., *Water and Environmental Law*. Halifax: Institute for Resource and Environmental Studies, Dalhousie University, 1981
–. *Group Politics and Public Policy*. Toronto: Oxford University Press 1986
Quarles, John. *Cleaning Up America: An Insider's View of the Environmental Protection Agency*. Boston: Houghton Mifflin 1976
Rabe, Barry G. 'Cross-Media Environmental Regulatory Integration: The Case of Canada.' *American Review of Canadian Studies* 19 (1989): 261-73
Rankin, Murray, and Peter Finkle. 'The Enforcement of Environmental Law: Taking the Environment Seriously.' *University of British Columbia Law Review* 17 (1982): 35-57
Richards, John, and Larry Pratt. *Prairie Capitalism: Power and Influence in the New West*. Toronto: McClelland and Stewart 1979
Roberts, John. 'Meeting the Environmental Challenge.' In Thomas Axworthy and Pierre Elliott Trudeau, eds., *Towards a Just Society: The Trudeau Years*. Markham: Viking 1990
Rose-Ackerman, Susan. 'Does Federalism Matter? Political Choice in a Federal Republic.' *Journal of Political Economy* 89 (1981): 152-65
Ross, Monique. 'An Evaluation of Joint Environmental Impact Assessments.' In Monique Ross and J. Owen Saunders, eds., *Growing Demands on a Shrinking Heritage: Managing Resource-Use Conflicts*. Calgary: Canadian Institute of Resources Law 1992
Rueggeberg, H.I., and A.R. Thompson, eds. *Water Law and Policy Issues in Canada*. Vancouver: Westwater Research Centre 1984

Rutherford, Barbara, and Paul Muldoon. 'Designing an Environmentally Responsible Constitution.' *Alternatives* 18 (1992): 26-33

Saunders, J. Owen. *Interjurisdictional Issues in Canadian Water Management.* Calgary: Canadian Institute of Resources Law 1988

Scharpf, Fritz. 'The Joint-Decision Trap: Lessons from West German Federalism and European Integration.' *Public Administration* 66 (1988): 239-78

Schattschneider, E.E. *The Semi-Sovereign People.* San Francisco: Holt, Rinehart and Winston 1960

Schneider, Anne, and Helen Ingram. 'Social Construction of Target Populations: Implications for Politics and Policy.' *American Political Science Review* 87 (1993): 334-47

Schrecker, Ted. *The Political Economy of Environmental Hazards.* Ottawa: Law Reform Commission of Canada 1984

–. 'The Canadian Environmental Assessment Act: Tremulous Step Forward, or Retreat into Smoke and Mirrors.' *Canadian Environmental Law Reports* 5 (1991): 192-246

Schultz, Richard J. *Federalism, Bureaucracy, and Public Policy.* Montreal: McGill-Queen's University Press 1980

–. 'Federalism and Telecommunications: Multiplication, Division and Sharing.' *Osgoode Hall Law Journal* 20 (1982): 745-61, 754

Scott, Anthony. 'Piecemeal Decentralization: The Environment.' In Robin Boadway, Thomas Courchene, and Douglas Purvis, eds., *Economic Dimensions of Constitutional Change.* Kingston: John Deutsch Institute for the Study of Economic Policy 1991

Scott, F.R. *Essays on the Constitution.* Toronto: University of Toronto Press 1977

Simeon, Richard. *Federal-Provincial Diplomacy: The Making of Recent Policy in Canada.* Toronto: University of Toronto Press 1972

Simeon, Richard, and Ian Robinson. *State, Society, and the Development of Canadian Federalism.* Toronto: University of Toronto Press 1990

Sinclair, William F. *Controlling Pollution from Canadian Pulp and Paper Manufacturers: A Federal Perspective.* Ottawa: Minister of Supply and Services Canada 1990

Skocpol, Theda. 'Bringing the State Back In: Strategies of Analysis in Current Research.' In Peter Evans, Dietrich Rueschemeyer, and Theda Skocpol, eds., *Bringing the State Back In.* Cambridge: Cambridge University Press 1985

Skogstad, Grace. 'Federalism and Agricultural Policy.' In Herman Bakvis and William M. Chandler, eds., *Federalism and the Role of the State.* Toronto: University of Toronto Press 1987

Skogstad, Grace, and Paul Kopas. 'Environmental Policy in a Federal System: Ottawa and the Provinces.' In Robert Boardman, ed., *Canadian Environmental Policy: Ecosystems, Politics, and Process.* Toronto: Oxford University Press 1992

Smiley, Donald V. 'An Outsider's Observations of Federal-Provincial Relations Among Consenting Adults.' In Richard Simeon, ed., *Confrontation and*

Collaboration – Intergovernmental Relations in Canada Today. Toronto:
Institute of Public Administration of Canada 1979
–. *Canada in Question: Federalism in the Eighties.* 3rd ed. Toronto: McGraw-Hill
1980
–. *The Federal Condition in Canada.* Toronto: McGraw-Hill Ryerson 1987
Sproule-Jones, Mark. *Public Choice and Federalism in Australia and Canada.*
Canberra: Australian National University 1975
Stein, Stanley B. 'An Opinion on the Constitutional Validity of the Proposed
Canada Water Act.' *University of Toronto Faculty Law Review* 28 (1970): 74-82
Stevenson, Colin P. 'A New Perspective on Environmental Rights After the
Charter.' *Osgoode Hall Law Journal* 21 (1983): 390-421
Stevenson, Garth. 'The Division of Powers.' In Richard Simeon, ed., *Division
of Powers and Public Policy.* Toronto: University of Toronto Press 1985
–. 'The Division of Powers.' In R.D. Olling and M.W. Westmacott, eds.,
Perspectives on Canadian Federalism. Scarborough: Prentice-Hall 1988
–. *Unfulfilled Union: Canadian Federalism and National Unity.* 3rd ed. St.
Catharines: Gage 1989
Stewart, Richard B. 'Pyramids of Sacrifice? Problems of Federalism in
Mandating State Implementation of National Environmental Policy.' *Yale
Law Journal* 86 (1977): 1196-1272
Stigler, George J. 'The Theory of Economic Regulation.' *Bell Journal of
Economics and Management* 2 (1971): 3-21
Stimson, James A. *Public Opinion in America: Moods, Cycles, and Swings.*
Boulder: Westview 1991
Struthers, James. *No Fault of Their Own: Unemployment and the Canadian
Welfare State 1914-1941.* Toronto: University of Toronto Press 1983
Thompson, Andrew R. *Environmental Regulation in Canada: An Assessment of
the Regulatory Process.* Vancouver: Westwater Research Centre 1980
–. 'Regulation as a Bargaining Process.' Paper presented to Boardrooms,
Backrooms and Backyards, a conference sponsored by the Canadian
Environmental Law Research Foundation, March 1982
Thompson, A.R., and H.R. Eddy. 'Jurisdictional Problems in Natural Resource
Management.' In W.D. Bennett, ed., *Essays on Aspects of Resource Policy.*
Ottawa: Science Council of Canada 1973
Thompson, Peter C. 'Institutional Constraints in Fisheries Management.'
Journal of the Fisheries Research Board 31 (1974): 1965-81
Tiebout, C.M. 'A Pure Theory of Local Expenditures.' *Journal of Political
Economy* 64 (1956): 416-24
Tingley, Donna. 'Conflict and Cooperation on the Environment.' In Douglas
Brown, ed., *Canada: The State of the Federation, 1991.* Kingston: Institute of
Intergovernmental Relations 1991
Toner, Glen. 'Whence and Whither: ENGOs, Business and the Environment.'
Mimeo, undated
Trebilcock, Michael, Douglas Hartle, J. Robert, S. Prichard, and Donald N.
Dewees. *The Choice of Governing Instrument.* Ottawa: Economic Council of
Canada 1982

Tremblay, André. 'La priorité des competences provinciales dans la lutte contre la pollution des eaux.' In Philippe Crabbé and Irene M. Spry, eds., *Natural Resource Development in Canada*. Ottawa: University of Ottawa Press 1973

Troyer, Warner. *No Safe Place*. Vancouver: Clark, Irwin 1992

Trudeau, P.E. 'The Practice and Theory of Federalism.' In Michael Oliver, ed., *Social Purpose for Canada*. Toronto: University of Toronto Press 1961

Tsebelis, George. *Nested Games: Rational Choice in Comparative Politics*. Berkeley: University of California Press 1990

Urquhart, Ian. 'Federalism, Ideology, and Charter Review: Alberta's Response to Morgentaler.' *Canadian Journal of Law and Society* 4 (1989): 157-73

Vanderzwaag, David, and Linda Duncan. 'Canada and Environmental Protection: Confident Political Faces, Uncertain Legal Hands.' In Robert Boardman, ed., *Canadian Environmental Policy: Ecosystems, Politics, and Process*. Toronto: Oxford University Press 1992

Victor, Peter A., and Terrence N. Burrell. *Environmental Protection Regulation: Water Pollution, and the Pulp and Paper Industry*. Ottawa: Economic Council of Canada 1981

Walker, Jack L. 'The Origins and Maintenance of Interest Groups in America.' *American Political Science Review* 77 (1983): 390-406

Warkentin, Mark. '*Friends of the Oldman River Society* v. *Canada* (Minister of Transport).' *University of British Columbia Law Review* 26 (1992): 313-29

Weaver, R. Kent. 'The Politics of Blame Avoidance.' *Journal of Public Policy* 6 (1986): 371-98

–. *Automatic Government: The Politics of Indexation*. Washington, DC: Brookings Institution 1988

Webb, Kernaghan R. *Industrial Water Pollution Control and the EPS*. Unpublished background study for the Law Reform Commission of Canada, May 1983

–. *Pollution Control in Canada: The Regulatory Approach in the 1980s*. Ottawa: Law Reform Commission of Canada 1988

–. 'Between Rocks and Hard Places: Bureaucrats, Law and Pollution Control.' In Robert Paehlke and Douglas Torgeson, eds., *Managing Leviathan*. Peterborough: Broadview Press 1990

Whittington, Michael. 'Environmental Policy.' In G. Bruce Doern and V. Seymour Wilson, eds., *Issues in Canadian Public Policy*. Toronto: Macmillan 1974

–. 'Department of Environment.' In G. Bruce Doern, ed., *Spending Tax Dollars: Federal Expenditures 1980-1*. Ottawa: Carleton University 1980

Wildsmith, Bruce H. 'Fisheries, Harmonization and the Economic Union.' In Mark Krasnick, ed., *Case Studies in the Division of Powers*. Toronto: University of Toronto Press 1985

Willis, L. Alan. 'The *Crown Zellerbach* Case on Marine Pollution: National and International Dimensions.' *The Canadian Yearbook of International Law* 26 (1988): 235-52

Wilson, Christina Anne. 'The Canadian Council of Resource and Environment Ministers as a Site for Elite Accommodation in Canada, 1963 to 1974.' M.A. thesis, University of Western Ontario, 1984

Wilson, James Q. 'The Politics of Regulation.' In James McKie, ed., *Social Responsibility and the Business Predicament*. Washington, DC: Brookings Institution 1975

–. *American Government*. 3rd ed. Toronto: DC Heath 1986

Wood, B. Dan. 'Principals, Bureaucrats, and Responsiveness in Clean Air Enforcements.' *American Political Science Review* 82 (1988): 213-34

Woodrow, R.B. 'The Development and Implementation of Federal Pollution Control Policy Programs in Canada, 1966-1974.' Ph.D. thesis, University of Toronto, 1977

Yergeau, Michel, and Jacques St-Denis. 'La protection de l'environnement: un survoi du cadre legislatif.' *Assurances* 56 (1988): 10-30

Young, R.A., Philippe Faucher, and André Blais. 'The Concept of Province-Building: A Critique.' *Canadian Journal of Political Science* 17 (1984): 783-818

Zaller, John R. *The Nature and Origins of Mass Opinion*. New York: Cambridge University Press 1992

Zerbe, Richard O. 'Optimal Environmental Jurisdictions.' *Ecology Law Quarterly* 4 (1974): 193-245

Index

Aboriginal groups: use of litigation to force environmental assessment of projects, 146; and pressure on federal government to act on environmental jurisdiction, 152

Aboriginal lands: affected by Al-Pac project, 147; as federal jurisdiction, 39, 50

Accords, federal-provincial, on environmental issues, 37, 103-7, 158, 174

Accountability: and Environmental Management Framework Agreement (EMFA), 160; of governments, for environmental protection, 175

Acid rain: control measures, and 'Green Plan,' 123; federal-provincial bilateral agreements on, 109-10; as jurisdiction of Environment Canada, 90; media coverage of, 85, 86; as transboundary issue, 44, 109-10

Agriculture, as federal jurisdiction, 36, 37, 39

Air pollution: and Canadian Environmental Protection Act (CEPA); 130; and Clean Air Act, 70-1; as federal jurisdiction, 45; neglect of federal jurisdiction concerning, 130; regulations, 99-100; as transboundary issue, 43, 45; US national standards, 15

Air Pollution Control Directorate, 100

Airports, as federal jurisdiction, 35

Al-Pac pulp mill project, 146-9, 152

Alberta: and Al-Pac project, 146-9; bilateral environmental accords, 105, 106; defense of environmental jurisdiction, 170; and emissions of carbon dioxide, 123; interviews for present study, 10; and national environmental standards,

143; objection to Canada Water Act, 72, 73, 74; objection to Canadian Environmental Assessment Act (CEAA), 136-7, 138; objection to Canadian Environmental Protection Act (CEPA), 129; objection to Fisheries Act, 1977 amendments, 94, 95; and *Oldman Dam* case, 48-9

Alberta-Pacific pulp mill. *See* Al-Pac pulp mill project

Anadramous fish, as federal jurisdiction, 38

Angus Reid, 118

Arctic Waters Pollution Prevention Act, 36, 63

Atlantic Accord, 158

Authority. *See* Comprehensive authority; Federal jurisdiction, environmental; Jurisdiction, environmental; Provincial jurisdiction, environmental; Restrictive authority

Automobile emissions, as federal jurisdiction, 40

Bacon, Lise, 150

Benefits: concentrated, 12; diffuse, 14; of environmental protection regulations, 13; of public policy, 12

Bertrand, Jean-Jacques, 75

Bhopal chemical spill, 117

Blais-Grenier, Suzanne, 90, 98, 120

BNA Act, 32. *See also* Constitution

Bouchard, Lucien, 121, 122, 123, 139, 147, 149, 150, 152, 170

Boundary Waters Treaty, 108

Bourassa, Robert, 149

British Columbia: bilateral environmental accords, 106, 158; defense of environmental jurisdiction, 170; dispute over 'equivalency,' 141; interviews for present study, 10; and national environmental standards, 154; objection to Canada Water Act, 72, 73, 74, 75, 80, 101; objection to Canadian Environmental Protection Act (CEPA), 129; objection to constitutional jurisdiction changes on environment, 78; objection to Fisheries Act, 1977 amendments, 94, 95; and *Oldman Dam* case, 49

'Buck passing,' between governments, in environmental area, 8, 20, 162, 174-5. *See also* Federal jurisdiction, environmental; Jurisdiction; Provincial jurisdiction, environmental

Bureaucrats: as different from politicians, 26-7; and interdepartmental conflict, 26, 172-3; interviews for present study, 10; provincial, and objection to Canada Water Act, 74, 75; and regulatory enforcement, 99, 113, 172

Caccia, Charles, 109, 132
Campbell, Kim, 158
Canada Environment Act, 97
Canada Metal case, 47, 130
Canada Water Act, 41, 63, 64-7, 69-70, 72, 73, 74, 75, 79, 87, 100-2, 108, 128, 163, 166
Canadian Council of Ministers of the Environment (CCME): and bilateral environmental accords, 155, 158; and Canadian Environmental Assessment Act (CEAA), 138; and Canadian Environmental Protection Act (CEPA), 142-4; Cooperative Principles for Environmental Assessment, 153; Environmental Management Framework Agreement, 159-60; and harmonization of environmental standards, 158-9, 167; Statement of Interjurisdictional Cooperation, 143-4. *See also* Canadian Council of Resource Ministers (CCRM); Canadian Council of Resources and Environment Ministers (CCREM)
Canadian Council of Resource and Environment Ministers (CCREM): and bilateral environmental accords, 105; evaluation of, 110-12; and Fisheries Act, 1977 amendments, 94; and

national environmental standards, 76; reduction of staff and budget of, 108
Canadian Council of Resource Ministers (CCRM): establishment of, 72; and national environmental standards, 72; objection to Canada Water Act, 74
Canadian Environmental Assessment Act (CEAA), 135-9, 153, 157, 163-4
Canadian Environmental Protection Act (CEPA), 52, 93, 115, 117, 128-33, 132, 140-2, 158, 163-4
Canadian Pulp and Paper Association (CPPA), 95-6
Canadian Wildlife Federation, 62
Canals, as federal jurisdiction, 36
Capital mobility: as constraint on provincial environmental protection, 21-2, 23, 29, 177; of polluting industries, 45
Carbon dioxide emissions, 123
'Carbon tax,' 122
CCME. *See* Canadian Council of Ministers of the Environment (CCME)
CCREM. *See* Canadian Council of Resource and Environment Ministers (CCREM)
CCRM. *See* Canadian Council of Resource Ministers (CCRM)
Census, as federal jurisdiction, 39
Central Canada Potash case, 112
CEPA. *See* Canadian Environmental Protection Act (CEPA)
Charest, Jean, 123, 151
Charter of Rights and Freedoms, and environmental protection, 35, 52
Chedabucto Bay oil spill, 56
Chemicals, standardization of testing requirements, 93
Chernobyl nuclear disaster, 117
Clark, Joe, 127
Clean Air Act, 45, 63, 70-1, 76, 79, 92, 97-8, 99-100, 102, 128
Close-ended questions, in public opinion measurement, 56, 57, 59-60, 82, 84
Coastal waters, as federal jurisdiction, 46
Collaboration model, of intergovernmental relations, 7, 8, 175
Competition: interprovincial, and national environmental standards, 165; interprovincial, for industrial investment, 21-4, 29; model, of intergovernmental relations, 7-8
Comprehensive authority, over environmental issues, 50

Conservative Party: and environmental protection, 90, 120-1; and 'Green Plan,' 157

Constitution: and Canada Water Act, 66, 75; and environment, report on, 77, 78; and environmental protection, 3-4; and Fisheries Act 1977 amendments, 95; interpretation by judiciary, 31-2; and jurisdiction, 18-19, 20, 31-2, 52, 91; Meech Lake Accord, 126-7; negotiations for renewal of, 76-9; Section 91(1A), legislative authority with respect to federal property, 36; Section 91(2), trade and commerce, 39-40; Section 91(3), federal taxation powers, 40-1; Section 91(6), census and statistics, 39; Section 91(10), navigation and shipping, 38; Section 91(12), fisheries, 37; Section 91(24), Indians and lands reserved for the Indians, 39; Section 91(27), criminal law, 41-2; Section 92(5), management and sale of public lands, 36; Section 92(10), local works and undertakings, 34; Section 92(10)(a), interprovincial works and undertakings, 39; Section 92(13), property and civil rights in the province, 34; Section 92(16), matters of a local or private nature, 34; Section 92A, provincial jurisdiction over natural resources, 34, 91; Section 95, agriculture, 39; Section 108, federal ownership of harbours, 36; Section 109, provincial ownership of land and resources, 33; Section 132, federal treaty powers, 38, 44

'Constitutional Powers to Control Pollution' working paper, 78

Constitutional Review Secretariat of the Privy Council, 77

Cooperative Principles for Environmental Assessment, 153

Copps, Sheila, 159

Costs: concentrated, 12, 14; diffuse, 13-14; of environmental protection regulations, 13-14; of public policy, 12

Cotret, Robert de, 122, 123, 145, 150, 151

Courts. *See* Judiciary; Litigation

'Cradle to grave' approach, to toxic substance control, 128

Criminal law: as federal jurisdiction, 36, 39; as instrument for environmental protection, 41-2, 71, 102-3, 130

Crown Zellerbach case, 44, 46-7, 51, 53, 143

Dams, as federal jurisdiction, 50. *See also* Oldman dam; Rafferty-Alameda dam

Davis, Jack, 67, 68, 70, 94, 98, 101, 104-5, 166

DDT levels, in wildlife, 56

Decima Research, 117

Department of Energy, Mines and Resources, 65, 74, 77

Department of Fisheries and Oceans, 94, 96-7, 99, 106-7, 129-30, 172-3

Department of National Health and Welfare, 70

Department of the Environment. *See* Environment Canada

Department of the Environment Act, 48

Dioxins: in Great Lakes fish, 85; in pulp and paper effluent, 117

Draft Framework for Environmental Assessment Harmonization, 153

Economic concerns, importance of, 59, 84, 118, 119, 123-4

Economic development. *See* Industries

Electorate. *See* Public opinion

Emissions: carbon dioxide, 123; and Clean Air Act, 71, 99-100; sulphur dioxide, 109-10, 123; vehicle, as federal jurisdiction, 40

Enforcement, of environmental standards: and bureaucrats, 26-7, 99, 113, 172; and Clean Air Act, 99-100; coordination among levels of government, 154; use of criminal law for, 41-2, 71, 102-3, 130; delegation to provinces, 103-7, 114; lack of, 15, 16, 102, 166-7; pressure for, with increased salience of environmental issues, 140

English-Wabigoon river system, 87

Environics, 117-18, 119

Environment Canada: use of bargaining with polluters, 103; and Canada Water Act, 88; and Canadian Environmental Protection Act (CEPA), 129-30, 140, 156; conflict with Department of Fisheries and Oceans, 96-7, 99, 106-7, 129-30, 172-3; creation of, 55, 70; and enforcement of Fisheries Act by provinces, 104-5; erosion of air pollution control capabilities, 100; objection to Al-Pac project, 147; and provinces' environmental jurisdiction, 86; reasons for lack of effectiveness of, 113-14, 115; reduction of staff and budget of, 157-8; regulatory functions, 96, 98-9, 164; specialization in acid rain and toxic substances, 90; Toxic Chemical Management Program, 90; White Paper on role of, 89

Environmental assessment: bilateral accords on, 158; Canadian Environmental Assessment Act (CEAA), 135-9, 153, 157, 163-4; court decisions, 144-53, 154; effect of court decisions regarding, 168

Environmental Contaminants Act, 90, 91, 92-3, 100, 102, 128

Environmental groups: and policy-making process, 115-16; use of environmental assessment process, 134-5; establishment of, 62; on federal environmental protection role, 51, 124-5, 126, 152, 176-7; and federal government independence, 175; and government funding, 27; influence of, 14-15, 115-16, 155, 168; interviews for present study, 10; use of litigation, 116, 142, 146, 160-1, 177; objection to Canadian Environmental Protection Act (CEPA), 132; objection to Meech Lake accord, 126; objection to weakness of 'Green Plan,' 122; and regulatory process, 103; as representatives of general public, 176; supportive of overlapping environmental jurisdiction, 106; watchdog role of, 160-1

Environmental impact assessment. See Environmental assessment

Environmental Impact Assessment and Review Process (EARP), 48, 49, 54, 133-4, 144-53

Environmental Management Framework Agreement (EMFA), 159-60

Environmental protection: and Charter of Rights and Freedoms, use by polluters, 35; and constitution, 3-4, 32, 76-9; as example of diffuse benefits and concentrated costs, 14; latent public support for, 82-3; politics of, 13-18. See also Enforcement; Environmental groups; 'Single window' approach, to environmental regulation

Environmental Protection Agency (US), 86, 112

Environmental Protection Service (EPS), 70, 96-7

Environmental standards: and Canadian Environmental Protection Act (CEPA), 167; consistency of, not achieved by federal-provincial accords, 107; for effluent discharge, 68-9; 'equivalency' concept, 129, 130-1, 140-1; federal, adoption by provinces, 154; federal-provincial bilateral accords on, 158-9; harmonization of, 88, 144, 156, 158-9, 174; and interprovincial competition for industries, 21-2, 165-6; minimum, requested by provincial governments, 73; national, 7, 129, 160, 167. See also Canadian Council of Ministers of the Environment (CCME)

'Equivalency': of federal and provincial environmental standards, 129, 130-1, 140-1; and harmonization of environmental standards, 144, 156. See also Canadian Environmental Protection Act (CEPA)

Exxon Valdez oil spill, 117

Federal Facilities Program, 99-100

Federal government: consultation with provinces on international agreements, 108; delegation of environmental protection role to provinces, 5, 29, 79-80, 162, 164-5; effect of public opinion on environment on, 5, 9, 63-4, 80, 113, 119, 163, 168-9; and environmental assessment legal cases, 151-3; global powers, 39-42; interviews for present study, 10; legislative power, 36-52; proprietary power, 36; retreat from role in environmental protection, 79-114; sectoral powers, 37-9, 52. See also Federal jurisdiction, environmental; Intergovernmental relations; Provincial governments; Salience, of environmental issues

Federal jurisdiction, environmental: advantages of, 7; 'advocacy approach' to environmental protection, 89; and areas of constraint on provincial governments, 34-5; attitude of federal government towards, 18-20, 54, 86-90; and bilateral accords with provinces, 105; and Canada Water Act, 64-7; and Canadian Environmental Assessment Act, 136; and Canadian Environmental Protection Act (CEPA), 129-32; and Clean Air Act, 71; comprehensive, 50; and constitution, 35-52; delegation of enforcement to provinces, 103-7; and Environmental Contaminants Act, 92; established by legal cases, 143; and Fisheries Act Amendments 1970, 68; future role of, in environmental protection, 155-61, 163; as indirect, 3, 19, 35; legislative powers, 36-52; limitations of, 52-3; and pressure by environmental groups, 51, 124-5, 126, 152, 176-7; proprietary powers, 36; and public opinion, 5, 9, 63-4, 80, 113, 119, 153, 163, 168-9; restrictive, 50; strengthened by 'equivalency' principle in Canadian Environmental Protection Act (CEPA), 131; supported by Canadian Environmental Protection Act (CEPA), 129; supported by judiciary, 32-3, 53; supportive role in environmental protection, 3, 108, 112, 157. *See also* Environmental protection; Judiciary; Provincial jurisdiction, environmental

Federalism, and public policy, 6-9

Federal-provincial relations. See Intergovernmental relations

First Ministers Conferences, 74, 75, 89

Fisheries: affected by Al-Pac project, 147; anadramous fish, as federal jurisdiction, 38; bilateral accords on, 158; conflict between Environment Canada and Dept. of Fisheries and Oceans, 96-7, 99, 106-7, 129-30, 172-3; as federal jurisdiction, 37, 50, 51, 52; as provincial jurisdiction, 37, 38, 91; as sectoral power of federal government, 36, 37. *See also* Department of Fisheries and Oceans; Fisheries Act, 74

Fisheries Act: 1970 amendments, 63, 67-70, 76, 79, 89, 163, 166; 1977 amendments, 90, 92, 93-6, 166; amendments opposed by provinces, 93-6; and bilateral accords, 158; enforcement of, 102, 104-5, 106-7; use by federal government to control water pollution, 37, 67-8; implementation of, 100, 163; jurisdictional dispute over, between Environment Canada and Dept. of Fisheries and Oceans, 99, 106-7

Fishing licences, as provincial jurisdiction, 37

Fjordbotten, LeRoy, 147

Forestry: and Meech Lake Accord, 126, 127; as provincial jurisdiction, 34, 91

Friends of the Oldman River Society, 51

Fuel additives, as federal jurisdiction, 40

Gallup polls, 57, 59, 60, 82, 117, 118

Game theory: and intergovernmental relations, 171-2; and political decision-making, 28

Georgia Strait, 92

Global powers, of federal government, 36, 39-42

Global warming, 44, 117

Good, Len, 122

Government. *See* Decision-making, political; Federal government; Federal jurisdiction, environmental; Policy, governmental; Provincial governments; Provincial jurisdiction, environmental

Grand Council of Crees case, 34, 40, 51, 137, 149-51. *See also* James Bay project

Grande-Baleine project. *See* James Bay project

Great Lakes: Canada-Ontario agreement on water quality, 105; pollution, as interjurisdictional environmental issue, 44

Great Lakes Water Quality Agreement, 108

Great Whale project. *See* James Bay project

Green, J.J., 67

'Green Plan,' 121-4, 156, 157, 164

'Green waves' in public opinion: effect of economic issues on, 17, 84, 118, 119; effect on federal claims to jurisdiction over environment, 63, 115, 166, 167

Greenpeace, 62

Harbours: as federal jurisdiction, 35, 36; Halifax, cleanup of, 121

Harmonization, of environmental standards, 88, 144, 153, 156, 158-9, 167, 174

Hazardous Products Act, 41-2

Hazardous wastes: media coverage of, 85-6; spills and accidents, and public pollution awareness, 117

Hydro Quebec: challenge of Canadian Environmental Protection Act over PCBs, 52; James Bay project, 40, 149-51, 152-3

Hydroelectric power generation: environmental impact assessment of, 40; as provincial jurisdiction, 34, 91

'Independence,' of federal government,

advantages of, 175
Indian lands. *See* Aboriginal lands
Industries: and Canadian Environmental
  Protection Act (CEPA), 132; and capital
  mobility, 21-2, 23, 29, 45, 177;
  favourable reaction to 'Green Plan,'
  122; and Fisheries Act, 100; and
  Fisheries Act amendments, 1977, 95;
  lack of compliance with environmental
  regulations, 102-3; objection to environmental protection regulation, 14;
  objection to overlapping environmental jurisdiction, 125; relationship with
  provincial governments, 6, 22-3, 176;
  subsidies for environmental protection,
  14, 15, 41, 109, 110, 164; support for
  'single window' environmental enforcement, 95-6, 106, 125, 129, 142, 158,
  159. *See also* Pulp and paper industry
Inland marine waters, as federal jurisdiction, 92
Interdepartmental Committee on Water,
  69
Interest groups: and collective action, 12;
  government support of, 27-8; industry,
  22-3; theory of, 15. *See also*
  Environmental groups; Industries
Intergovernmental relations: 1969-72,
  71-6; 1972-85, 108-12; 1985-95, 142-
  53; and attitudes towards federal
  jurisdiction, 86-90; use of bargaining to
  settle jurisdiction disputes, 32; and
  bilateral environmental accords, 174;
  and Canada Water Act, 65-7, 74-6; and
  Canadian Environmental Assessment
  Act (CEAA), 136-9; and Canadian
  Environmental Protection Act (CEPA),
  129, 140, 168; and Clean Air Act, 76;
  conflict during periods of salience of
  environmental issues, 162; and environmental assessment court decisions,
  144-5; and 'equivalency' principle,
  130-1, 132, 140-1, 141; and federal
  opposition to Al-Pac project, 147; and
  federal role in environmental protection, 142; and Fisheries Act
  Amendments 1977, 94-6; and game
  theory, 171-2; and 'Green Plan,' 122-4;
  and James Bay project, 149-51; models,
  7; and overlapping environmental
  jurisdictions, 7, 24-5, 29, 52-3; and
  public policy, 12
International agreements, on environmental issues, 108-10

International Boundary Waters Treaty, 38
International Joint Commission (IJC),
  108
Interprovincial Co-operatives case, 45-6, 47,
  53, 87, 91, 112
Interprovincial undertakings, as federal
  jurisdiction, 39

James Bay Agreement, 149-51, 152
James Bay project, 149-51, 152. *See also*
  Grand Council of Crees case
Jobs: loss of, as results of capital mobility, 23; as tradeoff with environmental
  concerns, 119
Judiciary: decisions on federal government's environmental authority, 164;
  as guardian of public environmental
  rights, 153-4; interpretation of constitution regarding environmental issues,
  31-55; and pressure on federal government to act on environmental
  jurisdiction, 152. *See also* Legal cases;
  Litigation
Jurisdiction, environmental: and constitution, 18-19; and government policy,
  18, 20-4; overlapping, of levels of government, 7, 24-5, 29, 30, 32, 52-3, 54.
  See also Federal jurisdiction, environmental; Intergovernmental relations;
  Provincial jurisdiction, environmental

Kerr, George, 74
Klein, Ralph, 138, 147

LaForest, Justice, 47, 49, 51
Lang, Otto, 63, 65, 74, 75
Laws. *See* Legislation
LeBlanc, Roméo, 96
LeDain, Justice, 46
Legal cases: *Canada Metal*, 47, 130;
  Central Canada Potash, 112; *Crown
  Zellerbach*, 44, 46-7, 51, 53, 143; *Grand
  Council of Crees*, 34, 40, 51, 137,
  149-51; *Interprovincial Co-operatives*,
  45-6, 47, 53, 87, 91, 112; *National
  Leasing Ltd.* v. *General Motors of Canada
  Ltd.*, 39-40; *Oldman Dam*, 34, 40, 47,
  48-9, 50-1, 52, 134, 135, 137, 164;
  Rafferty-Alameda Dam, 48, 51, 133, 134,
  135, 137, 142, 145-6, 146-7, 151-2, 164,
  173. *See also* Judiciary; Litigation
Legislation: Arctic Waters Pollution
  Prevention Act, 36, 63; BNA Act, 32;
  Canada Environment Act, 97; Canada

Water Act, 41, 63, 64-7, 69-70, 72, 74, 75, 79, 87, 100-2, 108, 128, 163, 166; Canadian Environmental Assessment Act (CEAA), 135-9, 157; Canadian Environmental Protection Act (CEPA), 52, 93, 115, 117, 128-33, 140-2, 158; Clean Air Act, 45, 63, 70-1, 76, 79, 92, 97-8, 99-100, 102, 128; Department of the Environment Act, 48; Environmental Contaminants Act, 90, 91, 92-3, 100, 102, 128; Fisheries Act, 37, 99, 100, 102, 104-5, 106, 158; Fisheries Act, amendments, 1970, 63, 67-70, 76, 79, 80, 166; Fisheries Act, amendments, 1977, 90, 92, 93-6, 166; Hazardous Products Act, 41-2; Northern Inland Waters Act, 36, 63; Ocean Dumping Control Act, 46, 91, 99, 102, 128; Omnibus Environmental Amendment Act, 100
Lévesque, René, 109
Liberal Party, 124, 157
Lincoln, Clifford, 129
Litigation: and federal environmental policy, 116, 134, 173; rare in prosecution of environmental offences, 102. *See also* Judiciary; Legal cases
Lobby groups. *See* Environmental groups; Interest groups
London Convention on Ocean Dumping, 1972, 92
Love Canal, 85

MacNeill, Jim, 77, 78
Manitoba: bilateral environmental accords, 105, 158; and *Interprovincial Co-operatives* case, 45-6, 87; and *Oldman Dam* case, 49; support for Canada Water Act, 72, 74
Marine pollution, as federal jurisdiction, 47, 53, 92
Market Facts, 60
McDonald, Lynn, 132
McMillan, Tom, 120-1, 133, 145
Media: coverage of environmental issues, 61, 62, 85-6, 116-17; as source material for present study, 10
Meech Lake Accord, 122, 126-7
Mercury pollution, 87
Migratory Birds Convention, 38
Mining, and Meech Lake Accord, 126, 127
Mississauga train derailment, 85-6

National Ambient Air Quality Objectives, 99
National emergency doctrine, and environmental crises, 43
National Energy Board (NEB), and James Bay project, 40
National Energy Program, 112, 122
National Leasing Ltd. v. General Motors of Canada Ltd., 39-40
Native lands. See Aboriginal lands
Natural resources, ownership by provinces, 3, 5-6, 19, 29, 32, 34, 91
Navigation, as federal jurisdiction, 36, 37, 38, 39, 52
New Brunswick: bilateral environmental accords, 105; interviews for present study, 10; and national environmental standards, 154; objection to Fisheries Act, 1977 amendments, 94, 95; and *Oldman Dam* case, 48-9; support for Canada Water Act, 74
New Democratic Party (Alberta), 146
Newfoundland: bilateral environmental accords, 37; objection to Canadian Environmental Assessment Act (CEPA), 137; objection to Fisheries Act, 1977 amendments, 94; and *Oldman Dam* case, 49
Nielson Task Force, 90, 112, 117, 120, 124, 128
Northern Inland Waters Act, 36, 63
Northwest Territories, and *Oldman Dam* case, 49
Nova Scotia: bilateral environmental accords, 37, 105; objection to Fisheries Act, 1977 amendments, 94, 95; support for Canada Water Act, 74

Ocean Dumping Control Act, 46, 91, 92, 99, 102, 128
Ocean pollution, as transboundary environmental issue, 43
Oil industry, taxation by federal government, 5
Oil spills, 56, 117
Oldman dam, 34, 40, 47, 48-9, 50-1, 52, 134, 135, 137, 164
Omnibus Environmental Amendment Act, 97, 100
'One window approach,' to environmental regulation. *See* 'Single window' approach, to environmental regulation
Ontario: bilateral environmental accords, 105, 106; defense of provincial envi-

ronmental jurisdiction, 170; and *Interprovincial Co-operatives* case, 45-6; interviews for present study, 10; and national environmental standards, 154; objection to Canada Water Act, 72, 73, 74, 75, 101; objection to Canadian Environmental Protection Act (CEPA), 129; objection to constitutional changes on environment, 78; objection to Fisheries Act, 1977 amendments, 94, 95

Ontario Water Resources Commission (OWRC), 74, 75

Open-ended questions, in public opinion measurement, 56, 57, 82, 117

Opposition parties: and Canada Water Act, 67; demand for stronger federal role in pollution control, 90, 124; objection to Canadian Environmental Protection Act (CEPA), 132; role in raising environmental issues, 63-4

Organization theory, and public policy, 12

Overlapping jurisdiction. *See* Jurisdiction, environmental

Paradis, Pierre, 150, 170

Parizeau, Jacques, 151

Park lands, as federal jurisdiction, 36

PCBs: as federal jurisdiction, 52; fire at Saint-Basile-le-Grand, 117, 140

'Peace, Order and good Government': and Canada Water Act, 66; as federal responsibility, 36, 39; and interjurisdictional environmental issues, 44; and international environmental matters, 38; invoked in Canadian Environmental Protection Act (CEPA), 130; judicial interpretation of, 45-52; limits of, 42-5; proposed amendment under Meech Lake Accord, 126

Pearse Commission, 99

Pépin, Jean-Luc, 65

'Permissive consensus,' on environmental issues, 84, 118

Pesticides, as federal jurisdiction, 39

Phosphates in detergents, as federal jurisdiction, 40

Policy, governmental: costs and benefits of, 12; effect of public opinion on, 5, 9, 63-4, 80, 113, 119, 153, 163, 168-9; and jurisdiction, 18, 20-4

'Policy entrepreneurs,' 14-15

Politicians: as different from bureaucrats,

26-7; objectives, 25-6, 169-71

Pollution: control, and intergovernmental relations, 71-6; interjurisdictional, 20, 43-4; priority of, in public opinion, 59-60, 82-6; taxes on, as environmental protection instrument, 40-1. *See also* Acid rain; Air pollution; Environmental protection; Global warming; Hazardous wastes; Soil pollution; Toxic substances; Water pollution

Pollution and Our Environment conference, 1966, 72

Pollution Probe, 62

Prince Edward Island: bilateral environmental accords, 37, 105; objection to Fisheries Act, 1977 amendments, 94

Provincial governments: competition for industry, 173-4; delegation of environmental authority to, by federal government, 5, 29, 79-80, 103-7, 114, 162; and federal subsidies for environmental protection, 41; interviews for present study, 10; and national environmental standards, 73, 76; objection to 'advocacy approach' to environmental protection, 89; objection to Fisheries Act, 1977 amendments, 93-6, 166; response to federal environmental legislation, 74-6; response to public demand for pollution control, 71; seen by environmentalists as less trustworthy, 125; support for 'single window' approach to environmental protection, 129. *See also* Federal government; Intergovernmental relations; Provincial jurisdiction, environmental

Provincial jurisdiction, environmental: advantages of, 7; and bilateral environmental accords, 105; and constitution, 3, 32-5, 91; constraints on, 34-5; defense of, 5-6; and economic development, 19; and environmental standards, 107, 162; and 'Green Plan,' 122-4; objection to Canadian Environmental Assessment Act (CEAA), 137-9; and ownership of natural resources, 3, 5-6, 19, 29, 165, 171; and policy-making, 20-4; preeminence of, during 1970s, 86; proprietary powers, as limitation on federal jurisdiction, 52; support for 'single window' approach to enforcement, 106. *See also* Federal jurisdiction, environmental; Industries; Provincial governments

Public opinion, on environment: 1969-72, 56-62; 1972-85, 82-6; 1985-95, 116-20; awareness of issues, in 1960s, 55; awareness of issues, in 1980s, 85-6, 115, 116-20; and collective action, 12, 16, 177; consultation of, for 'Green Plan,' 122; consultation of, regarding Canadian Environmental Protection Act (CEPA), 128; effect on government policy, 5, 9, 63-4, 80, 113, 119, 153, 163, 168-9; and federal/provincial jurisdictional conflict, 6; and 'Green Plan,' 121-4; influence of government on, 27-8, 171; measurement of, 56-62, 82-4, 117-20; objection to Environment Canada cuts, 120; problems in interpretation of, 83-4; shifts in, 16-17, 24-5, 124. *See also* Salience, of environmental issues

Pulp and paper industry: Al-Pac pulp mill, 146-9; dioxins in effluent, 117; interests of, and Fisheries Act amendments of 1977, 95-6; interviews for present study, 10; lack of regulation of, 22, 112; non-compliance with environmental regulations, 107, 140; objection to environmental standards, 64; regulation of, bilateral accords on, 158; subsidies for pollution abatement, 41, 103

Quebec: bilateral accord on pulp and paper regulations, 158; bilateral environmental accords, 106; defense of provincial environmental jurisdiction, 170; demand for provincial environmental jurisdiction in Meech Lake Accord, 126; and dispute over 'equivalency,' 141; and *Grand Council of Crees* case, 34, 40, 51, 137, 149-51; and *Interprovincial Co-operatives* case, 46; interviews for present study, 10; and James Bay project, 149-51; legal challenge of Canadian Environmental Protection Act (CEPA) over PCBs, 52; and national environmental standards, 143; objection to Canada Water Act, 72, 73, 74, 75, 101; objection to Canadian Environmental Assessment Act, 137, 138, 139; objection to Canadian Environmental Protection Act (CEPA), 129; objection to jurisdictional changes on environment in constitution, 78; and *Oldman Dam*

case, 48-9; revision of environmental statutes to match CEPA penalties, 154

Queen Charlotte Islands, 121

Rafferty-Alameda dam, 48, 51, 133, 134, 135, 137, 142, 145-7, 151-2, 164, 173

Railways, as federal jurisdiction, 39, 50

Regulations: definition, 13; lack of enforcement of, 15, 16, 102-3; as necessary 'stick,' in overcoming polluting behaviour, 14; non-enforcement of, 15, 16

Regulatory function: and Canada Water Act, 100; and Clean Air Act, 99; delegation of environmental protection to provinces, 5, 29, 79-80, 103-7, 114, 162, 164-5; and environmental protection, 13-14; of federal government, supported by Canadian Environmental Protection Act (CEPA), 130; and Fisheries Act, 100; inability to implement, by Environment Canada, 98-9; 'single window' approach, 95-6, 105-6, 142, 158, 159

Resources. *See* Natural resources

Resources for Tomorrow Conference, 1961, 72

Restrictive authority, over environmental issues, 50

Reynolds, John, 138

River pollution, as interjurisdictional environmental issue, 43, 44

Rivers, interprovincial, 87

Robarts, John, 74

Saint-Basile-le-Grand PCB warehouse fire, 117, 140

Salience, of environmental issues: decline in, 82-6, 113, 118, 119; prominence of, 57-61, 62, 117, 153, 164

Salmon, as federal jurisdiction, 38

Saskatchewan: bilateral environmental accords, 105, 106, 158; defense of provincial environmental jurisdiction, 170; and *Interprovincial Co-operatives* case, 45-6; and Joint Parliamentary Committee on Constitution and Environmental Protection, 79; objection to Canadian Environmental Assessment Act (CEPA), 137; objection to Fisheries Act, 1977 amendments, 94, 95; and *Oldman Dam* case, 49; and *Rafferty-Alameda Dam* case, 145-6; support for Canada Water Act, 72, 74

Sectoral powers, of federal government, 36, 37-9, 52

Service provision, as government function, 13

Sewage treatment facilities, subsidies for, 41, 109

Shipping, as federal jurisdiction, 38, 50

Sierra Club, 62

'Single window' approach, to environmental protection regulation, 95-6, 105-6, 129, 142, 158, 159

Smelters, subsidies for pollution abatement, 41

Soil pollution, addressed by Canadian Environmental Protection Act (CEPA), 130

Spending: as federal jurisdiction, 39; as government function, 13; subsidies for pollution abatement, 14, 15, 41, 103, 109, 110, 164

St. Clair River, 117

Stakeholders. See Interest groups

Standing Committee on the Environment and Sustainable Development, 156-7

Statement on Interjurisdictional Cooperation (STOIC), 143-4, 153, 158

Statistics, as federal jurisdiction, 39

Statutes. See Legislation

Stevenson, Justice, 49

STOIC. See Statement on Interjurisdictional Cooperation (STOIC)

Subsidies: for acid rain reduction, 109, 110; as 'carrot,' in overcoming polluting behaviour, 14, 15, 16, 103; for pollution abatement, 14, 15, 41, 103, 109, 110, 164

Sulphur dioxide emissions: control measures, and 'Green Plan,' 123; reduction of, 109-10

Supreme Court. See Legal cases

Task Force on Environmental Contaminants Legislation, 92

Task Force on Federal-Provincial Partnerships for Environmental Protection, 141, 143

Taxation: as environmental protection instrument, 40-1, 53; as federal jurisdiction, 39; as government function, 13; of oil industry, 5

Toxic Chemical Management Program, 90

Toxic substances: and Canadian

Environmental Protection Act (CEPA), 128; control measures, and 'Green Plan,' 123; evaluation of, 156; as federal jurisdiction, 39-40, 52, 53, 92, 130; list of, under Canadian Environmental Protection Act (CEPA), 140; mobility of, 43, 52, 53; occurrence of, in remote areas, 117; as specialty of Environment Canada, 90

Trade and commerce, as federal jurisdiction, 36, 39, 40, 52

Trucking, as federal jurisdiction, 39

United States: Clean Air Act, 97-8; Clean Water Act, 100; effluent discharge standards, 69; Environmental Protection Agency, 86, 112; and International Boundary Waters Treaty, 38; national environmental standards, 15; as origin of Canadian acid rain, 109; protest against Reagan's environmental policy reversals, 85; public concern with environmental issues, in 1980s, 118; welfare benefit cuts, effects of on neighbouring states, 21

Vehicle emissions, as federal jurisdiction, 40

Victoria Charter, 79

Voters. See Public opinion, on environment

Water pollution: and Canada Water Act, 64-7; and Canadian Environmental Protection Act (CEPA), 130; as federal jurisdiction, 37, 38; and Fisheries Act, 67-70

Water quality: as federal jurisdiction, 45-6; lack of enforcement of Canada Water Act, 100-2; national policy on, 65

Williston, Ray, 75

Winnipeg Centre for Sustainable Development, 121

Wood Buffalo National Park, 147

Working paper on 'Constitutional Powers to Control Pollution,' 78

Yukon, bilateral environmental accords, 158

Set in Stone by Chris Munro

Printed and bound in Canada by Friesens

Copy-editor: Anne Webb

Proofreader: Rachelle Kanefsky

Indexer: Annette Lorek